MIKE MEYERS' CERTIFICATION

Passport ☆

MCSE Planning a Windows® Server 2003

EXAM 70-293 Network Infrastructure

Martin C. Brown
Chris McCain

 OSBORNE

New York   Chicago   San Francisco
Lisbon   London   Madrid   Mexico City
Milan   New Delhi   San Juan
Seoul   Singapore   Sydney   Toronto

The McGraw·Hill Companies

McGraw-Hill/Osborne
2100 Powell Street, 10th Floor
Emeryville, California 94608
U.S.A.

To arrange bulk purchase discounts for sales promotions, premiums, or fund-raisers, please contact **McGraw-Hill/Osborne** at the above address. For information on translations or book distributors outside the U.S.A., please see the International Contact Information page immediately following the index of this book.

Mike Meyers' MCSE Planning a Windows® Server 2003 Network Infrastructure Certification Passport (Exam 70-293)

1234567890 DOC DOC 019876543

Book p/n 0-07-222569-6 and CD p/n 0-07-222571-8
parts of
ISBN 0-07-222570-X

Publisher	**Proofreader**
Brandon A. Nordin	Linda Medoff
Vice President & Associate Publisher	**Indexer**
Scott Rogers	Valerie Perry
Senior Acquisitions Editor	**Composition**
Nancy Maragioglio	Kelly Stanton-Scott and Tara A. Davis
Project Manager	**Illustrators**
Betsy Manini	Lyssa Wald, Kathleen Fay Edwards,
Project Editor	Melinda Lytle and Jackie Sieben
Emily Rader	**Series Design**
Acquisitions Coordinator	epic, Peter F. Hancik and
Jessica Wilson	Kelly Stanton-Scott
Technical Editor	**Cover Series Design**
Damir Bersinic	Ted Holladay
Copy Editors	
Sally Engelfried, Bob Campbell and	
Andrea Boucher	

This book was composed with Corel VENTURA™ Publisher.

About the Authors

Martin C. Brown, a professional writer for over four years, is the author of both the Perl and Python "Annotated Archives" and "Complete Reference" books (all four published by Osborne/McGraw-Hill), *iMac FYI* (Muska & Lipman), and 13 other published computing titles. His expertise spans myriad development languages and platforms—Perl, Python, Java, JavaScript, Basic, Pascal, Modula-2, C, C++, Rebol, Gawk, Shellscript, Windows, Solaris, Linux, BeOS, Microsoft WP, Mac OS, and more—as well as web programming, and systems management and integration. Brown has written columns for LinuxProgramming.com and ApacheToday.com. He is also a regular writer of white papers and "how to" guides for Microsoft on subjects such as migrating Solaris/Unix/Linux development and systems administration to Windows 2000 and 2003 Server product lines.

Martin draws on a rich and varied background as founding member of a leading UK ISP, systems manager and IT consultant for an advertising agency and an Internet solutions group, technical specialist for an intercontinental ISP network, database designer and programmer, and self-confessed compulsive consumer of computing hardware and software. In his formative pre-writing life, he spent ten years designing and managing mixed-platform environments. As a result, he has developed a rare talent for conveying the benefits and intricacies of his subject with equal measures of enthusiasm, professionalism, in-depth knowledge, and insight. When not writing, he develops data-rich websites and web-based applications for clients such as Hewlett-Packard, Oracle, and his own venture, Foodware.

Chris McCain is a Microsoft trainer and consultant specializing in Microsoft's core network operating systems and Microsoft SQL Server solutions. His enthusiasm for and expertise in these areas have led him to opportunities for authoring training courseware, in addition to many consulting projects, which he has undertaken. Chris complements the teaching aspect of his career with a strong consulting practice for which the clients are companies of all sizes. From Fortune 500 companies to the trendy retail shops of Beverly Hills, Chris has implemented networking and database solutions both large and small.

In 1999, Chris started his own consulting firm, and then moved to New York to join a major firm providing database consulting, data warehousing, and end-user training to large corporate clients. In 2001, Chris began training the core Microsoft exclusively. Today he is busy training, writing, and consulting, as well as being a founding member and developer of the National Information Technology Training and Certification Institute (NITTCI). NITTCI was developed to provide a strong resource for certification seekers and to certify individuals with a true working knowledge of information technology subject matter. As a senior member of NITTCI, Chris is responsible for leading the development of hands-on, job-task-based certifications for several industry-leading products. Chris currently lives in St Peterburg, FL with his fiancée, Stacy, and they are to be married in March of 2004.

About the Technical Editor

Damir Bersinic is an Infrastructure Consultant with Trecata Corporation, a system integration consultancy in Toronto, Canada. He has more than 20 years of industry experience and has worked with every Windows version since 1.0 in one way or another. He holds several Microsoft certifications, including MCSE, MCDBA, and MCT, and has also provided assistance to Microsoft in the development process of MCP exams. Damir has authored a number of titles on SQL Server, Oracle, Windows, and Active Directory. He is a database columnist for certcities.com and a regular contributor to *MCP Magazine*.

About LearnKey

LearnKey provides self-paced learning content and e-learning solutions to enhance personal skills and business productivity. LearnKey claims the largest library of rich streaming-media training content that engages learners in dynamic media-rich instruction complete with video clips, audio, full motion graphics, and animated illustrations. LearnKey can be found on the Web at www.LearnKey.com.

Dedication

To Sharon, for being there.

—Martin

To my mom and dad, who forged my past and helped me gain the tools I need to succeed in life. And to Stacy for helping me forge my future and helping me gain the tools I need to succeed in love.

—Chris

Acknowledgments

Despite the impression we authors try to give, there are, in fact, many people who work together to produce a book; and this is where we, as authors, get to list them all.

For my own part, I'd like to thank Thomas Willingham first for suggesting and then for recommending me for the project. I'd also like to thank him for all his work in the early stages, including his help in getting additional information and guides from his contacts in the certification and training departments.

While we're on that topic, I need to thank all those people at the certification and training department for their help, hospitality, and humor, and that includes Amy and Jim, the folks at Grandmasters (Richard and Ron), and the rest of the SMEs I met while there. I should also thank the receptionists at building 118 for not once laughing at my passport photo every time I signed in!

Over at Osborne, the biggest thanks need to go to Nancy Maragioglio, for believing in me in the first place, and for sticking with me through the project that was sometimes less than plain sailing. Also at Osborne, Jessica Wilson, for pushing and prodding in Nancy's absence, Emily Rader for turning manuscript into printed page, and the rest of the editorial and production staff that somehow turned what I typed into something readable.

Finally, I need to thank my co-author, Chris McCain, who did a stunning job on two chapters, in less than ideal circumstances.

—*Martin C. Brown*

Thanks to the publishers and editors Mike, Jessica, Betsy, and Nancy for the opportunity to work on such a successful series of books and to my fellow trainers Paul, Bill, Sam, Andrew, and Jeff, without whom I certainly would not be as well informed. A special thanks to those students of mine who have made my classes a learning experience for me as well.

—*Chris McCain*

Contents

Check-In

May I See Your Passport?

What do you mean you don't have a passport? Why, it's sitting right in your hands, even as you read! This book is your passport to a very special place. You're about to begin a journey, my friend, a journey toward that magical place called *certification*! You don't need a ticket, you don't need a suitcase—just snuggle up and read this passport—it's all you need to get there. Are you ready? Let's go!

Your Travel Agent—Mike Meyers

Hello! My name's Mike Meyers. I've written a number of popular certification books and I'm the President of Total Seminars, LLC. On any given day, you'll find me replacing a hard drive, setting up a website, or writing code. I love every aspect of this book you hold in your hands. Its part of a powerful new book series called the *Mike Meyers' Certification Passports*. Every book in this series combines easy readability with a condensed format—in other words, the kind of book I always wanted when I did my certifications. Putting this much information in an accessible format is an enormous challenge, but I think we have achieved our goal and I am confident you'll agree.

I designed this series to do one thing and only one thing: to get you the information you need to achieve your certification. You won't find any fluff in here—the authors, Martin Brown and Chris McCain, packed every page with nothing but the real nitty-gritty of the certification exam. Every page is packed with 100 percent pure concentrate of certification knowledge! But we didn't forget to make the book readable. I hope you enjoy the casual, friendly style. I want you to feel as though the authors are speaking to you, discussing the certification—not just spewing facts at you.

My personal e-mail address is mikem@totalsem.com. Please feel free to contact me directly if you have any questions, complaints, or compliments. If you'd like to contact Martin or Chris, they're available, as well, at mc@mcslp.com and hcmccain@yahoo.com, respectively. We all appreciate hearing from you—so please feel free to let us know what you think about this book!

Your Destination—Windows Server 2003 Network Infrastructure Certification

This book is your passport to the Planning and Maintaining a Microsoft Windows Server 2003 Network Infrastructure exam (Exam 70-293). Microsoft operating systems have become an industry standard, and the Microsoft Certified Professional program is one of the most respected certification tracks available to a computer engineer.

As you might suspect from the exam title, exam 70-293 focuses on planning and maintaining a Microsoft Windows Server 2003 network infrastructure. Topics covered on the exam include planning and implementing server roles and server security, network infrastructure, routing and remote access, server availability, network security, and security infrastructure.

Why the Travel Theme?

One of my favorite topics is the parallel of gaining a certification to taking a trip. All the elements are the same: preparation, an itinerary, and a route—even mishaps along the way. Let me show you how it all works.

This book is divided into eight chapters. Each chapter begins with an Itinerary, which provides objectives covered in each chapter and an ETA to give you an idea of the time involved in learning the skills presented in that chapter. Each chapter is broken down by real exam objectives, as published by Microsoft. Also, each chapter contains a number of helpful items to bring out points of interest:

Exam Tip	
Points out critical topics you're likely to see on the exam.	

Travel Assistance	
Provides you with additional sources, such as books and websites to give you more information.	

Local Lingo	
Describes special terms in detail in a way you can easily understand.	

Travel Advisory

Warns you of common pitfalls, misconceptions, and downright physical peril!

CHECKPOINT

The end of the chapter gives you two handy tools. The Checkpoint reviews each objective covered in the chapter with a handy synopsis—a great way to quickly review. Plus, you'll find end-of-chapter questions and answers to test your newly acquired skills.

But the fun doesn't stop there! After you've read the book, pull out the CD and take advantage of the free practice questions! Use the full practice exam to hone your skills and keep the book handy to check answers. When you're passing the practice questions, you're ready to take the exam—go get certified!

The End of the Trail

The IT industry changes and grows constantly—and so should you. Finishing one certification is just a step in an ongoing process of gaining more and more certifications to match your constantly changing and growing skills. Read the Career Flight Path (Appendix B) at the end of the book to see where this certification fits into your personal certification goals. Remember, in the IT business, if you're not moving forward, you're way behind!

Good luck on your certification! Stay in touch!

Mike Meyers
Series Editor
Mike Meyers' Certification Passport

PART

I

Server Security

Planning and Implementing Server Roles and Security

CHAPTER 1

	NEWBIE	SOME EXPERIENCE	EXPERT
ETA	5 hours	3 hours	2 hour

3

Planning is a one of those skills that is gained through a combination of knowledge and experience. In this chapter, we're going to teach you the ins and outs of planning for a Windows Server 2003 deployment. This is a brand new type of exam for Microsoft: it's the first planning exam they have ever had, and it's a new type of exam that has been developed with a number of key improvements over previous exams. Specifically, Microsoft has extended the question types from simple multiple choice to include hotspot and drag-and-drop–style answers.

Microsoft has also changed the way questions are introduced in the exam. Previous exams used a suite of questions that made up the exam. In order to combat the growing number of sites that provide a list of the questions and answers, the new exams consist of hundreds of questions, only a selection of which you will answer. That means to pass the exam, you'll actually need the knowledge provided in this book, rather than simply memorizing the right answers.

Finally, this is also one of the first exams designed from the start to address a common complaint of some of the earlier exams from the Windows 2000 MCSE, which was that it should test you on events and knowledge that will be required in the field. Therefore, by reading this book, not only should you be able to pass the exam, but you should also be able to apply many of the techniques and use much of your knowledge when you start your IT management job for real.

Throughout the exam, the primary concern is security, so throughout the book, we'll concentrate on planning different aspects of your Windows Server 2003 installation and how it affects the overall security of your installation. Although this will seem tiresome at times, our aim is to make it as entertaining and interesting as possible.

We'll also spend some time explaining why the security is so important. You might think it's obvious, but others won't. Technical and computer crime is on the rise, websites are broken into, industrial secrets are stolen, and in some cases criminal damage takes place. The meteoric rise of the Internet is in some small way responsible because it's opened up the borders of various companies in ways they never expected. It's also enabled unscrupulous individuals to study packets and information as it's transferred between companies over what is a public network.

In this chapter, we'll start with the basics of the operating systems, starting with the various editions, the security features of each version, and how this affects which edition you choose. We'll also cover how to use different core security systems to enforce and apply security settings on your servers and clients.

> ### Exam Tip
>
> These tips should help you identify what elements of each section will actually be tested on within the exam. Although all of the material in the book is potentially included, sometimes you need specific information about how the questions are structured and how a particular system is tested upon. Remember, in this exam Microsoft is looking for planning and analytical skills, rather than experience or knowledge of individual wizards, configuration, and administration tools. That means knowing the abilities, limitations, and technical architecture of the operating system and having the ability to apply that to build a plan for your network's infrastructure.

Objective 1.01

Evaluate and Select the Operating System to Install on Computers in an Enterprise

Windows Server 2003 is, like Windows 2000, split into a number of editions, each designed and targeted for a specific market and type of installation. As you plan your network, you'll need to know how to translate your organization's needs into a map of requirements for the operating system that will support your network.

In essence, these kinds of decisions are no different from any other you might make, from choosing dinner to choosing a new car. Okay, perhaps it's a bit different. When choosing dinner it's a question of likes and dislikes. When choosing a car, though, you need to think about a number of parameters, such as the type, the size, or the engine, before you get to the more human-like choices of colors, upholstery types, and whether you want a pair of dice dangling from the rearview mirror.

In this section, we'll look at the basic functionality and abilities of each operating system edition—it won't be an extensive summary and comparison, but it should be enough to enable you to differentiate between the versions and understand their key points. We'll also look at how to evaluate the needs of your organization and match one of the versions to your needs. Armed with this information, you should be able to make some decisions about the security implications of choosing the different versions.

Windows Server 2003 Editions

The Windows Server 2003 family consists of four distinct products:

- **Windows Server 2003, Standard Edition**   The basic edition, which supports the majority of features. This replaces the Windows 2000 Server and Windows NT 4 Server products.
- **Windows Server 2003, Enterprise Edition**   The same as the basic edition with support for additional processors, memory, and clustering. Replaces the Windows 2000 Advanced Server product.
- **Windows Server 2003, Datacenter Edition**   A specialized version of Windows Server 2003 designed with high stability and availability in mind. It replaces the Windows 2000 Datacenter Server product.
- **Windows Server 2003, Web Edition**   A new edition designed to provide basic web-serving functionality at a more cost effective price than using the full-blown Standard Edition product.

We'll have a closer look at some of the specific features of each edition before comparing features across all editions.

Standard Edition

Standard Edition (SE) supports the entire basic set of Windows Server 2003 features. It can act as a domain controller or public key infrastructure (PKI) server and provide core network services like Domain Name Serving (DNS), Dynamic Host Configuration Protocol (DHCP), and WINS,

The Standard Edition is aimed at the broadest range of applications, in particular file servicing, print serving, and low-demand application serving (such as Microsoft Exchange Server, SQL Server, or similar application-led tasks). It can also support basic terminal services, although its memory and processor limitations may make it less than ideal for larger terminal services roles. It's not capable of full clustering capabilities, but it does support network load balancing.

It should be clear that Standard Edition is ideal as an all-purpose platform for smaller environments, or as a server built into a group providing services in a larger network.

Technically, Standard Edition supports up to four CPUs in a Symmetric Multi-Processor (SMP) environment and up to 4GB of RAM. It can also address up to 4TB of disk space.

Enterprise Edition

The Enterprise Edition (EE) is intended for use in many of the same roles as Standard Edition, but it includes features designed to improve the reliability and scalability of these services. In particular, Enterprise Edition doubles the number of CPUs it can support to eight and the maximum RAM to 32GB. Enterprise Edition is also the first edition to support 64-bit processors.

Local Lingo

32-bit and 64-bit   Processors access memory and process instructions according to the width of the address that references the memory location. 32-bit processors can directly access up to 4GB of memory (tricks are used for values above this). A 64-bit processor can access a staggering 1.67 million terabytes of memory. 64-bit processors are not necessarily faster than their 32-bit counterparts, but the ability to address such large amounts of memory can increase the overall speed of an application by allowing more of the information to be directly available in memory.

Enterprise Edition supports Address Windows Extensions (AWE) that enable the operating system to reserve as little as 1GB for use by Windows, allowing the applications to use the remaining 3GB of the remaining memory. EE also allows memory to be added while the machine is running (hot-memory) on hardware systems that support it, and it allows non-uniform memory access (NUMA). Some systems use separate memory busses for separate processes; NUMA enables Windows to access these separate memory areas as one complete memory range (hence the support for 32GB of memory on 32-bit processor systems, 4GB for each of eight CPUs).

However, the primary improvements of this edition relate to additional functionality. Enterprise Edition supports clustering technology, allowing multiple servers to appear as one machine and automatically take over in the event of a failure. This works with clustered applications such as SQL Server Enterprise Edition and Exchange Server Enterprise Edition, as well as many applications and systems that do not directly include support for clustering technology.

Finally, EE extends the terminal services system with the Terminal Server Session Directory, which allows clients to reconnect to a terminal services system supported by a number of terminal services servers. For example, with eight terminal services servers, if one server fails, the Terminal Server Session Directory will allow clients to automatically reconnect to one of the remaining servers.

The Enterprise Edition is obviously all about maintaining the stability and reliability of your network services and should be used in situations where these parameters are most critical to your business needs.

Datacenter Edition

Datacenter is one of two editions of the operating system that are slightly different from the other versions. You cannot buy Datacenter Edition as a stand-alone product. Instead, it must be purchased as part of a combination of hardware and software from a supplier. The reason for this is that Datacenter Edition is sold only on hardware that has been specifically designed to work with the Datacenter Edition. Rules are much more strict about which hardware is supported, and specific solutions have to go through a huge range of tests. The aim is to provide you with a server that can remain up and running for 99.999 percent of the time—that's about 9 hours of unplanned downtime each year.

Travel Assistance

Downtime is classed as a problem that makes the machine unusable. It doesn't include the times when you take down the machine to perform some maintenance, install a patch, or change the hardware configuration.

The Datacenter program is 100 percent focused on reliability:

- All hardware included in a Datacenter server must meet rigid Microsoft standards and pass hundreds of compatibility and reliability tests, including everything from the processors and memory to the network cards, disk drives, and other components.
- All the device drivers much be certified and digitally signed by Microsoft. They must also have gone through similar testing procedures to the hardware—it can take months for a new piece of hardware to be certified for Datacenter Edition use.
- Customers cannot make unauthorized changes to the server hardware. All changes must pass the same suite of tests. Even when upgrading a four-CPU system to an eight-CPU system, you can only do so if the hardware has been certified in its eight-CPU configuration.

These rigid requirements, combined with the typical expense of a server that would make Datacenter Edition worthwhile to install, means that the Datacenter Edition is the least likely to be installed. It's possible you'll never ever come across a Datacenter Edition server in your entire career.

Web Edition

The Web Edition exists to fill a technological and price-related gap. The modern web server datacenter is not made up of single machines with a vast number of CPUs and memory. Instead, it's made up of stacks and stacks of smaller, one- or two-CPU processors with comparatively low amounts of RAM.

In this instance, using the Standard Edition would just be too expensive—in many cases more expensive than the hardware on which the OS is running. Some companies have instead switched to Linux and Apache, rather than Windows and IIS, to support their websites.

Microsoft has responded by producing the Web Edition. It provides enough of the operating system, IIS, and web application platform (ASP, ASP.NET) to allow it to serve websites and applications. It also includes the network load balancing, so that it can be used in a quasi-clustered environment.

However, it's also had a lot of technology removed, including Routing and Remote Access, terminal services, remote installation services, services for Macintosh, and Active Directory hosting. You can still connect to an Active Directory from Web Edition, but a Web Edition server cannot act as a domain controller.

Server Edition Comparison

To help you make decisions about which version you want to employ in your organization, we need to take a closer look at the specific differences, individual features, services, and abilities of each system. The basic requirements of each edition are listed in Table 1.1.

TABLE 1.1 Windows Server 2003 Requirements for Different Editions

Requirement/Edition	Standard	Enterprise	Datacenter	Web
CPU (32-bit)	133MHz	133MHz	400MHz	133MHz
CPU (64-bit)	N/A	733MHz	733MHz	N/A
Recommended CPU	P3 550MHz	P3 733MHz	P3 733MHz	P3 550MHz
RAM	128MB	128MB	512MB	128MB
Recommended RAM	256MB	256MB	1GB	256MB
Disk Space (32-bit)	1.5GB	1.5GB	1.5GB	1.5GB
Disk Space (64-bit)	N/A	2GB	2GB	N/A

Of course, the reality is that if you are installing Windows Server 2003, you'll probably also take the opportunity to convince management to buy you a new piece of hardware on which to install and run the new operating system, and it's getting increasingly difficult to find machines with processors running at less than 2GHz, let alone as slow as 550MHz. Memory and hard disk will be the issue here, but again, specifications of these parameters are also typically high, with most servers coming with 256MB and 40GB hard drives at a minimum. At the time of writing, both RAM and hard disk storage are cheap, with 256MB available for less than $100 and hard disks at an unprecedented 1GB/$ rate.

However, if you want to take advantage of Windows Server 2003 features and upgrade your existing hardware, you need to keep the figures in Table 1.1 in mind. I've successfully deployed Windows Server 2003 Standard Edition on a P3 700MHz machine. This operates as the domain controller, installation server, file server, and software update server for a relatively small network.

Exam Tip

Microsoft is likely to test you on the specifics of Table 1.1 so it's worth taking some time to remember the details. In particular, questions like "You have 10 Windows 2000 Servers that use Pentium III 600MHz processors. Which versions of Windows Server 2003 can you install on these machines?" may appear and then proceed to list the various editions to choose from.

When choosing a machine on which to install Windows Server 2003, you need to consider not only the current requirements, but also the future requirements and expandability. For example, if you know that you could support your company's e-mail facilities on 4-CPU server but expect to double your staff over the next two years, Standard Edition on a 4-way SMP box may be a limitation.

A full summary of the hardware requirements of the various editions of Windows Server 2003 is given in Table 1.2.

TABLE 1.2   Features and Hardware Limits for Different Editions

Feature/Edition	Standard	Enterprise	Datacenter	Web
Max RAM (32-bit)	4GB	32GB	64GB	2GB
Max RAM (64-bit)	N/A	32GB	512GB	N/A
Max CPUs (32-bit)	4	8	32	2

TABLE 1.2   Features and Hardware Limits for Different Editions *(continued)*

Feature/Edition	Standard	Enterprise	Datacenter	Web
Max CPUs (64-bit)	N/A	8	64	N/A
64-bit (Itanium) Support		X	X	
Hot memory		X	X	
Non-uniform memory access (NUMA)		X	X	

For more specific service-level features, you need to consult Table 1.3.

TABLE 1.3   Service Support Matrix for Different Editions

Service/Edition	Standard	Enterprise	Datacenter	Web
Directory Services				
Active Directory (Domain Controller)	X	X	X	
Active Directory (Member Server)	X	X	X	X
Identity Integration Server 2003 Support		X	X	
Security Services				
Internet Connection Firewall	X	X		
Public Key Infrastructure, Certificate Services, and Smart Cards	Partial	X	X	Partial
Terminal Services				
Remote Desktop for Administration	X	X	X	X
Terminal Server	X	X	X	
Terminal Server Session Directory		X	X	
Clustering Technology				
Network Load Balancing	X	X	X	X
Cluster Service		X	X	

| TABLE 1.3 | Service Support Matrix for Different Editions *(continued)* |

Service/Edition	Standard	Enterprise	Datacenter	Web
Communications and Networking Services				
Virtual Private Network (VPN) support	X	X	X	Partial
Internet Authorization Services (IAS)	X	X	X	
Network Bridge	X	X	X	
Internet Connection Sharing (ICS)	X	X		
IPv6	X	X	X	X
File and Print Services				
Distributed File System (DFS)	X	X	X	X
Encrypting File System (EFS)	X	X	X	X
Shadow Copy Restore	X	X	X	X
Removable and Remote Storage	X	X	X	
Fax service	X	X	X	
Services for Macintosh	X	X	X	
Management Services				
IntelliMirror	X	X	X	Partial
Group Policy Results	X	X	X	Partial
Windows Management Instrumentation (WMI) Command Line	X	X	X	X
Remote OS installation	X	X	X	X
Remote Installation Services (RIS)	X	X	X	
Windows System Resource Manager (WSRM)		X	X	

TABLE 1.3	Service Support Matrix for Different Editions *(continued)*			
Service/Edition	**Standard**	**Enterprise**	**Datacenter**	**Web**
.NET Application Services				
.NET Framework	X	X	X	X
Internet Information Services (IIS) 6	X	X	X	X
ASP.NET	X	X	X	X
Enterprise UDDI services	X	X	X	
Multimedia Services				
Windows Media Services	X	X	X	

Choosing the right edition or editions is therefore a case of matching your requirements to the list of available features. Within an enterprise environment, it's likely that you will use a combination of editions to build up your network infrastructure. For example, in a medium-sized network with 250 clients, you may use a number of Standard Edition solutions to provide basic domain controller, file, and printer server functionality.

In a larger network with 1000 machines, Enterprise Edition might be used to support an Exchange installation, with further Standard Editions to support the remaining file and print services. If you have an Internet connection and are supporting a number of websites, you might use Web Editions to support your web presence. In a vast enterprise class network, you might employ Enterprise Editions in a clustered environment for Terminal Services or Exchange and SQL Server.

The results of your choice should be a combination of the expected loading, the support for specific features—including CPU and memory support if you need a beefy machine to run a particular service—and the need for extended functionality such as clustering. In all other situations, Standard Edition is going to be adequate for most needs.

Identifying Minimum Configurations for Satisfying Security Requirements

Security is not just about making sure the sales department cannot see the files accounting is keeping on them. It's also about ensuring the security and stability of your network services and environment for your users. This means that not only do you need to take traditional security measures such as using passwords and considering file/folder security, but you also need to consider the stability of the system, its support for clustering technology, and its ability to withstand and, if necessary, recover from errors and problems that will affect your network.

With this in mind, you need to identify the minimum level of security required in your network, and you need to do it in such a way that it doesn't affect the running and operation of your network. For example, it's tempting to enforce the highest security for all your servers and services, but while this would be ultimately very secure, it would probably block or otherwise restrict the available options.

What you need is some sort of middle ground between no security at all and the maximum level of security. That mid-point will be the area where you get the best security while still supporting the services that you need to support. To find that mid-point, you need to create a basic level of security that can be applied to all your servers (and ultimately your clients) and then create security templates that can be used to secure specific server types and the services that they support.

We'll be covering the specifics of the process in this chapter, but you should know the five specific steps within the process:

- **Secure an initial installation** When you first create and install a new Windows Server 2003 computer, you need to secure the installation before you build onto that installation with additional security.
- **Create a secure baseline installation** The baseline installation is the core security settings that will be used across all your servers. With the baseline settings in place, you can specify additional settings for additional servers.
- **Design security for specific server roles** With the baseline in place, you can assign security settings for servers that provide file, print, IIS, and other services and tailor them accordingly.
- **Develop methods for updating systems** Keeping up to date with the latest patches should help keep your systems secure by plugging holes and faults in your OS. You need to apply these as carefully and efficiently as possible.
- **Test security** Once all the necessary systems are in place, you need to be able to test your security settings to make sure your systems are secure.

Objective 1.02   Plan a Secure Baseline Installation

You can plan the first two steps—securing an initial installation and planning a secure baseline installation—in one go. First, though, you must define the security policy that you are going to use on the servers and clients in your network.

Windows Server 2003 provides this functionality with security templates. The templates define specific security parameters that you can use to enforce basic security settings on new systems. The security templates are wide ranging, from configuring the basics of password policy through enforcing nightly backups and even network security settings.

In this section, we'll look first at how you can use templates to enforce the default security settings on new systems. Then we'll take a closer look at the specific client and server OS default security settings so that you know how to change these default parameters to match your own needs.

Travel Assistance

It's impossible to list all of the possible security settings and parameters that can be configured through the security template system. Although you shouldn't need it for the exam, you should be familiar with the various settings. Check the Windows Server 2003 site (www.Microsoft.com/windows2003) for more information.

Enforcing System Default Security Settings

There are a number of ways you can force a system to use and apply the default security settings. As it stands, Windows Server 2003 is already fairly secure during a standard installation. Most of the additional role-specific functionality, such as IIS, the DHCP service, and others, are not installed by default. Other simpler elements are also more secure. For example, the administrator password that you set during installation must adhere to the strictest settings (that is, it must be at least two nonalpha characters and at least six characters in length).

From a purely theoretical perspective, the easiest way to enforce the default security settings is to specify strict procedures to be used when installing the operating system, including

- Install from the original CD-ROM media or install from updated media that incorporates the latest service packs and security updates.
- Install only from verified installation files, either from a CD or network share. If using a network share, ensure that it can be accessed only by suitably trained and qualified staff.
- Configure only those roles and services that need to be supported by the server. Windows Server 2003 doesn't install most services by default. You can help maintain the security of the system by limiting those that are installed.
- Disable services that aren't needed, including those services that are installed by default that you do not need.
- Allow only trusted staff to install the system.

Not all of these suggested procedures can be followed, of course. In a distributed environment where servers may be installed across the company, it can sometimes be a nonadministrator or tech support specialist who performs the installation.

In this case, there are a number of alternative solutions:

- Use the scripting facilities of the Windows installer to automatically configure and control the server installation. All the user has to do is start or boot the server for the installation to take place. All the other elements are provided by the installation scripts.
- Use an isolated network for installation. Make the installation files available on a network share, and then provide secure access to this network share (read-only) to the user performing the installation.
- Create customized media that include the scripts and patches for automated installation.
- Use Remote Installation Services to control the elements that can be installed after the initial server software installation.
- Use disk imaging techniques to create an image of each type of server. Installation can then take place by simply applying the image to the server disk. The image can include all the necessary software, updates, and security settings.

One other tool that you can employ is the Group Policy system to apply security templates to the server. These are applied when the server joins an active directory domain—probably a required step for all server installations. Because the template is applied at a central level, it's impossible to override it. We'll be looking more closely at Group Policy and security templates in Objective 1.03, "Plan Security for Servers That Are Assigned Specific Roles."

Security Settings, Templates, and Default Security

Security settings can be applied across a network through the use of the Group Policy system and/or the security template system. The security templates are exactly that—a group of settings that specify basic security parameters. Windows Server 2003 comes with a number of default security templates designed for clients and servers, including specialized templates for specific server types and roles.

> ### Local Lingo
>
> **Group policies**   Settings that can be applied to computers in your network through the active directory system are group policies. The information is distributed to the clients automatically when the computer initially logs on to the domain, or it can be forced by using the gpupdate tool.

You can also create your own templates, either by using the supplied templates as a guide or creating brand new templates to suit your needs. These templates can be applied on an individual basis to machines with the secedit tool, or they can be applied through the Group Policy system. You can also set individual security parameters through the Group Policy system with or without a template as a base.

The security areas that can be configured through this system include

- **Account policies**   These are the computer security settings for accounts, including password policy (length, complexity, renewals), lockout policy, and Kerberos policy in domains on Windows 2000 and Windows Server 2003.
- **Local policies**   These allow you to configure who has local or network access to the computer and whether or how local events are audited, including security settings for audit policy, user rights assignment, and security options.

- **Event logs** These control security settings for the Application, Security, and System event logs. Event logs can be accessed using the Event Viewer.

- **Restricted groups** These allow membership control of restricted groups. Administrators are able to enforce security policy settings regarding sensitive groups, such as Administrators or Payroll.

- **System services** These control startup mode and security options (security descriptors) for system services such as DNS, DHCP, IIS, and others. You can use this to limit services on clients and servers even if the service has already been installed.

- **Registry** This is used to configure permissions for existing registry keys, including auditing information and the access permissions.

- **File system** This is used to configure security settings for file-system objects, including access control, audit, and ownership.

External Security

We once visited a company that was demonstrating the security of their systems. It was quite impressive. Users needed a smartcard to gain access to their computer, in addition to their login and password. Passwords were strict too, and rotated on a weekly basis, and their network used secure transmission. When we got to the server room, however, the door was propped open because the lock, an electronic one, had broken. It had been like this for months.

Despite all their security at the system level, just about anybody could walk into the server room and switch off, take down, or remove the servers.

This underpins a very basic principle: always start with the most basic security. In the case of your servers, that means making sure only authorized people can get to them. When it comes to the technical side of the security settings, the same basic rules apply: make sure the basics of the security system are in place and that the other security settings build on those basics.

Exam Tip

To be honest, Microsoft is unlikely to test you on this particular aspect of security, but we think it's an important concept to understand—technical security is only any good if the systems are also physically secure. It's a bit like your credit card security—having PIN numbers and a signature is all very well, but if somebody steals your card, you're in for trouble.

Default Templates

A number of default templates are included with Windows Server 2003. They serve two purposes. First, they enable you to apply default security settings for different systems. This can be useful in situations where you want to return a system or group back to the initial security settings applied when the OS was first installed. Second, they enable to apply specific security settings for different environments.

Travel Assistance

Templates are stored within the %SystemRoot%\Security\Templates directory as a series of .inf files. You should make sure that only administrators have access to this directory.

The list of templates and their effect on the various security parameters is shown in Table 1.4.

TABLE 1.4	Security Templates for Servers and Clients

Title	Template	Description
Basic Security	Basicwk.inf, Basicsv.inf, and Basicdc.inf	These are basic security templates, the contents of which match the default settings on Windows 2000 and Windows Server 2003 installations on NTFS partitions. The templates can be used to apply the settings to workstations (Basicwk.inf), member servers (Basicsv.inf), and domain controllers (Basicdc.inf).
Domain Controller	DC security.inf	When a server is promoted to a domain controller, this template is created and reflects the file, registry, and system service default security settings.

TABLE 1.4	Security Templates for Servers and Clients *(continued)*	
Title	**Template**	**Description**
Default Security	Setup security.inf	This is dynamically generated by the operating system when it is installed. It contains the default security settings, including file permissions for the operating system files, that are applied during the operating system installation. You should never apply this template through Group Policy as it will update all machines within the domain or OU with the default settings of the machine from which it was applied. For example, applying the template from a Windows Server 2003 machine across a Windows XP network would render the clients unusable.
Compatible	Compatws.inf	This contains the settings that will apply default permissions for workstations and servers for three specific user groups: Administrators, Power Users, and Users. Administrators are given the most power, Users the least. You should use this template when you want to secure your systems but also provide members of the Users group with the ability to run certified applications on the machine in question. This template should not be applied to domain controllers.

TABLE 1.4	Security Templates for Servers and Clients *(continued)*	

Title	Template	Description
Secure	Securews.inf and Securedc.inf	This templates applies increased security settings for the operating system in a manner that should not affect the way applications can be executed or how users interact with the system. In particular, it increases the security on Account Policy, auditing, and some registry elements. It also disables LAN Manager and NTLMv1 for authentication, which will limit the interoperability of operating systems; specifically, Windows NT 3.51, Windows 95, and Windows 98 should not have this applied.
Highly Secure	hisecws.inf and hisecdc.inf	A superset of the Secure templates, these apply additional levels of security and restrictions, particularly with respect to encryption and signing during authentication with servers and file shares. The result is a configuration that is only compatible with operating systems of Windows 2000 vintage or later. The Highly Secure configuration is provided for Windows 2000, Windows XP, or Windows Server 2003–based computers that operate in native (or pure) Windows 2000 or Windows Server 2003 environments only.
System Root Security	Rootsec.inf	Rootsec.inf specifies the root permissions; that is, it defines the default permissions for the root of the system drive. This template can be used to restore the root directory permissions if they are somehow modified.

TABLE 1.4	Security Templates for Servers and Clients *(continued)*	
Title	**Template**	**Description**
No Terminal Server User SID	Notssid.inf	The default file system and registry access control lists that are on servers grant permissions to a Terminal Server security identifier (SID). The Terminal Server SID is used only when Terminal Server is running in application compatibility mode. If Terminal Server is not being used, this template can be applied to remove the necessary Terminal Server SIDs from the file system and registry locations.

Objective 1.03

Plan Security for Servers That Are Assigned Specific Roles

When setting security parameters, you must have a method for applying them to your systems. You can use secedit on a machine-by-machine basis, but this is obviously quite a larger process if you have to apply the changes to a number of machines.

The easiest way to achieve the same results is to use group policies. Group Policy is a configuration system that is integrated and required with Active Directory and allows you to set specific parameters on all of the computers and/or users to whom it was assigned. Group policy can be applied at any or all of these levels, so you can define a domain-wide policy for basic settings and additional security settings for specific groups, such as domain controllers, member servers, and clients (Windows 2000 or later only).

The actual security settings either can be defined directly within Group Policy, or you can use one of the many security templates that we've already discussed. You can also create your own security templates to apply settings to your own groups of servers.

Taken together, you can use this system to apply security settings to specific server roles. Server roles actually have new meaning in Windows Server 2003: specific services are configured by enabling specific roles on each machine. Applying security to these roles is just a matter of creating a suitable template and applying that template at the right organizational level within the Group Policy system so that it is applied to the servers in question.

In this section, we're going to look at two areas: the effects of the Group Policy system and how it can be used, and how you can create your own specialized security templates for your server roles and specifications of your network.

Deploying Security Configurations

Now that you know what security settings to build and apply to your servers, we need to look at how you can apply those settings. In a well-managed network, you will almost certainly be employing Active Directory to provide authentication systems for your network.

Aside from the obvious finger-saving properties of only needing one password to access the network, Active Directory also provides a number of other facilities, including centralized information on the structure, design, and content of your network. It stores this structure and member information, so wouldn't it be nice to be able to configure settings across all of the computers that are, for example, a member of the web server group?

That's what Group Policy does. It creates a structure of settings for your computer that can be applied to groups of machines. Group Policy assigns these settings according to the members of a specific part of the Active Directory structure, such as an organizational unit (OU), domain, or subdomain. By default, these policies are inherited and cumulative across the network structure.

So, if you apply password security settings to an entire domain, all the computers within that domain will inherit those settings. If you apply the same policy only to members of the Sales OU, then only that OU's members will have the policy applied. Group Policy can be applied either on a computer or a user basis. This enables you to create a user-led policy that will be applied to the machine when a user logs in, a computer-led policy that applies to all the machines in a group irrespective of who logs in, or a combination of the two.

A group policy is made up of a number of Group Policy Objects (GPOs), and each GPO is a suite of settings applied to a computer or user. Multiple policies may be applied to the same user or computer at each level, except the local policy (which is only controlled by the local machine). There are a number of policies, and they are processed into the final group policy in the following order:

1. **Local policy**   Each computer has exactly one GPO that is stored locally and shared by all users of that computer for both computer and user Group Policy processing. The local GPO is stored on each system in the %SystemRoot%\System32\GroupPolicy directory.

2. **Site policy**   Any GPOs that have been linked to the site that the computer belongs to are processed next.

3. **Domain policy** Domain-wide policies are processed in the order specified by the administrator. The order is important because individual GPOs may alter previous settings.

4. **Organizational unit policy** These are the GPOs that apply at an OU level.

Travel Assistance

Additional information on Group Policy can be found on the Microsoft website at www.Microsoft.com/gp.

Creating Custom Security Templates

To enable you to apply security settings to specific server roles, you need to be able to create different templates that specify the security settings for specific groups of servers, according to their role and purpose within the organization.

To do this, you can create security templates or modify one of the existing templates to create a template specific to a server role. These templates can then be applied to the servers by importing the template into the Group Policy Objects that you create, which in turn will propagate the security settings to the servers.

Security Template Format

Security templates are text-based files. You can create templates either manually by creating a text file with Notepad, or, and this is the best method, using the Security Templates MMC snap-in.

Security Template Sections in the text file and the corresponding Group Policy area are listed in Table 1.5.

Account Security

There are some additional considerations you need to give to the different accounts that are configured in all client and server systems, such as the Local System account and the built-in user accounts. Some can be quite dangerous—the local Administrator built-in account, for example, has all the rights on the local machine (same as a domain administrator), including the ability to create local accounts and detach itself from the domain.

The local Administrator account cannot be deleted, but you can change its name, making it more difficult for a user to guess the account and break into it. You should also change the password of the local Administrator to something

TABLE 1.5	Group Policy Areas and Template Sections	
Policy Section	**Template Section**	**Description**
Account Policy	[System Access]	Sets password length, age, and complexity configured
Audit Policy	[System Log]	Sets lockout duration, threshold, and reset counter configured
	[Security Log]	Configures ticket lifetimes
	[Application Log]	Enables/disables recording of specific events
User Rights	[Privilege Rights]	Defines rights such as log on locally, access from network
Security Options	[Registry Values]	Modifies specific security-related registry values
Event Log	[Event Audit]	Enables success and failure monitoring
Restricted Groups	[Group Membership]	Administrators control who belongs to a specific group
System Services	[Service General Setting]	Controls startup mode for each service
Registry	[Registry Keys]	Configures permissions on registry keys
File System	[File Security]	Configures permissions on folders, subfolders and files

suitably complex,—definitely different from the domain administrator passwords. It's probably a good idea to also use different passwords on every server for the local Administrator accounts, or at the very minimum use different passwords for domain controllers and member servers.

Also ensure that the local administrator is not a member of the Domain Admins group. All these changes can be made through Group Policy, but it's a much better idea to do this on a local, individual basis so that you can adjust the information based on each server.

The Guest account, also created by default, is automatically disabled on both member servers and domain controllers, so you shouldn't need to give it any further thought. If it's been enabled, you should disable it because it presents a security risk.

Finally, consider the impact of service accounts. Your server's services are executed within the security context of its assigned service account. By default, most services use the Local System account, which has relatively low security clearance and abilities. Occasionally, services need to be installed with alternative account security—make sure you choose the account carefully and avoid using the local administrator or any domain accounts for services.

Configure Security for Servers That Are Assigned Specific Roles

Objective 1.04

Now that you know how you can apply security settings and policies to your servers and clients, you need to know how to apply them to individual servers. How do you choose what security settings to set for your web server, domain controller, or file server?

You can get some ideas and summary information by looking at the specific role of the server and then developing and applying a suitable policy. Before you apply these individual policies, however, you should install one of the two baseline policies:

- **Domain Controllers Baseline Policy (BaselineDC.inf)**   Required to set the baseline security policy for domain controllers.
- **Member Server Baseline Policy (Baseline.inf)**   Required to set the baseline security policy for member servers of a domain.

To apply further security settings, you need to understand the needs and potential problems with specific server roles.

Evaluating Security for Individual Roles

One of the new features of Windows Server 2003 is that many of the systems that were previously installed and enabled by default in Windows 2000 are not installed or configured in Windows Server 2003. This increases security by forcing administrators to specifically enable the functionality they need.

To enable different functionalities, you must configure Windows Server 2003 with one or more server roles. This installs and enables specific elements of functionality according to the role. Any server can have more than one role—it's a bit like giving a computer a number of personalities.

For example, IIS, a frequent source of security breaches and problems, is not installed by default into the Windows Server 2003 operating system; it must be installed after you install Windows Server 2003.

The roles are as follows:

- **File server**   Allows a server to share files and data across a network and sets up network shares.

- **Print server**   Enables you to share printers and use the printer spool mechanisms to provide centralized management of printers and print jobs.

- **Application server**   Installs Internet Information Services (IIS) 6 and related technologies such as COM+ and ASP.NET. Provides the basic functionality required to support websites and web applications, including XML and web services.

- **Mail server**   Enables the Simple Mail Transfer Protocol (SMTP) and Post Office Protocol (POP3) protocols to support basic e-mail distribution. POP3 and SMP provide a simple, Internet-compatible e-mail service that can be used for low volume e-mail-only communication within an organization.

- **Terminal services**   Enables the terminal services system to allow remote users to run applications on a central server but display the virtual desktop and interface on a local machine.

- **Remote Access/VPN server**   Enables the routing and remote access system to allow a server to route network packets (including to create a VPN) and allows clients to dial in to a server.

- **Domain controller**   Installs the Active Directory service as a server, making the machine responsible for storing and distributing Active Directory information and the authorization of user account information.

- **DNS server**   Enables the Domain Name Service for translating friendly network names into IP addresses and vice versa.

- **DHCP server**   Installs the Dynamic Host Configuration Protocol (DHCP) service that can distribute IP addresses to clients dynamically, eliminating the need to set TCP/IP parameters manually.

- **Streaming media server**   Allows you to manage and deliver Windows Media content to clients, including streaming video and audio over the Internet or an intranet.

- **WINS server**   Installs the Windows Internet Name Service (WINS), which maps IP addresses to NetBIOS computer names and vice versa.

The security requirements of your server will depend entirely on the roles configured. IIS provides support for providing websites to clients, typically over the Internet. Obviously, this means that its security requirements are more extensive than those for a DNS or DHCP server, which is accessible only to your internal LAN.

For security purposes, you need to group the service-specific server roles as defined within Windows Server 2003 into more generic roles. You can then create a security policy based on these generic roles that will apply to a server that has one of the service-specific roles. For example, DNS, DHCP, and WINS are all examples of a network infrastructure role that has different security requirements from a server running IIS.

Table 1.6 lists the various service-oriented roles and matches them to one of the member server roles. Domain controllers obviously have special needs and cannot be pigeonholed into one of the group role definitions, so you wont find it in the table. Also note that technically IIS is an application server role, but it also has special needs as a primarily public rather than private service.

Travel Assistance

Microsoft always advises that a domain controller should be kept separate from any type of application or IIS server because it becomes difficult to secure both the application and domain controller elements.

Securing Server Roles

Now that you know how service roles are allotted into their different roles, you can apply different security settings and facilities to them. We cover the specific issues of each role group in the next sections.

TABLE 1.6	Service Roles and Their Security Group Role Affiliations			
Service Role/ Server Role	**Application Server**	**File and Print Server**	**Infrastructure Server**	**IIS Server**
File server		X		
Print server		X		
Application server	X			X

TABLE 1.6	Service Roles and Their Security Group Role Affiliations (continued)			
Service Role/ Server Role	Application Server	File and Print Server	Infrastructure Server	IIS Server
Mail server	X			
Terminal services	X			
Remote Access/VPN Server			X	
DNS server			X	
DHCP server			X	
Streaming media server	X			
WINS server			X	

Application Server Roles

Application servers are used to provide application-led services such as SQL Server and Exchange. Both these systems, and many of the others that will also be installed on an application server, have their own security systems and requirements.

This makes it difficult to suggest any specific security requirements for servers supporting this service without also covering the specifics of the application server security. Using the baseline security policy for member servers provides the best basis on which to work.

IIS Server Role

IIS is an application and therefore should be part of the application server role, but it has special needs. IIS can be used for both internal (intranet) and external (Internet) application serving. Therefore, a server supporting IIS needs to protect itself from the client computers that can connect to them.

Windows Server 2003 installs IIS in a highly secure locked mode that should make it impervious from many of the most basic attacks. However, as you enable more features, particularly Web Distributed Authoring and Versioning (WebDAV) and the Active Server Pages (ASP and ASP.NET) components, you start to weaken the security by opening up more potential for break-ins and security breaches.

The baseline security policy for member servers should be sufficient for the main server components, but you will also want to use the IIS Lockdown tool and the Microsoft Baseline Security Analyzer to check the specific security of the IIS system and websites.

Note that there is also a Group Policy setting that can be used to disable the ability to install IIS. You can use this group policy on roles other than the IIS Server role to prevent these servers from enabling IIS. It does not affect existing installations, though, so if you have a specific server that needs IIS functionality but is part of another server role group, install IIS first, then apply the group policy to the OU for the group.

File and Printer Server Roles

File and print services provide a way of directly accessing and updating files on your server. This means that it can be difficult to secure servers supporting these roles without also limiting or disabling legitimate access to your server. A File and Print Server group policy is available that will secure your server without affecting services. The group policy also performs the following actions:

- Enables the Spooler service, which is used for printing.
- Disables the security policy setting Digitally Sign Client Communication (Always). If this is not disabled, clients will be able to print but not view the print queue. When attempting to view the print queue, they will receive the message, "Unable to connect. Access denied."

The file server element is the most difficult to secure effectively. You can disable the protocols that support the file service, Server Message Block (SMB) and Common Internet File System (CIFS) high-security environments, but this will effectively disable the service, even for legitimate users.

Irrespective of the Group Policy settings, you should also consider the effects of securing individual files and folders within the shared directories and ensuring that the various folders and directories are correctly configured with permissions and ownership.

Infrastructure Server Roles

Infrastructure servers have relatively simple security requirements. The main services that they provide are not particularly well known for their security exploits. They also do not normally compromise security through being enabled. In general, the baseline security template should be more than adequate.

Creating an Active Directory Structure and Deploying the Security Configuration

Apart from the overall makeup of your Active Directory structure, such as your choices for organizational and geographical elements within the directory, you need to be able to apply the various settings and policies at a server role level. This means creating a structure that enables you to apply the settings according to the different group roles that you defined in the previous section.

In addition, you need to consider subdivision of the roles and to differentiate between public and private IIS roles, specific application server implementations, and other subdivisions in the other roles, such as the sample shown in Figure 1.1.

 # Plan a Security Update Infrastructure

They used to have these adverts for car batteries that extolled the virtues of this new make of battery that you "could fit and forget," the implication being that you'd never ever need to worry about it again. Well, some people treat

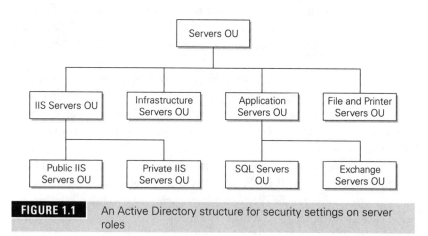

FIGURE 1.1   An Active Directory structure for security settings on server roles

their security in the same way. They set up their group policies, install their firewalls, and configure all their servers with the various security templates and think they are covered for every eventuality.

The truth, of course, is very different. Those car batteries weren't fit and forget, but they did last long enough that most people probably replaced their car before they had to think about the battery again. Your security's time lag isn't ten years like the battery, however. You really shouldn't go more than ten minutes without considering your system's security—at every point, each configuration change, new user, application, or system, the security should be right there at the top of the page of things to do.

The problem with computers is that they change. You don't set up a computer and hope that nobody uses it. More to the point, you don't ever believe that the computer is 100 percent guaranteed secure in the first place, no matter what it said on the box. You need to constantly review your security needs as well as your security settings and the effects of any newly discovered chinks in the security armor.

Doing this by hand would take ages, especially if you factor in all of your desktop and server machines. Microsoft provides two tools that will make your life significantly easier: Microsoft Baseline Security Analyzer and Windows Update. These deserve closer attention, so we'll look at the specific of these two below.

Microsoft Baseline Security Analyzer

Keeping your systems secure and safe from attack, malicious access, and unscrupulous individuals as well as protecting the files in the accounts department from those troublemakers in sales can be a full time job. In fact, in large companies it's fairly common to have someone whose sole responsibility is the security of your systems.

There are ways you can make your life easier when it comes to the security of your systems, including group policies and many of the simpler, nontechnological solutions covered in the "External Security" section of the this chapter. Sometimes, however, you want to be able to run a quick test and make sure that everything is safe enough to use.

Microsoft provides a tool for exactly this purpose, called the Microsoft Baseline Security Analyzer (MBSA). The MBSA checks one or more machines and the security settings for the core operating system and a number of other systems, such as IIS and SQL Server. You can use it on clients (Windows XP only) and servers (Windows NT 4, Windows 2000, and Window Server 2003). In all cases, its purpose is to identify misconfiguration errors that led to a security compromise.

Travel Assistance

All Microsoft downloads, including MBSA, can be obtained through the main Microsoft downloads page at www.Microsoft.com/downloads.

The specific areas that MBSA checks are

- **Windows operating system** Including guest account status, file system types, file shares, administrator group privileges, members, and many others.

- **Internet Information Server** Including virtual server directory configurations, sample applications (which should be removed in most instances), and general security settings on areas like the remote administration interface. It also checks if the IIS Lockdown tool has been used to check and secure the IIS installation.

Travel Advisory

The IIS Lockdown tool checks that default website settings and features have been switched off in versions of IIS prior to 5.1. It's not required for IIS 6, part of Windows Server 2003, because all of these features arrive already disabled.

- **Microsoft SQL Server (SQL Server 7 and 2000 only)** Including authentication mode, system administration account password status, and service account memberships.

- **Desktop application checks** Including checking IIS 5.01 and later security zone settings for each local user account and macro settings for Office 2000 and XP.

- **Security updates** Including checking the installed updates on each machine against the list either on the Windows Update site or with your local Software Update Services (SUS) server, if you have one installed. This checks for patches and updates against the core OS (for the platforms supported), Internet Explorer, Windows Media Player, IIS, SQL Server, and Microsoft Exchange.

MBSA can be used either through a GUI interface or a command-line interface, and you can run full blown MBSA scans or security update scans through the HFNetChk system. You can also scan a single machine or a group of machines, either by their Active Directory domain or by IP address range. It doesn't matter whether you are using a client OS or a server to run and originate the tests—the only requirement is that you must have Administrator authority for each machine that you want to test.

Through the GUI, once the tool has been used to test one or more machines, you'll get a list of the tests that were executed and an idea of the seriousness of each problem on a machine-by-machine basis. You can see a sample of the output, executed on a Windows XP machine, in Figure 1.2.

If you click the Result Details link, you'll be taken to web pages that give more detailed information, such as the list of missing updates or settings and information that were found to be suspect. Click the How To Correct This link to get information on how to fix the problem or where to download the patches in question.

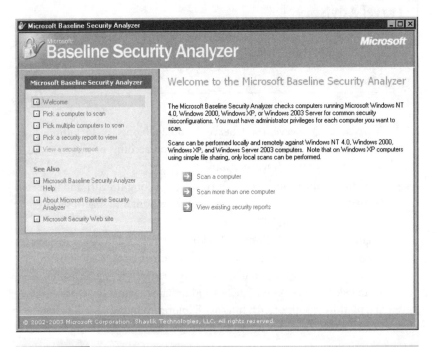

FIGURE 1.2   Microsoft Baseline Security Analyzer in action

Exam Tip

Make sure you know how to use MBSA and what elements it does and doesn't check before you go into the exam. You can get a full idea of the individual elements tested through the MBSA documentation page at http://www.microsoft.com/technet/treeview/default.asp?url=/technet/security/tools/tools/mbsawp.asp.

You should use MBSA regularly on your network to check for potential problems. Theoretically, there is no limit to the number of machines that you can check at any one time, but the checks do take some time to resolve. You should assume that the checks will take about 2 minutes per client and 5 minutes per server, although it could easily increase to 20–30 minutes on a web server with a large number of configured websites. That means you could check about ten servers and 120 machines in one 8-hour period.

Using MBSA once a month is not a bad idea, but you might want to use it more frequently on your servers or critical desktop machines. Remember that if you are using Automatic Updates, especially in combination with SUS, the most important aspect—security updates—will have already been covered. That's what we're going to be looking at next.

Patches and Updates

Security is not just about restricting users, setting file permissions, and employing network level tools like Active Directory. It's also about keeping your machine up to date with the latest patches and updates. With the best will in the world, it would be impossible for Microsoft to create such a complex and advanced system as Windows Server 2003 without there being a few problems.

These problems take a number of forms, but they basically fall into two categories: stability bugs and security bugs. Stability bugs affect the stability of your server that may, in turn, affect the stability and security of your network. For example, a stability bug could cause your server to fall over when an application tries to allocate itself a specific amount of memory, even if your server is technically able honor the request.

Security bugs are potentially more serious. Recent years have seen an increase in publicity about a number of worms and viruses to hit the Internet and be spread through Windows servers, particularly IIS. Most of these used an exploit in the operating system (particularly IIS) that allowed them to propagate across thousands of computers through the Internet in a relatively short space of time.

Local Lingo

Worms and viruses   A worm is a program that propagates itself over a network, while a virus is one that may propagate itself through a number of means, including a network, by copying itself to removable disks or spreading itself through e-mails. Not all worms and viruses are malicious or cause any serious damage, but even the relatively benign versions can be problematic.

Local Lingo

Exploit   Exploits are ways of attacking or bypassing the security of an operating system or application through a previously unknown or undocumented part of the system. The problem with exploits is that traditional security mechanisms, such as firewalls, frequently can't protect you because the exploit uses an otherwise legitimate method to contact your server.

The way to protect yourself from these, or recover from them if they have already happened to you, is to keep your systems up to date with the latest patches and security fixes.

Patch/Update Installation

Microsoft makes security and critical (stability) updates available on their website (www.Microsoft.com/downloads), which you can download and install as necessary. To keep up with the updates and patches though, you need to regularly check the site for updates. For a more automated solution, use the Windows Update or Automatic Update service. Alternative, more extensive sites and configuration can make use of a localized Software Update Service.

Whichever solution you choose, you should always test the patches and updates that are supplied. This is not because they may cause more problems than they solve (although this has happened) but because it may upset some part of your system or configuration in a way that neither you nor Microsoft can predict.

To give a good example, one of our clients used an undocumented feature (read that as "bug"—it's all about classification), which should have been removed, to provide a particular suite of functionality to their clients. Everything was working fine until a security patched "fixed" (read that as "eliminated") the feature and thereby rendered their software and solution unworkable. The client didn't realize this until the users complained that things had stopped working, and it took a little while to work out what had actually happened.

If they had tested the patch before blindly applying it to all of their servers, they would have been able to spot the problem and prevent the patch from being applied. This would have given them the necessary time to redevelop their application using the correct systems rather than a backdoor approach.

The same rules and restrictions should apply to your network—however much you do or don't trust a software supplier, you must test what they provide to you before blindly applying it to all your systems.

Windows Update

Windows Update was a feature of Windows 98 that has since been extended and expanded upon in more recent editions of Windows operating systems. Essentially, Windows Update is a website that enables you to check, select, download, and install specific updates to your machine.

To use it, visit the Windows Update site, which uses an ActiveX application to determine what is installed on your machine and what is available from Microsoft, thereby building a list of potential patches—as shown in Figure 1.3.

The problem with Windows Update is that it requires manual intervention to operate. Although this means you can exercise a level of control over which patches are installed, the down side is that as the number of servers and clients increases in your organization, it becomes more and more time consuming to use Windows Update to keep your systems up to date.

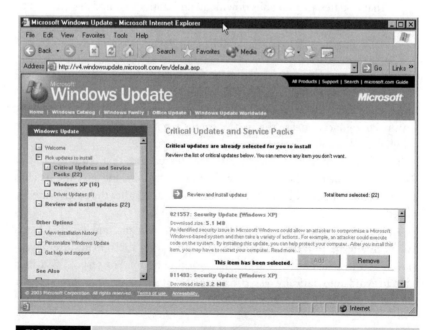

FIGURE 1.3   Using Windows Update

Automatic Updates

Automatic Update is a new feature built directly into Windows Server 2003 and Windows XP. Windows 2000 gained the ability to interface to the Automatic Update system with Service Pack 3, and it's also available as an installable patch on all previous editions of Windows down to Windows 95.

The Automatic Update system makes use of Windows Update technology to enable critical updates and security patches to be automatically downloaded to your machine. In its basic format, it doesn't automatically install them, but it notifies you that they are ready to be installed.

Travel Assistance

Automatic Update is disabled by default, but it's automatically enabled into the notification system after you have installed the OS and rebooted the machine once.

You can change this behavior by using the Automatic Updates control panel for pre-Windows XP systems or the System Control Panel for Windows XP and Windows Server 2003 machines. The configurable properties are

- How to download/install changes. There are three options: just notify that updates are available, download and notify that updates are read to install, or download and install the patches automatically.
- Download/check frequency and time of day.

You can either change these parameters manually on each machine (not recommended for those with full-time jobs), or you can use Group Policy to set these parameters throughout specific machines and organization units. The Group Policy location for this is Computer Configuration | Administrative Templates | Windows Components | Windows Update.

Through Group Policy you can also set how patches that require a restart should be handled : either automatically reboot the machine after the patches are installed, or notify the user that a restart is required after the patches are installed.

Which option you choose should depend on the machine and its role. Clients can normally be restarted automatically—providing the updates are downloaded and installed outside of normal working hours. For servers, you may want to avoid automatically restarting servers that are required to support your infrastructure. Mail servers (particularly those running Microsoft Exchange

Server), web servers, and domain controllers should be probably not be automatically rebooted.

Microsoft Software Update Services

The problem with Windows Update is that the system is entirely client driven. To select and install updates requires human intervention to visit the initial site, select the packages, and download the various components. Automatic Updates solve this by automating the download and installation of the vital updates that will keep your servers and clients stable.

In a relatively small network this is not an issue, but in a larger network with hundreds or thousands of servers and clients, the updating process can have a significant effect on your Internet connectivity and the overall stability of the network. The Automatic Update system also eliminates an element of control—the system downloads all updates that Microsoft has released, without giving you the opportunity to test the effects or even approve the installation unless you resort back to a human-driven interface. Again, this is time consuming and something that should be avoided. What, then, is the solution?

Software Update Services (SUS) enables you to create one or more servers within a network that download the critical and security updates. Your other servers and clients can then be configured (through Group Policy) to use your local server as their source for the updates. This means that updates are downloaded once and then distributed through to the rest of your network using your LAN, rather than tying up the Internet connection with multiple downloads of the same update.

Travel Advisory

SUS handles only the critical and security updates. Additional updates and software releases that are not deemed to present a potential stability or security risk are not included. You'll need to use other methods to distribute these updates to your clients and servers.

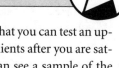

SUS also allows you to approve individual updates so that you can test an update and approve it for distribution to your servers and clients after you are satisfied that it will not affect your existing systems. You can see a sample of the approval window in Figure 1.4.

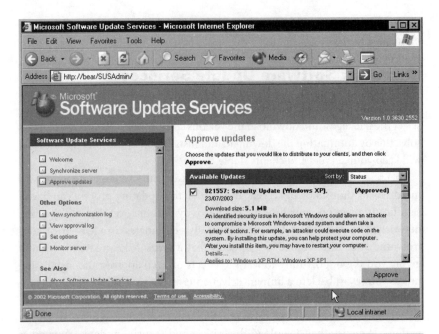

FIGURE 1.4 Approving updates through Software Update Services

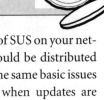

Travel Assistance

You can get more information on Microsoft Software Update Services at http://www.microsoft.com/windows2000/windowsupdate/sus/default.asp.

If you use SUS, however, you need to consider the impact of SUS on your network and your network design, as well as how updates should be distributed across your network. Taking the first issue in hand, SUS has the same basic issues as Automatic Updates—that means you need to choose when updates are downloaded and installed and whether machines automatically reboot without human intervention after the updates have been controlled.

Unlike the user-controlled automatic update system, the group policy that controls automatic updates also enables you to specify the name of the machine from which updates are downloaded. Because Group Policy is based on the organization structure of your Active Directory installation, you can specify different servers for different OUs. This leads to a number of network-oriented benefits of the SUS system.

The effect of SUS on your network depends entirely on the size and design of the network. It's tempting to install one server to provide SUS for the rest of your network, but in a large network this can create huge amounts of traffic and bottlenecks that will ultimately affect the performance of your network and your user's perception of the effectiveness of the IT department.

> ### Travel Advisory
>
> Our theory about system administration and users is that your users' perception of the system administrator and the IT department have more of an effect than hard data. For example, if your users complain about slow network speeds, you will be perceived as doing a bad job, even if you know that the network is running at 100 percent efficiency. Remember this when you prioritize jobs and plan your network—I guarantee it will make a difference!

You can do this through SUS because SUS appears to outside clients to be the same as the Automatic Update portion of Windows Update. If it didn't, clients wouldn't be able to use SUS just as readily as they use Microsoft's servers for Automatic Updates. The advantage of this design is that you can stack SUS servers within a network environment, reproducing the effect of caching the updates from the Internet, which will reduce the load on the network.

For example, Figure 1.5 shows a distributed SUS network using localized SUS servers for each department. This method reduces the potential load of 500 clients from each department (a total of over 1500 machines) from requesting updates from a single server, which would almost certainly saturate the network and have a significant effect on the performance of the server itself.

The secondary benefit of a structure layout is that the approvals system also works through the structure. If you have one server, called Bear, contacting Microsoft for updates, and all the other servers are contacting Bear for their updates, you can still manage which updates are approved for your network by using the approvals system on Bear. The SUS servers that contact Bear will only download updates that have been approved on Bear. The updates will also need to be approved on these servers, but this is a minor task once the main download and approval has taken place.

This last feature also enables you to control the way updates are distributed to different collections of machines. In Figure 1.6, for example, there's one central SUS server and two SUS servers downstream, one for clients and one for the web servers.

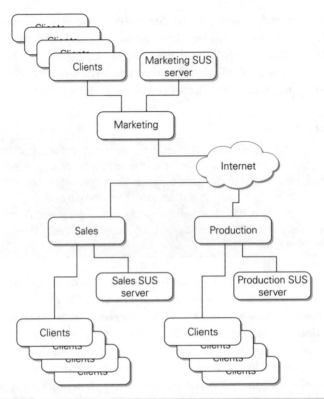

FIGURE 1.5 Localized SUS servers in a larger organization

By approving updates on the central server, the two servers downstream receive all the updates. However, updates to the web servers and updates to the clients can be independently controlled by approving individual updates on each of the downstream servers. This allows you, for example, to install patches for known exploits on the web servers immediately, as these are public facing, while waiting until further tests have been completed before approving the same update for your clients.

To summarize, when planning for using SUS you need to consider all of the issues pertaining to automatic updates:

- Your network size
- Your network layout
- Your update and patching policy on a departmental and/or role basis

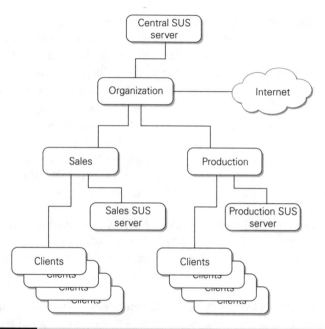

✔**Objective 1.01: Evaluate and Select the Operating System to Install on Computers in an Enterprise**   There are effectively four new versions of Windows Server 2003: Standard Edition, Enterprise Edition, Datacenter Edition, and Web Edition. You should be able to identify the differences between the versions and pick the one with the appropriate features and capabilities according to your needs.

✔**Objective 1.02: Plan a Secure Baseline Installation**   Before computers are deployed in the organization, a baseline security configuration for computers needs to be defined. A baseline can be implemented either during or after the initial installation of the operating system, applying security templates to computers that have similar security requirements. The default Security Templates can be used, or they can be a starting point for modifying a template specific to the environment.

✓**Objective 1.03: Plan Security for Servers That Are Assigned Specific Roles**   The services and applications that are installed on a computer depend on the role that was selected when the Windows Server 2003 was installed. Computers use different threat models dependent on their defined role. Designing security for computers with specific roles requires detailed knowledge and experience with the services or applications that run on the computers. The goal of security policies is to define procedures for configuring and managing security in the network environment. Group Policy can help implement the security policy for all workstations and servers in the Active Directory domains. Group Policy used with the OU structure can be used to define specific security settings for certain server roles.

✓**Objective 1.04: Configure Security for Servers That Are Assigned Specific Roles**   Once baseline policies have been installed, the servers will be significantly more secure. From this state, more specific settings may need to be enabled, adding additional security to the baseline policy.

✓**Object 1.05: Plan a Security Update Infrastructure**   Updating your machines with the latest patches and updates is at least as important as defining the original, as it ensures that your system is kept up to date. There are a number of tools that can help you in this task. The Microsoft Baseline Security Analyzer (MBSA) can identify outstanding patches that need to be applied to different systems. Windows Update can be configured on individual machines to automatically update a system with the latest patches and updates. If you want to centralize this service, either to reduce your Internet load or place a central point of control, you can use Software Update Services to download and distribute updates to your clients.

REVIEW QUESTIONS

1. You are the network administrator for a business that has 100 employees. You are responsible for implementing file and print services using Windows Server 2003. You want to implement a cost-effective solution with the possibility of growth, such as shared Internet connectivity. What version should you use?

   A. Windows Server 2003, Standard Edition

   B. Windows Server 2003, Enterprise Edition

   C. Windows Server 2003, Datacenter Edition

   D. Windows Server 2003, Web Edition

2. You are the network administrator for a healthcare facility. You are responsible for installing a server to run a database using Windows Server 2003. This is a very important database that needs to be as reliable and stable as possible. Your facility has a variety of hardware and software, and you don't want to get locked into a proprietary solution. What edition of Windows Server 2003 should you choose?

   A. Windows Server 2003, Standard Edition

   B. Windows Server 2003, Enterprise Edition

   C. Windows Server 2003, Datacenter Edition

   D. Windows Server 2003, Web Edition

3. You are designing a plan to create a secure baseline for your network. What is the first step for creating a secure baseline?

   A. Create security policy

   B. Create custom security templates

   C. Test security templates

   D. Deploy security templates

4. You are the network administrator for a magazine company that has 300 employees. You are responsible for the implementation of a secure DNS server. You have taken the steps for a secure installation and are using Group Policy to secure your servers. What type of server role template would you apply to the DNS server to ensure the appropriate Group Policy will be applied?

   A. Domain Controller

   B. Application Servers

   C. File and Print Servers

   D. IIS Servers

   E. Infrastructure Servers

5. You are the network administrator for a magazine company that has 300 employees. You are responsible for the implementation of securing domain accounts. To what location in the Active Directory structure does this group policy need to be imported to apply to all Domain Accounts?

   A. Site

   B. Domain

   C. Domain controller OU

   D. Member server OU

   E. User OU

6. You are the network administrator for a magazine company that has 300 employees. You have created a member server baseline security template that you want to apply specifically to the member servers in your Active Directory structure. What is the next step?

    A. Use secedit to import the policy to the Primary Domain Controller.

    B. Use secedit to import the policy to the primary member server.

    C. Import the template to the Group Policy Object at the Domain.

    D. Import the template to the Group Policy Object at the Member Servers OU.

    E. Import the template to the Group Policy Object at the Domain Controllers OU.

7. You are the network administrator for a magazine company that has 300 employees. You are tasked with the implementation of a Member Server Security Baseline. A security policy for the domain controllers has already been implemented. What would be the best location in the Active Directory structure for this Group Policy to be imported into to apply to member servers?

    A. Site

    B. Domain

    C. Domain controller OU

    D. Member server OU

    E. User OU

REVIEW ANSWERS

1. **A**   It's designed for small organizations and departments and provides file and print services and secure Internet connectivity.

2. **B**   Customers seeking higher levels of availability should choose Enterprise or Datacenter Editions, but because the Datacenter Edition offers a proprietary solution, the Enterprise Edition should be selected.

3. **A**   This policy contains all business and technical requirements for the computer, operating system, and applications.

4. **E**   Designed to increase security of servers acting as DNS, DHCP, and WINS servers.

5. **B**   This level is to address the common security requirements such as account policies and audit policies that must be enforced on all servers. Password and account policies will only affect domain accounts if the policies are set at the domain level.

6. **D**   After creating the template, it needs to be imported into a Group Policy Object using Active Directory Users and Computers.

7. **D**   Having all member servers in OUs by server roles is a good way to organize servers by function. If all member servers are contained in OUs under the Members Servers OU, that OU is the logical choice for placing this group policy.

Planning and
Implementing
TCP/IP

ETA	NEWBIE	SOME EXPERIENCE	EXPERT
	6 hours	4 hours	2 hours

"I am not a number, I am a free man!" is the famous cry of the Prisoner from the popular 1960s TV series. However, the reality in the networking world (and indeed the world in general) is that you *are* a number. Why? Because it's the easiest way to identify you, or your machine, in a short and relatively easy-to-store-and-exchange way. Think about the length of your address for a second: it probably takes up two or three lines at least, more if you want an international address. Now think about how you might refer to your machine within your address—you're getting up to something with quite a few lines in it. Now think about your phone number. It's probably 10 digits, possibly 13 or 14 if you include the international dialing code.

The same is true with your computer. Although it's fun to give it a name, even a name within a specific domain, the way computers really talk to each other is by using a numerical ID that can be used to identify an individual interface (network card, modem, or other network connection). Although there are lots of ways of using a numerical ID in this way, the most common and widely used—and therefore the one actually required for communication in a Windows Server 2003 network—is the TCP/IP address.

In this chapter, we'll look at the TCP/IP protocol and how it works so that you can design a network that uses the TCP/IP system. We'll also look at the DHCP protocol, which enables a server to dish out TCP/IP addresses, simplifying addressing and reducing the management workload of running a TCP/IP server.

 **Objective 2.01**

Designing a TCP/IP Network

If you pick up the telephone and dial your friend down the road in Seattle or your auntie halfway across the world, you probably don't think much about what's going on behind the scenes. However, behind the scenes there is a structure to the numbering system you use to contact these people, and each person you call has their own telephone number.

The same is true of machines within a network. In order for them to communicate with each other, they need to have a unique address. At a hardware level, the unique address is provided by the hardware ID (officially called the Media Access Control, or MAC, address) that is built into each network adaptor. The problem is that Ethernet—the most popular form of hardware networking—is not ubiquitous; that is, it doesn't support dial-up connectivity, for example. It's a bit like the serial number written on the bottom of your phone: it might be unique, but it's not very practical and it doesn't really have anything to do with the phone number that the phone might be connected to. You need a separate numbering scheme that is flexible and that works independently of the underlying hardware.

Travel Advisory

The Address Resolution Protocol (ARP) tracks the mapping between a hardware (physical) address and the IP address. This is used by the TCP/IP protocol stack to send an IP packet to the right physical address on the network. The arp command-line tool in Windows lets you view the internal ARP table.

At an OS and application level, however, you need a different numbering scheme. The most widely used and practical of these is generally referred to as the Transmission Control Protocol/Internet Protocol (TCP/IP) networking protocol. The address side of this is the Internet Protocol, which assigns individual machines a unique IP address that identifies them on the network. This is like your phone number. Although it's a fixed number that will always ring at your house, if you move, it can be mapped to another address or location. Working with IP is the Transmission Control Protocol, which enables two machines, each with its own IP address, to communicate and transfer information between each other. Built on top of TCP/IP are more-well-known protocols such the File Transfer Protocol (FTP) and Hypertext Transfer Protocol (HTTP).

Travel Advisory

A lesser used protocol, User Datagram Protocol (UDP), also uses the IP addressing protocol to identify hosts. Unlike TCP, which is based on having a logical connection between the sender and receiver, UDP works without any acknowledgement between the two hosts during communication. There is no guarantee with UDP that your packets reached their destination, but this has practical uses, such as ping and traceroute, with systems that don't want to flood or tie up networks with packets going nowhere. The Microsoft TCP/IP stack includes the ability to use the UDP protocol.

TCP/IP is the default networking protocol for Windows Server 2003 machines and is a required component for many of the protocols and services supported by the operating system, including Active Directory. It should also be the default protocol on your network across all your clients, servers, and other devices. As well as being an international standard and the communications protocol used on the Internet, TCP/IP is also an easily manageable and configurable network system that enables you to organize your network into individual subnets and to allow routing and communication between them.

Beyond the organizational and management capabilities of TCP/IP, there are a number of other advantages to using TCP/IP within the Windows OS, but the primary advantages are

- **Compatibility**   TCP/IP is supported by a huge range of devices, platforms, and operating systems. TCP/IP forms the basis of nearly every network in the world, and it's the protocol used on the Internet, enabling millions of networks and computers around the world to talk to each other.

- **Connectivity**   Because TCP/IP is so widely used, you can use it to connect to other machines and operating systems from your Windows Server 2003 machine. Good examples are the lpr printing protocol, used by many printers; Unix operating systems; and AppleShare IP, which enables you to share your folders with Apple Mac OS and Mac OS X clients.

- **Internet compatibility**   TCP/IP on your internal network allows you to connect your machines and clients to the Internet. You don't need to install any additional protocols or manage two different naming or addressing systems to provide both internal and Internet connectivity.

Designing a TCP/IP network involves a number of different steps, but the primary concerns are

- **TCP/IP infrastructure**   Using the design of your network as a guide, you can design your TCP/IP infrastructure to logically group devices together for easier management and identification. For example, you might choose to allocate all your servers an address within a specific range and your clients an address in another range.

- **Addressing scheme**   With your infrastructure plan in mind, you must now create an addressing structure. This might include subnetting (or dividing) your addresses into different networks and the use of public and private addresses to publicize and hide your network from the Internet.

- **Security**   The security of your network should be your primary concern. When you design your TCP/IP strategy, consider how it works with routers, firewalls, and internal security systems such as encryption and secure links.

- **Routing**   TCP/IP networks can be connected together by routing their packets from one network to another. We'll be looking at the issues of routing in Chapter 5.

Before we look at the specifics though, we need to look at the basic mechanics of the IP addressing system and how this affects how machines communicate with each other.

TCP/IP Basics

At the fundamental level, the key to TCP/IP's success is the IP address system and how this enables you to connect, distribute, route, and otherwise communicate information between machines. What follows is a quick guide to the mechanics of the IP protocol and addressing system that you should be able to use through the designing process.

The TCP/IP protocol fits into the International Organization for Standardization (ISO)/Open Systems Interconnect (OSI) seven-layer model. This defines the various layers within a networking system from the physical aspects (for example, the voltages used to denote a zero or one) up to the application level that defines how the network interacts with the user. The seven layers, from bottom to top, are physical, data link, network, transport, session, presentation, and application. The IP component of TCP/IP sits at layer 3, and the TCP component sits at layer 4.

The IP Address

You're probably already familiar with the format of an IP address: it's a string made up of four numbers, each separated by a period, such as 192.168.1.130. Each group of numbers is the decimal equivalent of an 8-bit binary number, known as an octet. An octet has a value between 0 and 255. This is because 8 bits gives you 2^8 (256, to save you getting out the calculator) combinations—we have to include zero, hence the top value of 255.

The binary format is important. Not only is it the default counting system used by computers, it also affects how other elements of the IP addressing system work. To convert a binary number to its decimal equivalent, you need a table like the one shown in Table 2.1. In this case, there are 8 columns, one for each bit of information. Each bit (from right to left) is a power of two, so 2^0 is 1, up to 2^7, which is 128. If you add up the values in row 1 where a value of 1 corresponds in row two, you get a value of 173.

TABLE 2.1	Converting Binary to Decimal						
128	64	32	16	8	4	2	1
1	0	1	0	1	1	0	1

Each IP address is made up of four octets, so an IP address is actually a string of 32 binary digits. Table 2.2 shows the IP address 192.168.1.130 in binary.

Exam Tip

It's unlikely that you'll be specifically tested on your IP math skills in the 70-293 exam, but that doesn't mean that you can ignore them either. Good design relies on you knowing the ins and outs of IP addressing and the effects of subnets, subnet masks, and other elements that we'll be looking at in this section.

IP Address Classes

With 256 possibilities in each part of the IP address, you have the potential to address 256×256×256×256 machines, or approximately 4.3 billion addresses. But addresses aren't given out randomly from one massive pool. Instead, the IP address space split the IP address system into a number of different classes. Classes come in three basic types, A, B, or C, with a number of other addresses allocated for different purposes.

To understand classes, you need to look back at the example IP address, 192.168.1.130. Each of the periods in this address has a purpose. When you look at a phone number such as 869-555-7848, you assume that certain elements of that number relate to areas or divisions and others relate to a specific telephone line and therefore a house or company.

The same is true of the IP address: the octets 192.168.1 define a network of computers, and the .130 octet identifies a single host, or machine, within that network. The first 3 bits of the first octet and the number of octets define which part of the address is used for the network and which is used for the hosts. This information in turn defines the class. See Table 2.3 for a basic summary of this information.

TABLE 2.2	A Full IP Address in Binary																														
128	64	32	16	8	4	2	1	128	64	32	16	8	4	2	1	128	64	32	16	8	4	2	1	128	64	32	16	8	4	2	1
1	1	0	0	0	0	0	0	1	0	1	0	1	0	0	0	0	0	0	0	0	0	0	1	1	0	0	0	0	0	1	0

TABLE 2.3				Network Classes			
Class	**Bit 1**	**Bit 2**	**Bit 3**	**Network Octets**	**Range**	**Networks**	**Hosts**
A	0	0	0	First only	1.0.0.0 to 126.255.255 .255	128	16.7 million
B	1	0	0	First and second	128.0.0.0 to 191.255.255 .255	16384	65536
C	1	1	0	First, second, third	192.0.0.0 to 223.255.255 .255	2 million	256

Now you can see why understanding the binary behind the system is important. Class A has 128 network combinations (actually 126, but two can't be used, as discussed in the upcoming Travel Advisory) because the remaining 7 bits of an 8-bit binary number leave only 128 possible combinations.

Travel Advisory

The 0.0.0.0 address can't be used due to IP addressing rules. This is true at all class levels, so the address 192.168.1.0 cannot be allocated to a host either. This reduces the *real* number of IPs available in each class.

Putting this into perspective, if you have been allocated an address in the Class B network range, you can create up to 16,384 different networks by using the first two octets of the address to define the network. Within each network, you can specify up to 16.7 million hosts. You can use this in your design plans to divide a network up into different elements, departments, and locations by using separate networks for each group, while still being able to identify individual hosts.

For example, you might use 192.168.1.*x* to hold hosts in the sales department and 192.168.2.*x* to hold hosts for the marketing department. These are two different networks, and you can identify up to 254 different machines within each network by allocating them a number between 1 and 254. So your sales department mail server might have the IP address 192.168.1.130. Hey, you've found your machine!

Travel Advisory

You might be wondering why you don't have 256 available addresses in that network. The reason is that two addresses in every network are reserved: 0 is the address for the network as a whole and 255 is the broadcast address for the network. We'll look in more detail at these in a moment.

The remaining addresses (those above 224.0.0.0) are allocated for special purposes, and the 127.0.0.0 address range is used for the special "loopback" addresses, which always point back to the original host—that is, the current machine—even if you don't know the machine's IP address.

Private Address Classes

There are a number of addresses that you can use on an internal network—that is, a network that's not connected directly to the Internet. You can use these addresses to set up your network and then use systems like Network Address Translation (NAT) or proxy servers to provide your connectivity to the Internet without having to have a public IP address. We'll look at Internet connection methods in Chapter 5. Three address ranges are available, each within a different class so you can define different networks and hosts within your network according to your needs. The internal ranges are as follows:

- **Class A**   10.0.0.0
- **Class B**   172.16.0.0 to 172.31.255.255
- **Class C**   192.168.0.0 to 192.168.255.255

For example, if you wanted to create a network using a Class C network address, you would use the 192.168.0.0 range.

Travel Assistance

The Internet Connection Sharing (ICS) and Network Address Translation (NAT) system uses the 192.168.0.0 range to connect client computers to the Internet through a gateway machine.

Subnets

The problem with the class system is that although it's neatly divided into networks and hosts, it's still possible to have too many addresses available to you when you are trying to create nice, tight little groups of computers. You can get around this by creating a subnet. A subnet divides a network with a number of potential host addresses and divides it up into a number of smaller subnetworks.

For example, imagine a Class C network with 254 potential hosts that you want to divide into a number of subnets so that you can put sales and marketing into their own groups. To create a subnet, use the same basic principle that created the class system in IP addresses, but use it on one of the small ranges.

Say, for example, you have a Class C network of 192.168.1.0 that you want to split into two. To do that, you use the first bit of the last octet to specify one subnet of 128 hosts (because using that first bit to split the network in two reduces the number of host bits to 7). You now have two networks, 192.168.1.0 to 192.168.1.127 and 192.168.1.128 to 192.168.1.255.

You can repeat the exercise by borrowing more bits. If you use 2 bits to specify the network, you get 4 networks of 64 hosts each. Three bits would create 8 networks of 16 hosts. Each time you borrow a bit, you double the network and halve the number of hosts.

> **Travel Advisory**
>
> In fact, you lose two addresses for each additional network you create, because the first and last addresses in each subnet are again used to define the network as a whole and the broadcast address for the network. Thus, a subnet that is defined by borrowing two bits might have a network address of 192.168.1.64 and a broadcast address of 192.168.1.127.

Technically, subnets are also created if you use a Class A or B address to define one or more networks within the entire allocation range. For any type of subnetting to work, though, you need to tell the computer how the subnet is defined, and that's where the subnet mask comes in.

Subnet Masks

Once you created a subnet, the subnet mask tells the machine how the subnet is organized. The combination of the machine's address and its subnet mask enables the machine to determine which subnet it's a part of. With this information, it can also determine whether other hosts with a given IP address are within the same network. It then determines whether the machine can be contacted directly, or whether it needs to send the packet to a router on the network to reach its destination.

The way it does this is to AND the binary representation of the IP address with the subnet mask. A subnet mask defines which bits are used to identify a network. So, for a Class C network, the first three octets (24 bits) are used to define the network address. The corresponding subnet mask (or just netmask) has all 24 bits switched on, resulting in a netmask of 255.255.255.0.

Local Lingo

AND This is a logical operator that works at a binary level. The result is true (equal to 1) only if both input values are also true. Thus, 0 AND 0 equals 0, 1 AND 0 equals 0, and 1 AND 1 equals 1.

Given a Class C host address, such as 192.168.1.130, the machine can determine the network component by ANDing the IP address with the network mask. You can see this in Table 2.4.

The result, in decimal, is a network address of 192.168.1.0.

You can repeat this again with a subnet that is a division of a Class C address. Let's say you used the first two bits of the last octet in the 192.168.1.0 network for a subnet. You'd then need to determine the network for your IP address of 192.168.1.73. With two bits being used for the subnet mask, its value will be 255.255.255.192. Table 2.5 contains the last octet calculation. This results in a network address of 192.168.1.64.

It should be obvious from all of this that a subnet must be a binary multiple—you can't decide to have a subnet of 111 addresses just because that's how many you need. You can only have a subnet that is 256, 128, 64, 32, 16, 8, or 4 addresses. Nor can you have only one or two addresses in a class subnet, because you need a minimum of two addresses for the network and broadcast IPs.

TABLE 2.4   Using AND to Determine a Network from an IP and Mask

IP	1	1	0	0	0	0	0	0	1	0	1	0	1	0	0	0	0	0	0	0	0	0	1	1	0	0	0	0	0	0	1	0
Mask	1	1	1	1	1	1	1	1	1	1	1	1	1	1	1	1	1	1	1	1	1	1	1	1	0	0	0	0	0	0	0	0
Result	1	1	0	0	0	0	0	0	1	0	1	0	1	0	0	0	0	0	0	0	0	0	1	0	0	0	0	0	0	0	0	0

TABLE 2.5   Determining Subnet of a Class C Address

IP	0	1	0	0	1	0	0	1
Mask	1	1	0	0	0	0	0	0
Result	0	1	0	0	0	0	0	0

You can also use higher subnets within the IP address structure. For example, if you want to use two Class C IP networks, you can put them logically into the same network by using a subnet mask of 255.255.254.0.

Travel Advisory

Networks and their masks can also be written like this: 192.168.1.0/24. The number after the slash is the number of bits used to define the network, in this case 24, which leaves 8 bits for an address, and hence a Class C network. 192.168.1.0/26 leaves 6 bits, or 64 hosts, while 192.168.1.0/23 gives 9 bits, or 512 hosts.

Variable-Length Subnet Masks

One of the problems with subnets and their masks is that they restrict what you can talk to. Say you want to be able to create one big network but also restrict certain hosts to a specific group, all within the same network. Essentially, rather than using the same subnet right across your network, you'd use different subnets within the same network address space, producing a variety of different subnets of different sizes. You can do this using variable-length subnet masks (VLSM).

Default Gateways and Routing

When you send information to another machine by opening a connection through its IP address, your machine needs to determine where the machine is. You already know that it does this by using the subnet mask to determine its own network and uses this information with the destination IP address to find out that machine's location.

If the machine is local, the TCP/IP protocol stack resolves the IP address of the machine to a hardware Ethernet address (using the information cached by the ARP system) and sends the packet out on the network.

If, however, it determines that the destination machine is not within the local network, it instead forwards the packet to the default gateway—usually a router or machine configured as a router, which forwards the packet on to another router, or the destination, by using the same IP address/subnet mask determination.

This is how your machine, with an IP address in your local range, can talk to a machine halfway round the world—the packet is forwarded between routers that should know the route to the destination. The same is true of an internal network separated by routers. Figure 2.1 shows a simple routed network.

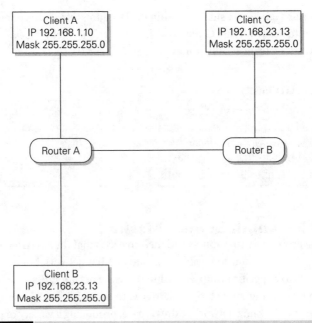

FIGURE 2.1   Routing and default gateways

Each client is connected to a router, and the router's IP address is configured as the default gateway for each client. For Client A to communicate with Client B, it must have a default gateway configured—in this case, Router A—which then checks the IP address and netmask configured for the router's own ports to determine that Client B is reachable directly from this router. To reach Client C, the packet must be forwarded to Router A, which then forwards it to Router B, which then forwards it on to the client.

Without a default gateway address, your machine will determine that the destination host is unreachable because it has no way of sending the packet on to a device that can send it on to its destination.

TCP/IP Implementation

There are lots of different ways you can organize your TCP/IP network, but your primary concerns should be

- Security
- Ease of communication
- Usability
- Manageability

Because you can organize computers into different logical networks through IP addressing, this also raises a number of other key points:

- TCP/IP is a logical addressing system and protocol and ignores the underlying hardware. You can have multiple machines connected to the same physical piece of hardware—a hub or switch, for example—but with different TCP/IP networks. If they are not on the same IP network, they can't talk to each other, physically connected or otherwise. This means that your hardware network (which we'll discuss in Chapter 4) and TCP/IP network are largely separate entities. The areas where they converge are routers and gateways, which provide both logical and physical connections between two or more networks.

- You need to subnet your networks according to the physical structure of the network. Your physical structure will probably match your typical organizational layout anyway. For example, creating different subnets for your sales and marketing departments is an obvious move if they are already physically separate.

- Be sure to choose an IP addressing scheme that matches your expected capacity, and allow for expansion. If you have 250 machines and choose to use a single Class C address, you'll have only four spare IP addresses to play with. Better to use two Class C addresses and a subnet that incorporates them both into the same network. Similarly, when subnetting a Class C, don't subnet down to the number of bits you need, always use one more. If you have 30 machines, it might be tempting to subnet down to just 5 hosts, but you should use 6 and give yourself 32 additional addresses to play with.

If you keep all of this in mind, you should be able to create a manageable and practical network that is also easy to extend.

Designing a Structured Addressing Scheme

Before you start assigning IP addresses to machines, you need to think about which machines should be given which addresses, whether you are going to use DHCP, whether to use subnets, and whether you need public addresses (that is, addresses available to the Internet) or can get by with private addresses only.

There are two parts to the addressing scheme decision. The first is the model you'll use to assign addresses. The second is whether you will use public or private IP addresses within your scheme.

> ### Travel Advisory
>
> TCP/IP design and the physical structure of your network are very closely linked. Typically, you'll create structures that merge or involve both structures. Microsoft likes to separate out the two because technically they can be completely independent of each other. Practically though, it's impossible to think about one without the other. We'll be looking at the physical side in Chapter 4.

Addressing Model

You can make your life easier by creating a structured IP address assignment model. This specifies which machines will be given which addresses. More specifically, it helps you choose specific ranges for specific machines, which enables you to make decisions about subnets, your IP addressing scheme, and whether you need to use DHCP.

To summarize, the choices you need to make are

- Whether to use static or dynamic addressing
- Which address allocation you'll be using
- Whether to use of subnets

The structured design, once completed, will help you identify your networks, identify your machines within those networks, and locate and organize services according the structure model.

Static or Dynamic Addressing   Dynamic addresses are given out by the Dynamic Host Configuration Protocol (DHCP). A DHCP server uses a pool of addresses that it can assign to machines on a first-come, first-served basis, when they ask for it. For more information on designing a DHCP infrastructure, see Objective 2.02, "Designing a DHCP Infrastructure."

Static addressing is manually and specifically giving a machine an IP address. For example, you will probably want to give your servers and routers a static IP address so their IP address is consistent. It's also a requirement for certain network services to have static IP addresses, including the DHCP server, DNS servers, WINS servers, and the Active Directory domain controllers. Other servers not running these services, including file and print servers, can use dynamic addressing, although by convention, usually all servers are given static IPs.

Address Allocation   You need to choose a method for assigning addresses to your networks and individual machines. This will depend partly on your physical network layout, but you should also keep in mind your security and organizational concerns. Microsoft identifies four primary allocation methods that apply at a network level:

- **Random address allocation**   Here you just give out an address or range at random from a pool of those available. Using this scheme is usually lethal because it makes network management more difficult. This is shown in Figure 2.2: you can see how it would be impossible to determine where a host was just by looking at its IP address unless you also kept a list of the locations and organization handy.

- **Allocation by organization chart**   This is where you separate the network by different departments, as shown in Figure 2.3. While better than random allocation, this can start to become unwieldy as you increase the number of networks. For example, given the network 10.68.2.0, can you be sure at which geographical location it's located, even if you can identify it as a sales network?

- **Allocation by geographic location**   This uses specific locations to organize the system, as shown in Figure 2.4. This is better than organization chart allocation, but it still becomes unmanageable with larger networks.

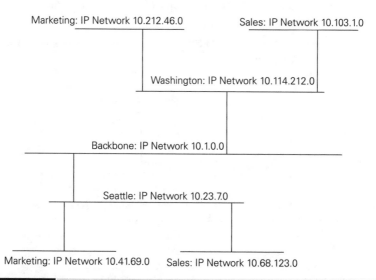

Marketing: IP Network 10.212.46.0

Sales: IP Network 10.103.1.0

Washington: IP Network 10.114.212.0

Backbone: IP Network 10.1.0.0

Seattle: IP Network 10.23.7.0

Marketing: IP Network 10.41.69.0

Sales: IP Network 10.68.123.0

FIGURE 2.2   Random address allocation

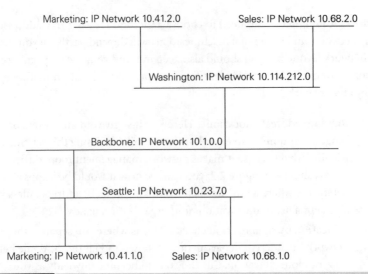

FIGURE 2.3 Organization chart address allocation

- **Allocation by topology** Essentially, this is a mixture of the previous two strategies. Most larger companies use this strategy. You organize your network according to the hardware layout, and in most companies that matches the geographical and organizational structure. The advantage of this system is that it's easy to identify a machine by its IP address in terms of location, department, and even the network hardware that it's connected to. You can see an example of this in Figure 2.5.

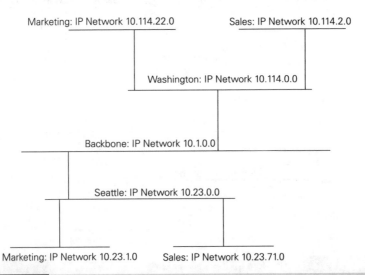

FIGURE 2.4 Geographic address allocation

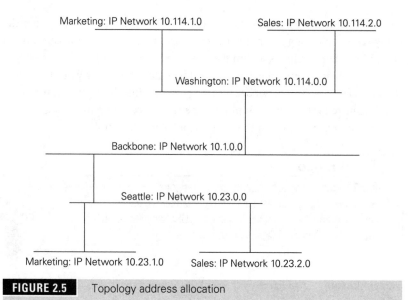

Marketing: IP Network 10.114.1.0   Sales: IP Network 10.114.2.0

Washington: IP Network 10.114.0.0

Backbone: IP Network 10.1.0.0

Seattle: IP Network 10.23.0.0

Marketing: IP Network 10.23.1.0   Sales: IP Network 10.23.2.0

FIGURE 2.5   Topology address allocation

Ultimately, the aim of network allocations is to make your network easy to understand and identify and also to make it easier to route packets through the network. For example, using the random addressing model, you'd need extensive routing tables within the routers to know the next router in the chain to contact when moving from the sales office in Washington to the marketing department in Seattle. With a topology-based system, you only need to tell the routers the next address level to contact for it to reach its destination.

The same identification rules also apply to individual machines in the network. If you always use the first 20 addresses for routers and static devices and the next 20 for servers, you know that the address 10.2.45.107 is a client and 10.87.13.3 is a router.

Subnets   Subnets are designed to help you organize your machines, as you've already seen with the network address allocation strategies. But subnets are also a security and performance feature. Two subnets cannot talk to each other without a router, and that means that you can isolate traffic between the two networks. This is true even if the routers are connected to the same hub.

The performance aspect comes into play because routers only broadcast traffic according to the destination. If two networks are connected by a router, only those packets required to exchange information between the two sides will be transferred. This isolates the traffic created locally on the two networks. This can be used to great effect with very busy networks, such as a multimedia or publishing systems, separating the traffic they create from the networks and capacity required for other machines within the company.

Layer 3 switches are an extension of this philosophy. They work just like a standard network switch, but because they can monitor the TCP/IP traffic, they can maximize performance on physical networks according to the logical network structure. We'll look at this in more detail in Chapter 4.

> **Local Lingo**
>
> **Layer 3**   Networks are notionally organized into a number of separate layers, from the lowest physical aspects up to the highest application level communication. The model used is the ISO/OSI Seven Layer model. Layer (or level) 3 is the TCP/IP packet layer.

Sample Design   The easiest way to put this into perspective is to look at a typical network and then demonstrate the IP addressing scheme for this site. For this example, we'll use a company called Fabicab. They have almost 1,000 machines, including 100 servers, and they are split into five departments: sales, marketing, production, dispatch, and accounts. Each department has approximately 180 machines in it.

The first step is to decide which devices should have a static address and which should have a dynamic. Static addresses should always be used where the IP address of the device needs to remain constant, even across reboots. Generally all servers, routers, and other core network equipment should have a static address, while all clients and machines that do not require a static address use dynamic addressing.

It's also clear in this example that you could logically split the individual departments into a number of subnets. Some of those departments have their own servers, so you also need to give some thought to the internal structure of each subnet.

For example, so that you can quickly determine whether a given IP address is a server or a client, you should allocate the first 20 addresses within each subnet to be used only for routers. You can also allocate a further 30 addresses for other fixed IP devices such as servers or printers. The remaining addresses can be assigned dynamically to the clients. The exception to the rule is the main backbone network, where you can allocate nearly all the addresses in the network to servers and other static IP devices. The resulting structure is given in Table 2.6.

TABLE 2.6	Example TCP/IP Addressing Structure			
Subnet	**Role**	**Router IPs**	**Server IPs**	**Client IPs**
1	Core	10.0.0.1–10.0.0.20	10.0.0.21–10.0.0.254	None
2	Sales	10.0.1.1–10.0.1.20	10.0.1.21–10.0.1.40	10.0.1.41–10.0.1.254
3	Marketing	10.0.1.1–10.0.1.20	10.0.1.21–10.0.1.40	10.0.1.41–10.0.1.254
4	Production	10.0.2.1–10.0.2.20	10.0.2.21–10.0.2.40	10.0.2.41–10.0.2.254
5	Dispatch	10.0.3.1–10.0.3.20	10.0.3.21–10.0.3.40	10.0.3.41–10.0.3.254
6	Accounts	10.0.4.1–10.0.4.20	10.0.4.21–10.0.4.40	10.0.4.41–10.0.4.254

Public and Private Addresses

There are two types of addresses that you can allocate to your machines: public and private. In a nutshell, a public address is available on the Internet and a private address is used only within your company. This is like the difference between your company's public telephone number and your internal extension number.

There are some rules for determining whether to use an internal or external IP address:

- If you use a direct connection to the Internet, you must use public addresses.

- If you use an indirect connection such as a proxy server or NAT, use private addresses.

- If your organization is not connected to the Internet, use private addresses rather than valid public IP addresses. This way, if you later connect to the Internet using an indirect connection, you will not need to change addresses already in use.

Public Addresses   Public addresses are those that are publicly accessible over the Internet. Usually, you'll use a public address if you want to have your own presence on the Internet, say for a website, or if you are hosting your own mail server that will receive e-mail directly from the Internet.

The problem with public addresses is that there are only a limited number of public IP addresses available and these are given out very selectively, usually only to large companies with a need, or to ISPs who may, in turn, distribute these to their own clients in small subnets.

Public addresses are not, however, required for access to the Internet. You can use a private addressing scheme through a service called Network Address Translation (NAT). This hides your private addresses behind one or more public addresses and allows clients on the private side to access the Internet through a single public address. NAT is included in Windows Server 2003 as part of the Routing and Remote Access Service (RRAS). NAT is also used by Internet Service Providers (ISPs) to provide connectivity through dial-up, cable modem, and digital subscriber line (DSL) connections.

If you have a direct connection to the Internet, that is, one through a leased line such as T1, T3, or another fixed digital connection, they will usually require a public address as these systems are attached to the Internet using directly connected hardware routers.

Private Addresses   Private addresses are used when you do not need connection to the Internet, or when you want to separate the internal and external portions of your network. You can still be connected to the Internet through NAT or a proxy service. Private addresses use one of the private address class ranges specified earlier in this chapter in the section "Private Address Classes."

The main benefit of private addresses in your internal network is that you can exercise complete control over the network structure, creating your own subnets and organizational structure. You also gain access to potentially unlimited numbers of IP addresses, allowing you to create a network of many thousands of machines, all of which could have Internet access, behind as few as one public IP address.

Security Basics

IP does not have any inherent security mechanisms, making it easy for some users to spoof their IP address in order to gain access to your network and/or your network services. There are a number of solutions available to help prevent these tricks from affecting your network.

Local Lingo

Spoof   To mimic an address is to spoof it. Spoofing a network address allows a malicious attacker to appear to be within your network, even though they are physically outside of it, thereby bypassing many simple firewalls and address-based security systems.

There are also more general issues with security, such as providing secure connectivity between your servers, securing the connectivity of wireless clients, and protecting the security of your network as a whole from other parts of your LAN, your WAN connections, and the Internet.

For communication on your internal network between servers and clients, the solution is to use Internet Protocol Security (IPSec). This secures the information stored within IP packets as they are transmitted over the network, which can be used either to secure your network traffic generally or to support secure, encrypted links between specific servers on your network, including over a WAN or routed connection. IPSec is the most efficient method for securing communication on your network because it works at the lowest communication level.

Wireless networks provide a number of security risks that should be addressed. Security of your wireless network as a whole can be handled by restricting access to specific devices, encrypting the links, or using IPSec to secure your links.

Protecting your IP network from outside attacks at your various IP borders requires the use of one or more firewalls. These protect your network by controlling the IP addresses and ports that can be used in different parts of the network.

For more information on all of these issues, refer to Chapters 5 and 6.

IP Multicasting

IP multicasting allows a machine to send network packets that are then sent to a multicast address and potentially picked up by all IP clients within the multicast scope. This is used for a number of systems, including the registration and peer-to-peer systems such as WINS. Most commonly, however, IP multicasting is used for multimedia applications such as videoconferencing, live Internet video broadcasts, and audio/video streaming.

There are no specific problems or concerns when designing your network to support multicast traffic—Windows Server 2003 incorporates the necessary technology and support to enable multicast solutions. However, if you are broadcasting multicast traffic onto the Internet or expect to be able to use multicast traffic from the Internet on your internal network, there will be routing issues. See Chapter 5 for more information on these issues and how to resolve them.

Understanding IPv6

The current IP addressing system is more than 30 years old, and in some respects the age is beginning to show. One of the biggest recent problems, or so it seemed, was address space. Four or five years ago there was talk, particularly among the ISPs, that we were running out of IP addresses to allocate to companies on the Internet. Part of this was because until then most computers that wanted an Internet connection had to have a public IP address.

Recent changes, such as the introduction of NAT, the use of firewalls and proxy services, and a more specific machine/purpose–led approach (whereby only machines that actually require a public IP address, web servers, and mail servers, for example, are given one) means that the available address space is less of an immediate worry.

However, the addressing problem combined with other issues inspired the introduction of a new standard, IPv6, which addressed all these issues. Among the key points, beyond the increase in address space, are

- Improved security
- Improved performance
- Better integration with security measures such as firewalls
- Automatic IP address allocation (without systems like DHCP)
- Better integration with the DNS system for resolving IP addresses to and from names

Windows Server 2003 and Windows XP include support for IPv6, although lack of wider support for IPv6 makes it difficult at this time to use it for anything other than testing. Table 2.7 details the differences between IPv4 (the current implementation) and IPv6.

TABLE 2.7   Key Differences Between IPv4 and IPv6

Feature	IPv4	IPv6
Source and destination address length	32 bits (4 bytes)	128 bits (16 bytes)
IPSec support	Optional	Required
QoS support	Some	Better

TABLE 2.7	Key Differences Between IPv4 and IPv6 *(continued)*	
Feature	**IPv4**	**IPv6**
Fragmentation	Hosts and routers (slows router performance)	Hosts only
Checksum in header	Yes	No
Options in header	Yes	No (moved to extension headers)
Link-layer address resolution neighbor messages	ARP (broadcast ARP request)	Multicast neighbor solicitation messages
Local subnet group membership management	Internet Group Management Protocol (IGMP)	Multicast Listener Discovery (MLD) messages
Default gate discovery	ICMP router discovery	ICMPv6 router solicitation and router advertisement messages
Broadcast usage	Yes	No (Local link scope all-nodes multicast address)
IP address configuration	Manual, DHCP	Automatic (does not require manual or DHCP)
DNS name queries—host name to IP Address	Uses A records—maps host names to IPv4 address	Uses AAAA records—maps host names to IPv6 addresses
DNS reverse lookup queries—IP Address to Host name	User pointer (PTR) resource records—maps IPv4 address to host names	User pointer (PTR) resource records—maps IPv6 address to host names
DNS reverse queries	Uses IN-ADDR.ARPA	Uses IP6.INT
Minimum MTU	576 bytes	1280 bytes

Returning to the IP addressing issue, the new 128-bit standard enables you to address 2^{128} IP addresses, or approximately 3.4×10^{38} addresses. That's a staggering 5×10^{28} addresses for each person on the planet. Although that might seem like a lot, with predictions that everything from computers to cars to washing machines will have their own IP addresses, it's not such a high number.

Objective 2.02 Designing a DHCP Infrastructure

TCP/IP relies on each machine within the network to have a unique IP address, but giving out addresses and other configuration information to a number of machines quickly becomes tiresome. A small number in a small network—say, under 25 machines—is just about manageable. But what happens if you need to change the IP addresses of all the machines? How about a default gateway, DNS server, or netmask change?

If you average 5 minutes per machine, 25 of them will take you over two hours. Change that to 100 machines, and you're talking about a full day's worth of configuration changes—not to mention the interruption to the users' work. Increase that to 250 machines and you're looking at the best part of a week, once the inevitable interruptions come into play.

Much easier would be some system that enables you to automatically hand out an IP address when one is needed by a client, without any form of intervention necessary on your part. That's where the Dynamic Host Configuration Protocol (DHCP) comes in. DHCP will do that for you, keep a record of what it does, and allow you to change things without having to visit each client to make those changes.

Using DHCP, however, requires some careful design to make sure that you can deliver DHCP addresses to all of your machines and still be in control of the process. Also, your network design may drive certain aspects of your DHCP design. In this section, we'll have a look at these design issues.

Exam Tip
DHCP is not officially a component of the exam, but the use of DHCP is a recommended best practice when deploying a TCP/IP network, so you should be aware of the main issues and advantages of DHCP within a TCP/IP network design.

Benefits of DHCP

The main benefit of DHCP is that it removes the need to manually configure and allocate individual IP addresses. The DHCP server gives away an IP address when asked and then frees it up when it's no longer required. That means that you no longer have to configure each machine or keep a record of the IP addresses you've given to different machines.

DHCP does more than that, though. It also provides information to clients on the subnet mask (another vital component), the default gateway, the DNS servers, and WINS servers—they can all be configured with the DHCP system.

Better still, because the DHCP server is a centrally managed resource, you can change the IP addresses, DNS servers, default gateway, and other information all from the same server. If anything changes, you won't need to go around to every client in the company and change the information—it'll all be done automatically the next time your clients start up and ask for an IP address.

Manual IP Allocation

As we've said, keeping track of an entire network that uses manual IP addresses is a major task, and the larger your network, the more complex this becomes. However, there are times when automatic allocation will not work or is ill advised. Although it's tempting to move to a dynamic solution such as DHCP in this situation for all hosts on your network, there are certain devices and services on your network that cannot be set up this way.

In particular, the following hosts should be configured with a manual address:

- Domain controllers
- DHCP servers
- DNS servers
- WINS servers
- Routers
- Non-Windows hosts that do not support DHCP
- Public Internet servers (web, e-mail, and so on)

In addition, many administrators prefer to use manual addressing on other servers in your network, including file, print, and e-mail servers. This is not absolutely necessary, as these can be configured with fixed IP addresses allocated through the DHCP service by using "reserved" addresses. However, a fixed IP address makes it possible for servers to boot up ready to run, even in the event of a failure of DHCP servers or parts of the network.

You can mix and match manual and dynamic IP allocation, but it's best to split your allocations of manual and dynamic addresses within a specific range. For example, you might configure your network to use static addresses from 192.168.1.1 to 192.168.1.50 and dynamic addresses from 192.168.1.100 to 192.168.1.199.

DHCP Mechanics

DHCP works because the client is configured to send out a broadcast packet on the Ethernet network before an IP address has been allocated. This packet is received by the DHCP server, and a response is sent back to the client with the assigned IP address and other information. This is then used by the client to set the parameters on the TCP/IP stack and in turn to configure its own network interfaces, DNS server addresses, and other information.

The address assigned is either a dynamic address or a reserved address. A dynamic address is one taken from a pool of available addresses, called a scope; a different address may be given to the same physical client each time it asks for an address. Reserved addresses are the same IP address for each network card (according to their MAC address).

Dynamic Addressing

Dynamic addressing is the standard DHCP system, where clients are given an IP address from a pool (or scope) of available addresses. Dynamic addresses are given to clients on a first-come, first-served basis: the next available IP address is given out when it is requested.

Of course, if you did this without some way of freeing the addresses when the client finishes with them (that is, when they shut down or restart), the IP address scope you configured would run out of addresses fairly quickly. DHCP gets around this by selling a lease, or right, to use the IP address for a given period, rather than giving out an IP address and forgetting about it.

When the client is given the IP address, it's also given the lease period; it's the client's responsibility to renew the lease before it expires. If the client fails to renew (because it's been shut down, for example), then the server frees the IP address allocation and makes it available for another machine to use.

This is a bit like hiring equipment and lanes at a bowling alley. You've rented the equipment and lane for a set period, and the owner records that information on the computer, so that the staff know when an alley will become free. If you decide you want to stay for another round, you have to go and request an extension.

With DHCP, the client requests a renewal when half the original lease period is up. If it fails to get a response from the server, it tries again when half of the remaining time is left, and continues until it's able to renew the lease. If it runs out of time, it keeps the IP address but continues to request a renewal every hour. For example, if the lease time was 12 hours, the client might try at 6 hours remaining, 3 hours remaining, 1.5 hours remaining, 45 minutes remaining, and then return to retrying to renew the lease every hour.

Reserved Addressing

Reserved addressing combines the flexibility and manageability of DHCP with the control and stability of manual IP addressing. Essentially, you configure the DHCP server to allocate an IP address to a given MAC address. Then, when the machine using the network with that hardware address requests an IP address from the server, it's given the same address each time.

This enables you to set an IP address for a machine just as if you'd done so through a manual configuration process, and it still allows you to change the address or subnetting scheme from the same central DHCP server. Unlike dynamic addressing, reserved addresses are provided without a lease, so the client does not have to request to update the address when the lease expires.

Travel Advisory

Another benefit of reserved addressing is that you can use it to document your network structure without having to create a separate record of the information.

Deploying DHCP

DHCP obviously reduces the complexity and management overheads of a typical fixed IP network, but you have to be careful how you deploy and configure the servers in your network. There are two main issues to resolve in the deployment of a DHCP solution:

- **Server configuration**   This includes elements such as the lease times, performance, and integration with other services.
- **Server location**   This affects your DHCP design and, to an extent, your network and TCP/IP design.
- **Server availability**   You need to make sure that your clients can obtain an IP address through DHCP when they request one.
- **Subnet effects**   This changes the location, configuration, and availability parameters as a whole, depending on how your subnets and network is designed.

We'll take a closer look at these different aspects in this section.

DHCP Server Configuration

The configuration of your DHCP servers will affect many different aspects of your overall design. In all cases, you need to consider the impact of your design on your network performance, the speed and performance of the machine or machines serving your DHCP service, and the location of the machines in relation to the clients they are serving.

Although it's tempting to throw caution to the wind and place servers everywhere, the reality is that you need to keep costs down and make the best use of the hardware and equipment available.

Luckily, in most respects DHCP is a fit and forget service (a service that you can just install and then never again have to worry about). Aside from monitoring the server as part of your general administration, you shouldn't ever have to do much more than provide the machine with the usual courtesy and encouragement that you give to all your servers.

Server Performance   Although DHCP is a relatively low-overhead service, with larger networks you may find that only one server doesn't allow you to respond to all client requests. DHCP requires a lot of general network communication and a significant amount of information to be checked when a new IP address is requested: remember, DHCP must look up the scope and which IP addresses are available, not to mention checking that an existing lease is valid and extending it.

That little bowling alley owner with the computer works very hard most of the time, but imagine the load on the server first thing in the morning when everybody switches their machines on—in a 250-client network, assuming people arrive and switch on over the space of an hour in the morning, that's a request rate of one IP address every 14 seconds, and that load will be repeated when the lease is renewed.

There are a number of solutions to the problem of handling large numbers of simultaneous registrations before you need to resort to using additional servers and splitting your DHCP configuration:

- **Extending the lease duration**   You can reduce both network loading and server loading by extending the lease duration given to clients. Although this won't affect the periodic loading on the server, you can use it to extend the lease beyond the typical uptime of the machine. For example, if your clients shut down each day, there is no reason a lease cannot be given for 24 hours because it will automatically be renewed when the client is shut down and restarted. You can also create multiple scopes and then stagger the lease period across each scope to reduce all your clients renewing at the same time.
- **Increasing RAM**   The more physical RAM you have available, the more information can be cached by the DHCP server service, which

not only speeds queries but also helps to reduce the loading on the
server's hard disks.

- **Increasing disk drive speed**   A significant amount of space is required
  to store and back up the DHCP configuration. The longer it takes to read
  and write the configuration (including the current lease allocations) the
  slower your server will be to respond to requests. Changing the disk
  drives to faster units or using RAID disks to speed access will improve
  general DHCP server performance.

> **Travel Advisory**
>
> The DHCP service includes a number of System Monitor counters
> that you can use to monitor performance.

DHCP Integration   DHCP integrates with a number of core components in
Windows Server 2003. Specifically, it coordinates with DNS, to enable dynamic
updating of the DNS system with respect to the IP address allocated to individual machines, and with Active Directory, if you are using AD-integrated zones
with the DNS service. For more information on this, see Chapter 3.

Server Availability

The problem with DHCP is that because it is responsible for distributing IP addresses and other information, a DHCP failure can cause catastrophic problems. There are a number of different solutions available to alleviate this:

- **Split-scope configurations**   These configurations use two (or more)
  machines with different IP address scopes that are responsible for
  responding to IP address requests. For example, you might have two
  servers, one with a scope of 192.168.1.100–149 and another with
  192.168.1.150–199. Any machine requesting an address checks in with
  the DHCP server that answers first. If one server is unavailable, the
  other is still available to supply DHCP addresses.
- **Clustered DHCP servers**   These servers use the Microsoft Clustering
  Service to provide backup. With clustering, multiple machines are
  configured to provide the same services, but only the server is active—
  in the event of a failure, responsibility is automatically transferred to
  another server.
- **Standby servers**   These servers are configured identically to existing
  DHCP servers, but the DHCP service is disabled. When the existing

DHCP server fails, the standby server's DHCP service is enabled by hand by the administrator. Although this is a manual process, it does enable a backup DHCP service on a machine that may already be dedicated to another task; this is therefore a good use of resources when additional servers or equipment is unavailable.

Server Location

You need to consider the location of your DHCP servers carefully in your network design because their placement will affect the availability, performance, and management of your DHCP system. There are three basic DHCP infrastructure design layouts: distributed, centralized, and combined.

A distributed DHCP layout has two or more DHCP servers spread about the network. Each server is responsible for a particular subnet within your network and is placed logically within the network structure, as shown in Figure 2.6.

In a centralized structure, one server is responsible for dishing out IP addresses across all the subnets in use at a location. However, in this sort of structure, you need either routers that support DHCP/BOOTP relaying (that is, routers compliant with RFC1542), or DHCP Relay Agents employed on the subnets to distribute addresses. You can see this in action in Figure 2.7.

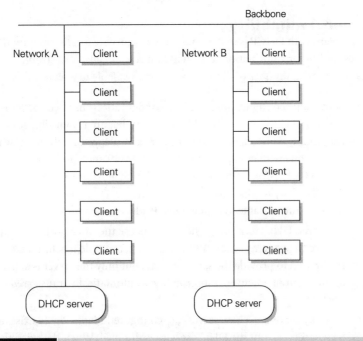

FIGURE 2.6   A distributed DHCP server structure

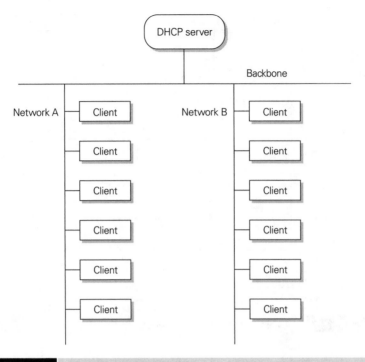

FIGURE 2.7   A centralized DHCP server structure

In a combination structure, you use centralized servers within specific locations—for example, you might use a single server to handle three or four smaller departments and their subnets, while using single, distributed servers for the remaining larger subnets, as shown in Figure 2.8, where there are individual DHCP servers for Networks A and B, but a combined server for E, F, and G, and another combined one for C and D.

A final part to the plan should be the effect of the network structure itself on the location of different servers. For example, if you have a distributed network structure using WAN connections to connect separate offices, then using a centralized structure is probably a bad idea because it will place additional loads on lower-speed and higher-cost network links. The role of separate subnets and routing configuration will have a similar effect.

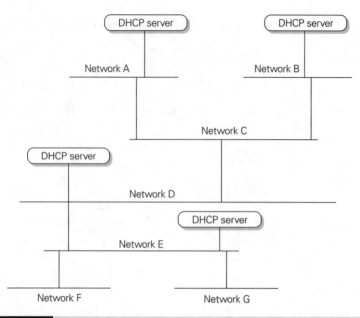

FIGURE 2.8 A combination DHCP server structure

Exam Tip

If you have multiple DHCP servers, they should each be configured with a different scope to prevent different servers giving out the same IP address. A good question is one that provides multiple DHCP scopes and expects you to notice where the duplicate IP address problem is occurring.

Supporting Multiple Subnets

If you have multiple subnets within your network, then you need to give more thought to the location and placement of your DHCP servers. If you are using a single, centralized DHCP server, you must ensure that your routers are able to relay DHCP/BOOTP messages correctly to computers on the other subnets.

If your routers do not support DHCP/BOOTP relaying, you should use a DHCP Relay Agent on each subnet to relay DHCP requests between the local subnet and the central server. Alternatively, you can use multihoming (using multiple network cards) to provide a DHCP server presence across more than one subnet while still using the same central server.

Travel Advisory

The DHCP Relay Agent Service is available only on Windows Server 2003, Windows 2000, and Windows NT 4. For Windows Server 2003 and Windows 2000 machines, the Routing and Remote Access component must be installed to support DHCP relaying. Windows NT 4 provides DHCP Relay Service through the network configuration.

Remember, using a single server for so many machines is a potential point of failure, and two or more servers, either centrally managed or spread over the subnets, is a better choice.

IP Allocation with APIPA

When DHCP configuration is enabled and a DHCP server cannot be located, Windows Server 2003, Windows 2000, and Windows XP machines revert to using Automatic Private IP Addressing (APIPA) to allocate an IP address to the machine. This selects a random IP address in the range 169.254.0.1 to 169.254.255.254 using a 255.255.0.0 netmask.

Computers using APIPA addresses are therefore only able to communicate with other APIPA addressed machines. They also cannot be used within a routed network because there is no way to determine the address of a router on the network.

However, APIPA can be used as an alternative to DHCP when a DHCP server is not available and routing is not required.

CHECKPOINT

✔**Objective 2.01: Designing a TCP/IP Network**   When you start the TCP/IP design process, a number of design decisions about your network infrastructure must be made; for example, you might decide to plan your IP infrastructure based on a hierarchical network design model for enterprise-wide scalability. After you decide what design model to follow, you must also choose between hardware- and software-based routers and decide whether to use static routing or dynamic routing protocols. You must design a structured model for IP address assignment that fits your current networking environment and accommodates growth. You must also decide if you will use public or private IP addresses, or a combination of both.

After you make these decisions, you will need to consider security issues for an IP network. For higher availability and load balancing, you can include redundancy in your network design. Decide whether you need to use technology enhancements such as IP multicast to optimize server workload and network bandwidth. You might start deploying IPv6 on certain network servers or clients, and, if so, decide how you want to manage IPv6/IPv4 coexistence.

✔ **Objective 2.02: Designing a DHCP Infrastructure**   DHCP is a system that greatly simplifies the management of a TCP/IP network by removing the need to individually hand out static IP addresses and gateway, DNS, and other information. For any network with more than ten clients, DHCP is a must. Because the gateway, DNS host, and other information is controlled and supplied by a central server, it means that changes to the information can be made across your network without having to visit each individual machine. Planning a DHCP infrastructure requires you to install a server that is capable of handing out addresses within a specific range and, if necessary, to give out fixed IP addresses to servers and clients that need to retain a static IP address while still getting their IP configuration information from the central server. You also need to consider the effects of large numbers of clients requesting a DHCP address, as well as the effects of the IP addressing scheme you use to separate fixed and dynamic addresses assigned to clients and servers.

REVIEW QUESTIONS

1. You are a consultant, brought in to design a three-tier model WAN for a company. You have the following information about the company:
   - There are currently three separate geographic locations.
   - There is a LAN at each location that encompasses 3–5 buildings at each site.
   - Each site needs Internet connectivity.

   You want to implement a simple, inexpensive IP addressing scheme, with the possibility of growth. What type of addressing strategy would you use on the internal network for this company?

   A. Public

   B. Private

   C. VLSM

    D. Subnetting for the correct number of networks and hosts

2. You have installed private addressing on your company's internal network. You set the router up with the appropriate public address and private address. You want your users to be able to access the public network, so what technology do you need to implement?

    A. VLSM

    B. Dynamic routing

    C. NAT

    D. DHCP

3. You have set up your internal network using DHCP for IP address configuration and you notice that the DHCP server is starting to get slower. What can you do to help optimize the DHCP server?

    A. Upgrade to a faster hard drive.

    B. Install an additional network card in the DHCP server to load balance network requests.

    C. Implement Bootp forwarding on the routers.

    D. Verify the DHCP server is authorized in Active Directory.

4. You have been given a Class C address. You have two networks with about 100 clients per network. What do you need to do to organize the addressing for these two networks within the Class C address?

    A. Install a DHCP server.

    B. Install a router that is RFC 1918 compliant.

    C. Implement Bootp forwarding on the routers.

    D. Implement subnetting.

5. Why would it be beneficial to implement a router in a LAN or WAN? (Choose two.)

    A. To create a DMZ

    B. For security purposes

    C. To create broadcast domains

    D. To speed up Internet access

    E. To enable split-scope configuration on your DHCP server

6. You have implemented DHCP on your network. On which network computers will you probably have to manually configure TCP/IP addresses?

    A. DNS server

    B. DHCP server

    C. Windows XP Professional

    D. Windows NT 4 Workstation

    E. Windows 2000 Professional

7. You have implemented centralized DHCP on your routed network. Most of the routers are new, but there are some that you are not sure of. Your network has five subnets. The DHCP server is on subnet 2, and the clients on subnet 4 are unable to get IP addresses. The rest of the subnets, 1, 2, 3, and 5 are able to lease addresses. What would you look at first to troubleshoot this issue?

    A. Check the NAT server.

    B. Verify the DHCP server is authorized in Active Directory.

    C. Verify the scope on the DHCP server is properly configured.

    D. Verify the router is RFC 1918 compliant.

    E. Verify the router is RFC 1542 compliant.

REVIEW ANSWERS

1. **B**   Using a private addressing scheme is less expensive than using public addressing, and the scheme can be designed to accommodate virtually unlimited growth. Public addressing relies on your getting three separate public IP address allocations instead of just one, and it would not accommodate a suitable amount of growth. Subnetting (and therefore VLSM) applies only if you have already decided on a public or private addressing scheme.

2. **C**   This device translates IP addresses from private network addresses inside an organization to public addresses outside the organization. The others provide background services for your network but do not make associations for public and private networks.

3. **A**   As clients boot up and request an IP address from the DHCP server, reads and writes occur on the DHCP server hard drive to check the DHCP database. Increasing the speed of the hard drive will allow an address to be retrieved from the database more quickly, and thus allow the processing of more addresses.

4. **D**   Creating subnets allows you to borrow bits from the host ID for the network ID. This allows you to create more networks that contain fewer hosts.

5. **A** **C**   Screened subnets or DMZs are created within the private network, protecting important data. Broadcast domains are typically bounded by routers, because routers do not forward broadcast frames.

6. **A** **B**   Addresses are configured manually for domain controllers, DHCP servers, DNS servers, WINS servers, routers and non-Microsoft hosts that do not support DHCP.

7. **E**   This RFC outlines how a router is able to forward DHCP requests.

Planning a
Host Resolution
Strategy

	NEWBIE	SOME EXPERIENCE	EXPERT
ETA	2–4 hours	1–2 hours	1 hour

On the whole, humans aren't very good with numbers. Think about how many phone numbers you really know, that is, those you can actually dial without having to think about. You'd be surprised how few you actually remember—it's probably less than 20. But if I asked you to name the people in your high school or college class, you could probably name many of them. Probably most people in your office, too, not to mention numerous celebrities, film stars, pop stars, and politicians.

Why is that? Because it's a name. For some reason, we humans remember names much more easily than numbers.

The same is true out there on the network. Probably nobody (well, except the administrators) remembers that you can reach a famous company's website on 207.46.134.190. But everybody knows that Microsoft.com points to their website. IP addresses don't exactly roll off the tongue!

This causes something of a problem, though: how do you resolve names into the IP addresses that you know the computers are using behind the scenes? Within Windows there are two solutions: Domain Name System (DNS) and Windows Internet Naming System (WINS). WINS is a Windows-only system that has a few benefits when used on an internal network. Many of the original advantages of WINS, however, have been transferred to DNS, which can also be used on the Internet and in an integrated format with the Active Directory (AD) system.

The exam concentrates highly on the security aspects of the network design within Windows Server 2003, but it's important to understand the underlying issues so that you can appreciate the security implications as well as the general needs and requirements of the DNS and WINS systems.

Objective 3.01 Planning a DNS Strategy

D NS works on a very simple system that was designed with distributed networks such as the Internet in mind, but it can be used equally well in medium- to large-sized LAN environments.

Windows Server 2003, like Windows 2000 before it, uses DNS extensively: it is the default name resolution system and an integrated part of Active Directory. AD now uses the DNS domain name structure as the basis of its own naming system. Where Windows NT used a single word for its domain name, for example, MCSLP, in Active Directory the same domain would be known by its DNS-style name of mcslp.com. AD can also update the DNS information based on the allocation of IP addresses through DHCP and can help to organize the information stored within AD and its DNS records.

Overview of DNS

DNS was originally designed to provide the name resolution facilities for the TCP/IP protocol. DNS works on a system of top-level domains, such as .com, .net, or .co.uk, and the main organizational level domains within these, such as Microsoft.com, which is known as a domain name, as is Amazon.com, bbc.co.uk, and other such Internet domains that you're familiar with. The domain does not map to a given IP address; it is a container for the individual machines and resources within the network.

Machines within the domain are given a specific name, which then maps to their allocated IP address. For example, the address 192.168.1.1 might map to the name workstation.mcslp.com. This name is known as a Fully Qualified Domain Name (FQDN).

Domains can also be further subdivided by additional classifications within the main domain. For example, the sales department of mcslp.com might be contained within the subdomain of sales.mcslp.com. The FQDN for a workstation within that subdomain would then be workstation.sales.mcslp.com.

Domain Zone Files

Domain information is stored within a zone file (or the corresponding structure within AD). There are two main types of zone file supported by all DNS implementations, a third supported only by Windows 2000 and Windows Server 2003, and a fourth supported only by Windows Server 2003. The first two are the primary and secondary zone files. The third is an Active Directory–integrated zone. The fourth zone type is the stub zone, which can also be Active Directory integrated. Within these four main types there are also two subtypes: the forward zone file maps names to IP addresses, and a reverse zone file maps IP addresses to names.

The primary zone file holds all of the authoritative information for a domain. There can be only one machine and one zone file per domain for this information. This creates a potential single point of failure because one machine can be responsible for handling the primary domain information.

However, to help spread the load of requests, primary domains can be shared with other servers. These zone files are known as secondary domains, and they are read-only (because they can only be updated from the primary zone file and the primary domain server). The zones themselves are distributed from the primary server to another through a zone transfer. Zone transfers occur when the primary server sends an update notification to the secondary domain servers—the time between updates is configured within the zone file itself.

There are two types of zone transfer, the full zone transfer (AXFR) triggers the secondary server to request a full copy of the entire zone file from the primary server. The incremental zone transfer (IXFR) exchanges only the changes since the last transfer were sent to the secondary servers.

The AD-integrated zone causes the zone file information to be stored within the AD database. This provides a number of benefits:

- Zone transfers are no longer required because the zone information is exchanged with other AD servers as part of the AD database.
- There is no longer a single point of failure because the information can be distributed and updated through any AD domain controller.

The downside is that only domain controllers with the DNS service enabled can host AD-integrated zones and therefore respond to DNS queries. However, other servers that are not domain controllers can host secondary zones based on an AD-integrated zone and respond to queries.

Understanding Queries

DNS is a distributed service. What makes it so useful is that an individual server is not only knowledgeable about its own domains (whether primary, secondary, or AD integrated), but it can also suggest alternative servers that know the answer.

To use the phone number analogy again, if you want to speak to Bob Smith, you can look up his phone number in your authoritative server—your address book—to see if you have his number. If you don't, you might have the phone number of somebody at the same company who does know Bob's number, and you can ask them for it.

The DNS system works in the same way. If a client requests an IP address based on a name from a server and the server doesn't know it, then it can forward the request on to a machine that does know it—for example, if you are trying to resolve the name of an Internet website, your server will probably forward the request on to your ISP's DNS server.

There are two important points here: the first is the idea of authoritative servers and the second is the format of the request itself. An authoritative server is one that knows it is authoritative for the domains it hosts. Therefore, if you ask a server that is authoritative for the mcslp.com domain for an IP address for the FQDN workstation.mcslp.com, it knows that if it doesn't have the address, the name is invalid and it will return a failure.

DNS requests are sent by the client in two different ways, iterative and recursive. Iterative queries request information from a server and ask them to provide the best information they can. Typically this means that if the hostname is in the server's cache, or it is authoritative for the domain, it returns the response directly. If it isn't, it returns the address of a server that might have the information. A recursive query follows this information. Most queries are therefore a combination of the two systems: an iterative to find out if a server knows the answer, and a recursive to force the server to resolve the address. The two request types may be made either by the client or the server, which may also send its own iterative or recursive queries on to other servers to try to answer the original query.

You'll see this more clearly if you actually walk through the process of a client communicating with its name server to resolve the address for www.microsoft.com.

Local Lingo

Name server A name server is a computer running a DNS service set to answer queries.

---

1. The client checks its own cache to see if it has resolved the name recently but doesn't find anything.

2. The client sends a recursive query to its primary name server.

3. The name server checks its database and cache, doesn't find anything, and sends an iterative request to a root server for the .com top-level domain.

Local Lingo

Top-level domain These are the core domains used on the Internet, such as .com, .net, and country-specific domains such as .uk and .au.

Local Lingo

Root server Root servers hold information about the domains within a top-level domain and the authoritative servers responsible for them.

---

4. The root server responds to the DNS server with the IP address of the DNS server that is authoritative for the Microsoft.com domain.

5. The DNS server sends an iterative request to the DNS server for the Microsoft.com domain to resolve the address www.Microsoft.com. It uses an iterative request because it already knows that the Microsoft.com DNS server is authoritative for the domain.

6. The Microsoft.com DNS server returns the IP address to the DNS server.

7. The DNS server returns the IP address to the client.

You can see this perhaps more clearly in Figure 3.1—the numbers on the arrows refer to the steps in the preceding list.

Mapping DNS to an Internal Network

How does all this fit in with planning and design an internal DNS network? Well, the same basic principles remain: as the size of your network increases, it's likely that you will need to increase the number of DNS servers and zone files, both to keep machines logically separated and to help reduce the traffic crossing your network through the use of the DNS system.

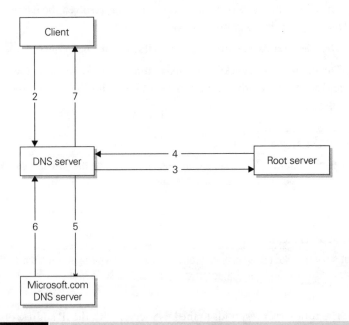

FIGURE 3.1 The DNS name-resolving process

For example, in a network with thousands of computers, it's unlikely (and impractical) that you'll want a single server responsible for DNS queries. You'll also have to come up with an interesting naming scheme within a single zone to ensure that names are not confused and do not collide with each other—for example, if you wanted to provide separate file servers within two departments.

This means you need to plan the location and distribution of your servers so that you can resolve names while also reducing background network traffic in the form of requests. You also have to consider the security implications (because zone files are distributed among servers) and how your DNS service will integrate with AD and other third-party DNS solutions, including those provided by your Internet Service Provider.

Stub Zones

Stub zones are essentially a small copy of the copy of the zone file for a primary domain that only contains the resource records necessary to identify the site of authority (SOA) for the domain in question.

This can be useful in situations where you want to be able to resolve or connect specific domains and resources but do not want a machine to act as either a domain controller or full secondary zone host for the domain in question. This means that when a client requests an address from a server hosting a stub zone, the information is resolved using the SOA servers for the domain. This ensures that the information is always the most up to date rather than cached or gleaned from a secondary name server that may be using an older version of the DNS zone records.

The main benefits of a stub zone are as follows:

- **Delegated information remains current**   By updating the stub zone for child zones regularly, the servers will maintain up-to-date records on the SOA for a zone and also maintain reliable sources for resolving queries on a zone.

- **Improve name resolution**   Because stub zones resolve queries through the recursion system, not by forwarding requests, you can improve the reliability of queries by sending requests directly to the machines that have the most up-to-date information.

- **Simpler administration**   By using stub zones, you can continue to have localized name servers within departments that resolve company-wide addresses without the need to manage secondary domains across a number of different servers.

Exam Tip

Stub zones are not a solution for load balancing. If you need to spread the load over a number of machines, you must continue to use secondary servers to host domains and provide resolving queries.

Plan a DNS Namespace Design

Your namespace design is how you logically divide up your network and identify individual machines. There are a number of issues here:

- **Root domain name choice**   You need to choose the name of your root domain name, which may be a private domain or a domain that is directly responsible for your appearance on the Internet.
- **Subdomain name choice**   If you have a larger network, you may want to separate your primary domain name into a number of subdomains. This can be done by geographical location, role, or a combination of the two, or any other scheme you deem suitable.
- **Active Directory integration**   If you want to combine your DNS namespace with your AD design, you must consider its implications on your AD design.
- **Internal/external requirements**   If you have an external Internet presence, you must think about how to separate the internal and external names within your network.

We'll have a look at each of these requirements in this section.

Exam Tip

Occasionally, Microsoft likes to slip in questions based on this type of relatively straightforward design choice, often combined with the Active Directory, group policy, or other settings; for example: You want to apply group policy settings based on a given domain or subdomain structure, so how should you name and organize the following network?

Root Domain Name Choice

The root domain name choice is probably the easiest of the choices to make. In fact, if you have an Internet-registered domain name, the decision has been made for you. This is because you can use your Internet domain as your internal DNS name and even for your AD domain name.

If you plan to get an Internet domain name, it's best to register the name with one of the various domain name registrars. They will be able to advise you which names have been taken and allow you to register with one of the many top-level domains, such as .net, .com, or the country-specific domains.

If you don't have a registered domain name and have no plans to get one, or you want to create a local domain, then you should use the top-level domain suffix of .local to identify the domain as local rather than part of the public Internet domain name space.

> ### Travel Advisory
> Remember when choosing an Internet-compatible name that it can contain only uppercase and lowercase letters, numbers, and hyphens. Windows Server 2003 also supports other characters, including extended ASCII and Unicode characters to retain compatibility at a NetBIOS level. However, these characters can only be used in an all Windows Server 2003 environment.

Subdomain Name Choice

You should only use subdomains either if you need to logically divide your network for identification purposes, or if you are integrating with AD and want to divide the network up according to specific groups or divisions.

The divisions serve two purposes. First, they make it easier to distribute DNS servers and resources around the network—for example, you can create a sales domain and then have all sales machines talk to a dedicated sales domain DNS server. Second, they act as a mental aid—remember, the point of the naming system is to help us poor Homo sapiens recognize machines.

If you know, for example, that a computer is in the sales department in the Seattle office, the FQDN is probably something like sales.seattle.mydomain.com. It works in reverse, too: if you have an entry in your event log indicating a problem with a machine with an FQDN of pr.fr.mydomain.com, it's a good bet that it's a machine located in the PR department of the French office.

The size and complexity of your network will define the most appropriate naming system based on a combination of different factors, including, but not limited to

- **Network size**   If your network is divided into a number of Class C networks with routing between them, it may make sense to create a new subdivision for each network group.
- **Geographical structure**   If your network is spread over a wide area, you probably already have network divisions configured according to IP addresses. You can logically group these by state, county, and country accordingly.
- **Organizational structure**   Dividing your network by your organization structure, such as sales, marketing, IT support, and so on, can be a useful way of identifying machines.

All of these different solutions, combined, are shown in Figure 3.2. Note that we've used a combination of country and state level divisions here.

Active Directory Integration

The same rules apply to the AD naming structure as to the DNS naming structure. AD domains can be identified and subdivided into the same structure as the DNS domains. The easiest way to design the DNS system is to first design the AD structure and then to include the DNS system to help support the AD structure and the machines within it.

For example, with an Internet domain of Microsoft.com, you might choose to subdivide your organization through a combination of geographical and organizational subdomains, such as us.Microsoft.com and sales.us.Microsoft.com.

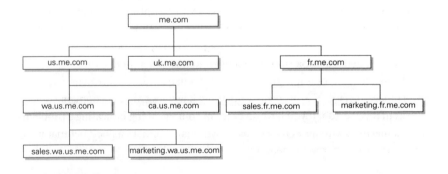

FIGURE 3.2   DNS subdomains by organization and geographic layout

Using your public, registered, Internet domain name for your AD structure guarantees that your name will be unique, both globally and within the public Internet namespace. You can also use the same naming format to add further subdivisions and departments.

For smaller companies, it probably makes sense to use a simpler design, perhaps using only one domain and AD. However, keep in mind that AD design also implies group policy and other settings, and you may still want to use AD and DNS domains to help organize this.

Internal/External Separation

If you have a public presence on the Internet, it can be a good idea to split your internal and external namespaces. This enables you to publicize your public addresses without publishing your private addresses to the world. It also means that you can apply filters and security access based on the internal and external subdomains, making administration significantly easier.

The split can be a simple case of using the public domain name as the root for external names, that is, mydomain.com, while using a subdomain for all of your internal clients, such as corp.mydomain.com. Or you can use separate internal and external subdomains—for example, internal.mydomain.com and external.mydomain.com—just be aware that if you have a public presence you may want to have simplified addresses for specific hosts—www.mydomain.com for example.

Plan Zone Replication Requirements

When you separate your network into a number of different zones, chances are you'll need to replicate the zone information among one or more servers to help reduce the loading on a single machine. You'll also need to think about the localized demands of your network: if it's split into a number of subdomains, different network segments, and so on. DNS zone replication therefore comes down to network traffic and bandwidth.

Of course, if you've already logically divided your DNS system into different locations or departments or both, you can easily identify where the different server should be located.

There are some general rules that can be applied to DNS design:

- You should provide two DNS servers for each locality to allow one primary and one backup secondary server for clients to resolve addresses.

- You should provide at least one DNS server within each physical location if they are separated by WAN links, or one DNS server per major subdomain or subnet in a larger organization.

- Each DNS server should contain zone information for all domains that need to be resolved by that subdivision. For example, if your site holds two domains, then each server should have copies of both zone files.

- When using AD-integrated zones, each DNS server should contain a copy of the _msdcs.forestrootdomain zone, as this holds details about the servers for a domain, including the domain controllers, and domain information.

Exam Tip

A common DNS-related question is, "Why can't this user contact their domain controller?" You need to know that the _msdcs.forestrootdomain contains vital AD data that must be replicated—without it, secondary servers won't respond to queries.

You can see these rules in action for a basic DNS domain (that is, non-AD-integrated) in Figure 3.3.

Within an AD-integrated domain you have to take into account the effects of the AD data. First, additional domain controllers for the same domain or within the same domain tree automatically share DNS information, but secondary servers (not domain controllers) must replicate the core zone information and the _msdcs.forestrootdomain information. You can see an example of this in Figure 3.4.

Plan a Forwarding Configuration

When a DNS server doesn't know the IP address for a given name (that is, it's not authoritative for the domain), the server forwards the request to another DNS server for resolving. This is called forwarding and you will need to plan the forwarding configuration very carefully depending on your domain configuration and setup.

There are two basic types of forwarding: delegation, when a specific subdomain within a zone is delegated to the responsibility of another server, and standard, which sends queries that cannot otherwise be resolved by the current server to another server.

DNS is designed to reduce the amount of information flowing around a network, and, in general, your forwarding configuration will also depend on your network layout and your zone replication requirements. It will also depend on

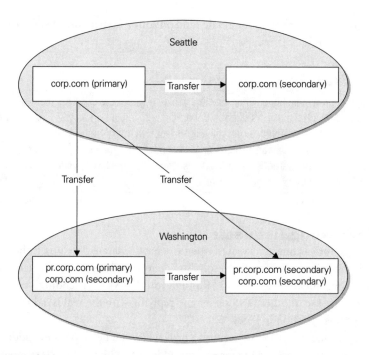

FIGURE 3.3 Primary and secondary servers in a native DNS domain

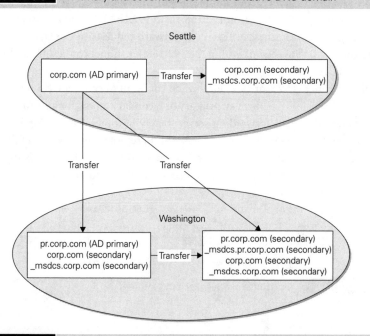

FIGURE 3.4 Primary and secondary servers in an AD-integrated domain

your DNS structure and subdomains and on your AD structure, if you are using AD-integrated domains.

Exam Tip

Expect a few questions about the DNS design of your network. That means understanding the effects of both forwarding and delegation on your design. In a nutshell, use forwarding when you want to resolve addresses outside the local scope—whether subnet or DNS subdomain—and use delegation from parent servers to child subdomains to allow logical divisions within a DNS namespace.

Forwarding Requests

Standard forwarding can be used when you have separate domains, rather than subdomains, that you want to resolve or when you want to resolve external addresses over the Internet. It works through your DNS server sending a recursive DNS request to another DNS server and replying with the real IP address. You can see this in action in Figure 3.5.

Forwarding can also work within a LAN when you need to resolve addresses across subnets by setting the forwarding address to a higher DNS server within your network structure. For example, as shown in Figure 3.6, you would set the DNS address for the clients on 192.168.1.*x* to 192.168.1.10 and then set the forwarding address on the DNS server to forward requests to the DNS server at 192.168.10.10. Now clients within the 192.168.1.*x* subnet can resolve addresses across the rest of the network.

Forwarding servers are also ideal when you want to create a DNS server that has no responsibility, either as a primary or secondary server, for a given zone. In this configuration, a forwarding server merely becomes a cache for DNS requests on the local network. You can use this in remote offices where a full DNS service is not required but you want to reduce the network traffic being forwarded over a WAN link for the purposes of resolving domain names.

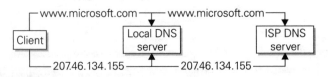

FIGURE 3.5   Forwarding requests to the Internet

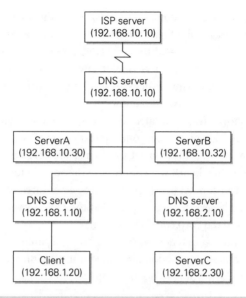

FIGURE 3.6   Forwarding requests in a LAN

Conditional Forwarding

Conditional forwarding enables you to send requests to other namespaces that are outside of your own zone and would not normally be accessible through the Internet. For example, if you were partners with another company and needed to resolve names within their network, you could use conditional forwarding to resolve the addresses. The same situation applies when one company is recognized by a number of different names. Conditional forwarding eliminates the need to act as a secondary domain name server for those domains.

For example, imagine one company with two namespaces, mcslp.com and mcwords.com. Rather than having servers within mcslp.com act as secondary domains for the mcwords.com domain, the servers could be configured to provide conditional forwarding to the mcwords.com domain.

The benefit of conditional forwarding is that it continues to resolve addresses with the SOA servers for a domain and does not rely on updates to the secondaries. This helps ease administration and returns the most up-to-date information when the domains are queried by clients.

Delegation

Delegated forwarding is generally automatic and happens when a subdomain is handled by another server. The delegation occurs by having name server (NS) records within the parent domain that point to the name server for the subdomain. Whereas regular forwarding works to resolve addresses outside the scope—usually an IP subnet—of the local DNS server, delegation works to resolve addresses outside the name scope of DNS server. This means that you must have a separate resolving strategy, using either a centralized DNS server or the forwarding system to forward requests.

Figure 3.7 shows two delegated domains, sales.corp.com and marketing.corp.com. There are no current zone replications in effect. For ClientA to resolve ServerA.marketing.corp.com, it has to ask the corp.com DNS server to resolve the address. If ClientB wants to resolve the address for ServerA.marketing.corp.com, it can contact the corp.com DNS server directly, or it can ask the sales.corp.com DNS server to do it, provided the DNS server is configured to forward requests to the corp.com DNS server.

The reason for this is that delegation works from a parent domain down to a subdomain but not across subdomains, so you must either ask at the highest level or configure forwarding to do the asking for you.

Plan for DNS Security

There are a number of security issues with the DNS system, but the two most important are securing your DNS system from the public Internet and updating and providing DNS information. The first is easy to resolve if you think logically about the requirements of your internal clients and your external presence on the Internet, if there is one.

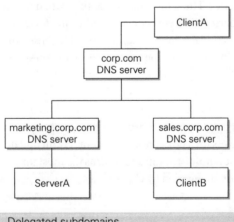

FIGURE 3.7   Delegated subdomains

The second issue is more difficult to resolve because it involves all areas of the DNS server. For example, how you secure the server, how dynamic updates are handled, and how information is exchanged between DNS servers, particularly if AD is involved, all come into play.

There are a number of ways your security can be breached if you do not take care of this:

- *Incorrect information is provided to your clients.*   If the DNS zones have been updated by another server or malicious client, your clients may end up communicating with the wrong machine. For example, if your DNS service is compromised, users could then connect to what they think is your intranet server, when in fact it's an external site that could have captured a number of passwords.

- *Someone acquires a complete list of all your configured servers and IP addresses (called "footprinting") or acquires the entire zone file.*   This is a good way of gathering all of the information about your network without much effort. Once someone has an approved list, they can try to contact and communicate with the different machines directly, even using known exploits where necessary. The information can also be used to spoof or imitate a given IP address, allowing a malicious user to access your network as if they were a local user.

- *Denial of service attacks can render your servers useless by flooding them with requests.*   This can prevent your genuine clients from picking up information, or it can bog your servers down enough that they crash or not respond correctly when they run out of capacity.

Local Lingo

Denial of service (DoS) attack   A DoS attack is one that doesn't rely on directly affecting the system or service but instead floods the system with so many apparently valid queries that it prevents genuine users from getting through. This is a bit like someone continually talking to you while you are having a conversation with someone else: it limits your ability to communicate, without going as far as actually wiring your jaw shut or stuffing cotton in your ears.

Exam Tip

The exam is hot on security, so it's likely that you'll be asked how you can secure your DNS installation. Make sure you are aware of why DNS security is important (as just covered) and how you can ensure its security.

There are a number of specific concerns relating to security that you need to be aware of:

- **Security of the DNS resolving process**   Controlling how your internal clients and your public clients on the Internet resolve addresses within your domain or domains.

- **Security of the DNS server**   Preventing malicious attacks on your server and preventing users from accessing or updating information that they shouldn't have access to.

- **Zone security**   Ensuring DNS zone information is not updated from dynamic clients or the database corrupted in the process.

- **Client security**   Your clients should be talking to the right server.

I'll cover each of these concerns in the next sections.

Security When Resolving Addresses

When designing a DNS system, you need to be able to resolve internal addresses and external addresses and also, if necessary, publish your public presence on the Internet. Obviously, the moment you include the Internet in your equation, you need to think about the security, not only in terms of preventing or restricting your internal clients from accessing the Internet, but also to prevent external users from accessing areas of your network that you do not want them to access.

There are four scenarios involving the different combinations of internal resolving, external (Internet) resolving from the internal network, and the publicizing of your public presence on the Internet. We'll look at each combination and its recommended solution next.

Exam Tip

You may be asked to suggest one of the alternatives in this section based on the requirements of the network.

Internal Resolving Only   If your clients only need to resolve names within the internal network with no resolving of Internet names, then you should disable all forwarding and configure your server to handle the resolving for the root and top-level domains.

Internal and External Resolving (No Public Presence) With internal clients that need to communicate with the Internet for resolving purposes but do not have an Internet presence, you can use forwarding on your DNS servers to send the requests to your ISP, as shown in Figure 3.8.

For more secure access, another alternative is use a proxy service, such as Microsoft's Internet Security and Acceleration (ISA) server, as shown in Figure 3.9. The ISA server or servers can be configured to resolve Internet addresses, so while the clients continue to talk to the DNS servers to resolve internal addresses, they can talk to the proxy server to resolve Internet addresses for web browsing.

Internal Resolving with Public Presence If you have internal resolving requirements and have a public presence on the Internet but don't need to resolve Internet addresses, the easiest method is to completely separate your internal and external DNS servers. The internal server handles all internal traffic, while the public server handles the serving of your Internet domain and presence. You can see this in action in Figure 3.10.

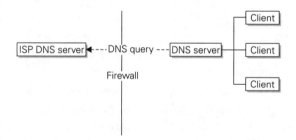

FIGURE 3.8 Using forwarding from an internal DNS server for queries

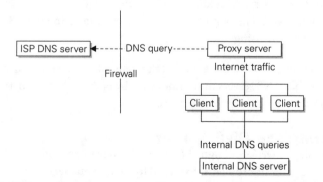

FIGURE 3.9 Using a proxy server for communication with the Internet

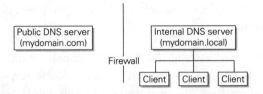

FIGURE 3.10   Using separate internal/external DNS servers

In this situation in Figure 3.10, there is no communication between the internal and external servers. However, the same principles of an internal-only DNS server apply: you must configure your internal server to host the top-level and root domains.

Internal and External Resolving with Public Presence   There are a number of different solutions to choose from if you want an internal DNS server, an Internet presence, and the ability to resolve Internet addresses on your internal network. Most rely on a combination of the solutions we've already discussed. We recommend one of the following three solutions:

- Split the DNS namespace between external (public) machines and internal (private) machines. For example, with the public domain mydomain.com, your public presence would remain within mydomain.com, but your internal servers would be within the internal.mydomain.com subdomain.

- Split the DNS service between internal and external DNS servers. The external servers not only publicize your presence and allow public clients to access your network, but also resolve requests for your internal clients. This is similar to the non-public presence solution, with the addition that your internal servers forward their requests to the external DNS servers for resolving public addresses, as shown in Figure 3.11. The same solution could use a proxy server, as demonstrated in Figure 3.9, for Internet browsing.

- Split the DNS, but use a firewall that only allows the internal and external DNS servers to communicate by opening UDP and TCP port 53 between the two DNS servers.

Securing the DNS Server

Unsurprisingly, DNS is designed to be a relatively open system, but that can lead to a number of problems if you fail to secure your server from potential

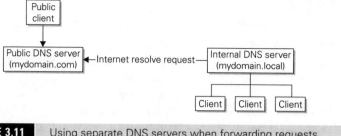

Using separate DNS servers when forwarding requests

attack. You can secure the server using a combination of the server settings and, if you're using AD, the discretionary access control list (DACL) for AD.

The four problems you can address directly through the settings for the DNS server service are as follows:

- **Interface exposure**   The more interfaces your machine has, the more likely it will be affected by a potential problem. This is particularly true on a server that has separate internal and external interfaces. You can control which network interfaces and IP addresses support DNS lookups.

- **Cache pollution**   Deliberately badly formatted resolving requests can pollute the name cache space, which can then return bad or false information to clients. The server provides the Secure Cache Against Pollution setting to prevent this.

- **Recursion**   Not an obvious problem, but the default recursion option for a server can be abused by allowing the recursion to cause a denial of service (DoS) attack. Switching the recursion off should not affect the operation of your server because it will continue to communicate directly with DNS servers to resolve addresses without recursion.

- **Root hints**   If you have an internal-only DNS server, you should configure the root hints—used to resolve authoritative domains on the Internet—so that it points only to your internal servers.

If your server is running AD and acting as a DNS server, you should use the discretionary access control lists to restrict different levels of access to only those people who specifically need it. Table 3.1 lists the default, and recommended, security settings.

Group or User Names	Permissions
TABLE 3.1 Default Permissions for Users and Groups Accessing the DNS Server Service	
Administrators	Allow: Read, Write, Create All Child Objects, Special Permissions
Authenticated Users	Allow: Read, Special Permissions
Creator Owner	Special Permissions
DnsAdmins	Allow: Full Control, Read, Write, Create All Child Objects, Delete Child Objects, Special Permissions
Domain Admins	Allow: Full Control, Read, Write, Create All Child Objects, Delete Child Objects
Enterprise Admins	Allow: Full Control, Read, Write, Create All Child Objects, Delete Child Objects
Enterprise Domain Controllers	Allow: Special Permissions
Pre-Windows 2000 Compatible Access	Allow: Special Permissions
System	Allow: Full Control, Read, Write, Create All Child Objects, Delete Child Objects

Zone Security

There are three main areas of security and integrity of the zone data: dynamic updates, browsing, exchanging zone information during a replication.

Dynamic Updates   Dynamic updating is a complex issue. Since Windows 2000, clients running Windows 2000, Windows XP, or Windows Server 2003 have been able to register their configured computer name against the IP address they have been allocated (either statically or through DHCP) directly with a DNS server through a system called Dynamic DNS. This is a separate system from that which automatically registers DHCP allocations to the DNS server at the server end.

Travel Assistance

For more information on the dynamic update protocol, check out the online webcast at http://support.Microsoft.com/servicedesks/webcasts/wc050301/wcblurb050301.asp.

The problem with Dynamic DNS is that it potentially lets any client register its configured name and address to the DNS server, and this information could overwrite or update information in the DNS namespace. Windows Server 2003 allows secure updates, which provides two key benefits:

- The ability to grant the permission to modify zones and recourse records to specific users and groups. For example, you could allow dynamic updates only from computers when the user logs in and is a member of the Administrators group.
- The ability to protect zones and resource records against unauthorized modification.

You can set secure updates within the DNS servers Properties dialog box.

Exam Tip

Secure updates rely on the fact that only the computer that created the resource record can update the information within it. If you are using DHCP to perform DNS updates on behalf of the client computer, this can be a problem. You can resolve this by adding the DHCP server to the DnsUpdateProxy group.

Security from Browsing   If you have a public presence on the Internet and do not protect your private DNS space (through the use of separate internal/external servers), it will be possible for external users to browse your internal domain and discover information, IP addresses, and server details remotely. It's best to secure yourself by separating your internal and external domains using one of the methods already described.

Also, be aware that unless it is configured to prevent it, a public server can respond to requests from another DNS server to share its DNS zone files. Within Windows Server 2003 and Windows 2000, you can configure your DNS server to exchange only its entire zone file with servers explicitly listed as name servers (that is, with NS records) within your domain.

Security When Exchanging   Directly related to the previous problem and just as important is the security of exchanging DNS zone files within an organization to reduce the risk of an internally sourced attack. You can protect your DNS servers by allowing only specific IP addresses, or hosts listed as NS/SOA, for the domain to actually request and transfer the information.

DNS Client Security

Without careful monitoring, it's possible for clients to start using alternate DNS servers. This can lead to the wrong IP address being returned when a name is looked up. There are two ways this can be controlled:

- **Use DHCP**   The most obvious solution is to force your clients to use DHCP for their IP and DNS allocation.
- **Restrict the DNS server**   You can configure Windows Server 2003 to resolve only for clients within a given IP address range.

Examine DNS Interoperability with Third-Party DNS Solutions

You may need to be able to integrate your Windows Server 2003 domains with an existing DNS name server. In most situations, the other server will be running an implementation of the BIND DNS server. Windows Server 2003 is compatible with the following BIND implementations:

BIND 4.9.7
BIND 8.1.2
BIND 8.2
BIND 9.1.0

These are the implementations that have been tested and confirmed as working with Windows Server 2003, although other implementations, including other DNS servers, may also work.

There are a number of subissues relating to the compatibility, which we discuss in the next few sections.

Zone Transfer

Zone transfer with other BIND-oriented DNS servers should work without any major issues. Windows Server 2003 defaults to fast domain transfers when exchanging domain records. BIND versions of 4.9.7 and lower do not support these fast transfers, which may lead either to corrupted zone information or nonexistent zone information. You can configure slow zone exchanges by checking the Bind Secondaries box in the advanced server properties.

AD Compatibility

Only BIND versions of 8.1.2 or later support the necessary requirements for deploying AD. If you can't upgrade to this version, then consider migrating any existing DNS server data to a Windows Server 2003 installation and disabling the older servers.

If you are not using BIND, look for the following standards supported by your DNS server implementation:

- The SRV resource record, required to enable AD to specify the location of specific services within a domain
- Dynamic updates

DNS Integration Implementations

If you have to integrate into an existing DNS structure, rather than creating a completely new DNS structure, simply create a new subdomain within your current DNS namespace to hold your AD domain. For example, if you have a domain of Microsoft.com, you might create an AD subdomain called windows.Microsoft.com. To do this, you must delegate responsibility for the windows .Microsoft.com domain within the parent domain zone file to the AD server.

Objective 3.02 Planning a WINS Strategy

The Windows Internet Naming Service (WINS) was the original default method for resolving names into IP addresses within a Microsoft network. Unlike DNS, which resolves FQDNs into an IP address, WINS resolves NetBIOS names into IP Addresses. Although WINS has been replaced with DNS as the primary name resolving service, it is still in use within some networks with older Windows-based computers; it has a generally lower overhead than DNS.

Planning a WINS strategy relies on choosing whether to use NetBIOS and WINS in your network, how this relates generally to your name resolution strategy, how to replicate WINS information, and using the local rather than network-based Lmhosts file for WINS name resolving.

> ### Exam Tip
>
> WINS is being phased out, with sections of the WINS and NetBIOS system already removed from the 64-bit versions of Windows Server 2003. As such, WINS in Windows Server 2003 is seen as a compatibility system, rather than an ideal solution. Questions on WINS in the exam are likely to focus on whether WINS is actually required, the use of an Lmhosts file, and the replication of WINS databases.

When to Use WINS

If your network is entirely populated by machines running Windows 2000, Windows Server 2003, or Windows XP, there should be no need to run WINS services or even to use the NetBIOS protocol within your network.

However, if you have a mixture of newer and older Windows machines, including Windows 95, Windows 98, and Windows NT, you should use both WINS and DNS within your network. The older machines will use WINS as the default method for resolving names within the local network and within specific domains. For example, when accessing a UNC path such as \\server1\fileshare, the server1 name will be resolved by WINS on all but the latest machines.

One other consideration is other operating systems in your network that may be able to register themselves through the WINS service. For example, Unix servers running the Samba application (for file and printer sharing), Mac OS servers running AppleShare server, and Mac OS X all support the ability to register themselves through the WINS service. Although all of these systems also support direct TCP/IP connectivity and can be manually registered within AD or a DNS zone file, it is worth considering the lower administration overheads of WINS.

NetBIOS

NetBIOS is the underlying protocol that provides support for the WINS service. WINS is primarily a broadcast service, but it can also be used in registration mode (where a client registers its address with a WINS server). WINS is designed to work with the NetBIOS over TCP/IP (NetBT) standard.

NetBIOS is a session-level protocol that communicates between devices on the network. WINS is merely an extension of the NetBIOS system that enables NetBIOS name/IP address registration to be stored within a server and then distributed to specific clients—just like a DNS server—for resolving NetBIOS names. The main difference between NetBIOS/WINS and DNS is that the registration information is not divided into domains.

This limitation means that NetBIOS is suitable only for resolving names used within a network segment. You can share information across segments by using WINS replication, but you may run into name clash issues. There are also a number of security issues related to the use of NetBIOS that are covered later in this chapter in the "Security Issues" section.

NetBIOS Name Registration

When you switch on a machine it attempts to register its name and IP address with a WINS server. This is done either through a broadcast message, which the WINS servers must pick up, or a directed message (if the WINS server is configured on the client). If the name does not already exist in the WINS database, it's updated accordingly.

However, if the name does exist, the WINS server communicates with the existing machine to check if the registration should remain. If the originally registered machine responds, the WINS server sends a negative registration response to the new machine. If the registered machine does not respond, the entry is cleared from the database and the new machine is added to the records.

Travel Advisory

Generally, machines will register themselves more than once to enable them to register as different types of host. For example, a single machine may register itself as a domain controller, file server, or WINS server, but all are the same server. The WINS service and NetBIOS system allow a machine to register itself in different ways so that other computers can look up a machine of a specific type.

As you might expect, if WINS servers are configured, direct registration is used in place of broadcast, with the primary server being contacted first. If the primary server cannot be contacted, the remaining servers are contacted until a registration can take place. If no servers can be contacted, the registration is repeated at ten-minute intervals until registration has completed. The WINS server used for registration is rotated every hour

Renewals are handled by the client along similar lines to the DHCP renewal system. The first renewal is requested when 50 percent of the renewal interval has expired. As with the initial registration, renewals are requested every ten minutes with a rotation every hour of the WINS server.

Burst Mode Handling

To help handle very large registration loads with a DHCP server, Windows Server 2003, Windows 2000, and Windows NT 4 support a system called burst mode handling. These very high loads can occur after a power or network failure when a large number of machines come back online at the same time.

Burst mode is initiated when a burst queue threshold value is reached for the number of active requests. Up until the threshold, registrations are handled normally. After the threshold, burst mode handling is enabled.

Burst mode handling enables a server to handle very high loads of registrations by immediately responding to the client with a positive response (indicating successful registration) but with a very low time-to-live (TTL) figure, forcing clients to re-register with the server after a relatively short period, presumably when the loading is much lighter.

The actual TTL figure varies, according to the number of registrations received. For example, if the burst threshold was 500 registrations, then the TTL figure for the next 100 registrations would be 5 minutes; for the next 100 it would be 10 minutes; for the next 100 it would be 15 minutes, and so on, with 5 minutes added for each new block.

Once the TTL expires, the clients re-register, but because they are re-registering in batches of 100 units every 5 minutes, the server can respond with proper registrations.

The Lmhosts File

If a WINS server is not available, the system may fall back on the Lmhosts file; this is the NetBIOS equivalent of the main hosts file that backs up DNS lookups. The Lmhosts file is located in %systemroot%\system32\drivers\etc and should not have an extension.

The format of the file is straightforward:

```
192.168.1.10    server1
```

The character between the IP address and the name should be a TAB.

Additional entries should be on their own line. The only problem with the Lmhosts file is that it's primarily used to populate the NetBIOS cache on a client with address information. By default, hosts in the Lmhosts file are removed from the NetBIOS cache after 15 minutes if the address is not used.

Travel Advisory

The Lmhosts file is accessed sequentially, so you should place the addresses used most frequently at the top.

You can get round this by using the #PRE tag against each name. This will force the address to be preloaded and never expire from the cache. For example, you can change the preceding to

```
192.168.1.10    server1 #PRE
```

Travel Advisory

Place preloaded hosts at the bottom of the file because they are read and loaded only when the TCP/IP service is initialized. They shouldn't ever be loaded again, so they can be loaded last.

Another extension tag can be used to associate a given name/address with a domain. For example, to log server1 as part of the mcslp.com domain:

```
192.168.1.10    server1 #PRE #DOM mcslp
```

The Lmhosts file is still an effective way of distributing NetBIOS lookup information, especially for static addresses like your primary servers. If you use NetBIOS heavily, we recommend you supply a copy of the Lmhosts file to your clients to act as a final backup in case either the WINS servers or the broadcast service fail to operate. The easiest way to do this and keep it manageable is to use the #INCLUDE directive in the local Lmhosts file to refer to an Lmhosts on a UNC share. For example, you could distribute the following file,

```
192.168.1.100    server5 #PRE
#INCLUDE \\server5\public\lmhosts
```

and then keep the lmhosts file on server5 up to date with the latest information.

Name Resolution

The registration and resolution of WINS information within a NetBIOS environment depends on the node type of the machine you are using. There are four different node types, and these use four corresponding modes to resolve the information. These node types and the resolving mechanisms they use are summarized in Table 3.2.

TABLE 3.2   NetBIOS Node Types

Node Type	Description
B-node (broadcast node)	Broadcasts its name for registration and uses broadcasts to aid in resolution of names.
P-node (peer node)	Queries a WINS name server for resolution. All P-node computers must have a WINS server configured so they can resolve queries.

TABLE 3.2	NetBIOS Node Types *(continued)*
Node Type	**Description**
M-node (mixed node)	Combines B-node and P-node, first using broadcast mode to resolve an address and then using peer mode to request an address from a WINS server.
H-node (hybrid node)	Similar to M-node, but checks a WINS server first, then tries broadcast mode.

Exam Tip

Microsoft still expects you to know the different NetBIOS node types and the way they affect how hosts are resolved.

The default node type in Windows 2000, Windows Server 2003, and Windows XP is hybrid (H-node). You can determine the current node type by using the ipconfig /all command. Note that the default node type will change to a B-node if no WINS servers are configured.

Exam Tip

WINS server information can be distributed through the DHCP service, in much the same way as DNS server addresses are. You can also specify the node type through DHCP.

The resolution of a name on an H-node is as follows:

1. The client checks to see if the name queried is its local NetBIOS computer name. If it is, it returns its own IP address.

2. The client checks its local NetBIOS name cache. Names are cached by the client for 10 minutes.

3. The client forwards the NetBIOS query to its primary WINS server. If the primary WINS server fails to answer the query, the client will try to contact other configured WINS servers in the order they are listed and configured for its use.

4. If it still hasn't been resolved, the client broadcasts the NetBIOS query to the local subnet. Any machine on the network with the NetBIOS name in the broadcast can respond to the query and return its IP address.

5. The client checks the Lmhosts file for a match to the query if it is configured to use the Lmhosts file and the file exists.

6. The client tries the Hosts file and then a DNS server.

Travel Advisory

Windows 2000, Windows Server 2003, and Windows XP computers will use DNS to resolve the hostname first if the name is longer than 15 characters or contains a period (which signifies a DNS domain).

Resolution in other modes follows the same basic sequence. In fact, ignoring the specifics of the WINS system, you can apply a more general sequence of name resolution using both WINS and DNS and the two host files like this:

1. Determine if the name is longer than 15 characters or if it contains periods (.). If so, query DNS for the name.

2. Determine if the name is stored in the remote name cache at the client.

3. Contact and try configured WINS servers to attempt to resolve the name using WINS.

4. Use local IP broadcasts to the subnet.

5. Check an Lmhosts file to see if Enable LMHOSTS Lookup is enabled in the Internet Protocol (TCP/IP) properties for the connection.

6. Check a Hosts file.

7. Query a DNS server.

If you are using WINS, you should either ensure that your WINS servers are available (see the next section, "Plan a WINS Replication Strategy"), or use an Lmhosts file for resolving your key servers and machines within your network.

Plan a WINS Replication Strategy

One difference between WINS and DNS is that because WINS information can be replicated across servers and individual machines can register with any valid WINS server, the information will be exchanged between WINS servers within the replication group. A single WINS server is actually able to support a comparatively high number of clients for registration and resolving purposes.

However, for redundancy and fault tolerance reasons, it can be a good idea to install more than one WINS server so that the WINS service is always available.

WINS replication can be used in this situation as the replication syncs between the two servers and both servers can update their local copy before exchanging the updated information with the other.

Replication Types

When you set up replication, the information is exchanged between replication partners in one of three ways: push, pull, or push and pull:

- **Pull partners**   Request updates from a replication partner at specific intervals, by default every 30 minutes. This type of partner is ideal where you want a server to act as an additional resolving server without providing registration services. Pull partners can also be used where the WINS database needs to replicated across a slow network link. The downside is that the exchange interval can mean that WINS services are not copied in time for them to be used.

- **Push partners**   Notify replication partners when the number of changes to the local database exceeds a given figure. Push partners are best used on fast networks where the consistency of the database is paramount because the updates can be sent almost as soon as the local database is updated.

- **Push/pull partners**   Use a combination of the two systems, automatically requesting updates from replication partners at given intervals and pushing updates as required.

All types of replication can use the persistent connections (enabled by default) that maintain the connection between WINS servers, which makes synchronization faster by removing the need to open the connection each time.

Exam Tip
Except in special circumstances, you can generally use push/pull technology to keep two servers synchronized with each other.

Automatic Partner Discovery

Automatic partner discovery allows WINS servers to automatically discover their replication partners by using the multicast address 224.0.1.24 to broadcast their existence on the network. All WINS servers discovered with this method are set to push/pull mode with a pull interval of two hours.

Because it relies on a special broadcast address, this method cannot be used across routers unless you specifically add the 224.0.1.24 address to the router. You'll also need to add a multicast scope to your DHCP server if you are using one to allocate a multicast address.

Replication in Larger Networks

Replication should also be used if you have a number of network segments or a larger network—perhaps even distributed over a wide area network (WAN)— and you want to minimize the network traffic of communicating to a central WINS server.

The best solution in all these situations is to use a centralized WINS server that then uses push/pull replication to a number of satellite servers that provide localized registration and resolving services. Figure 3.12 shows the basic layout, in this case in a multisegment network.

The same network diagram can be used with multibranch networks: just replace the network hubs displayed in Figure 3.12 with a WAN connection, and you'll have a diagram suitable for multibranch networks.

Database Management

The WINS database should be pretty much self-managing, and it's unlikely that you will ever need to do any serious maintenance on the database unless you get corruption or disk failure of some kind. In these cases, you can either restore from a backup, or re-create the database because it will be automatically re-created by the machines when they re-register themselves again.

However, occasionally you'll have problems with a running WINS installation. It's possible, for example, that a registered entry can become stuck within the database, long after it should have been released. You can resolve this by scavenging the database to remove registrations that have expired or been released but not removed from the server database.

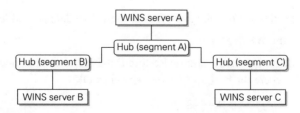

FIGURE 3.12   Using WINS replication in a larger network

In this section, we'll look at the basics of database management for the WINS service.

Scavenging the Database

Scavenging removes entries in the WINS database that should have been automatically removed. You can scavenge addresses manually, but this is obviously a time consuming process. Ideally, you should set your server to scavenge the database automatically. You can normally do this as infrequently as once a week; on a busy server you may want to scavenge addresses daily.

The scavenging intervals are controlled on a server-by-server basis by modifying the settings in the server properties.

Backing Up the WINS Database

Backing up the database can help bring your WINS server back to use as quickly as possible in the event of a corruption or other failure. You set the backup directory for the WINS database through the server properties. Once you have configured the backup directory location, the information automatically backs up every 24 hours. Automatic database backups can also be triggered when the service is stopped or when the server is shut down properly. You can also manually back up the database whenever you need to.

Remember that even once it's backed up, you should also consider keeping a copy of the WINS database on another machine or backed up using your usual backup system.

Restoring the WINS Database

You should restore the WINS database in the event of a corruption that cannot be resolved using the scavenging technique. Restoring a WINS database is relatively easy:

1. Stop the WINS service. It may take a number of minutes for the service to stop.
2. Delete all the WINS database files in the WINS database folder.
3. Open the WINS Manager.
4. On the Action menu, choose Restore Database, and then choose the folder where the backup files are kept; click OK.
5. Start the WINS service again.

Deleting (Tombstoning) an Entry

Occasionally, registrations will remain in the database and you'll want to manually delete them. You do this by selecting the appropriate entries from the list of Active Registrations and choosing Delete. You can opt to delete the record from the current server, but the details may reappear after the database is replicated with other servers. To resolve this, you must "tombstone" the entry, which deletes the version on the server and marks the entry for deletion when the information is next replicated with the other WINS servers.

Even when deleted, the entry is not actually removed from the server. To physically remove the entry, you must use the scavenging technique already mentioned or wait for the extinction interval to expire. This interval is configured on a server-by-server level within the server's properties.

Checking Database Consistency

You should regularly check the consistency of the WINS database to ensure that it has not become corrupted. Corrupted databases can exhibit a number of problems, including, but not limited to, failure to register entries and invalid responses when queried. You can manually check the database consistency through the WINS Manager.

You can also automatically verify the consistency by configuring the server properties accordingly. Typically, you should automatically check the consistency every 12 hours, and perhaps as frequently as every one or two hours if your servers handle a high numbers of registrations.

Security Issues

WINS and the NetBIOS naming system is not the most secure of protocols, largely because it was never designed with security in mind, and it was certainly never envisaged as having to cope with networks of the size now common in many environments. The world in which WINS was created was also a safer place, where hackers and crackers were rare and the idea of a network connected to the Internet was relatively uncommon, particularly at the client level.

The primary problem with WINS is that it's an unauthenticated protocol. Machines name themselves, whether or not a user a logged on to the network, and it's possible for one machine to register a name that clashes with another without any redress. This can cause horrendous problems. Imagine two machines, one a client and one a server, called fileserver—if the server crashes and the client manages to register itself, future requests by other clients may try to access the client rather than the server.

Protecting yourself from this is easy:

- Prevent unauthorized access to your network. Ensure your firewall is configured to block unnecessary access and make sure that users are not attaching their own computers and peripherals to the network. Also ensure that any wireless networking devices are suitable secured.
- Enable WINS logging and study the logs to ensure clients are correctly registering themselves with addresses within the expected range.
- Use Network Monitor to capture and examine the raw packets that make up a WINS request if you suspect an attack. You should be able to determine from that the physical Ethernet address of the machines on the network and therefore the machine originating the attack.
- Use static WINS addresses for your servers. Static addresses cannot be overwritten, so it should be impossible for a user to use this method to update your server with an alternative address.
- Restrict who can enable, configure, and disable the WINS service on your server. You must be a member of the Administrators group to manage the WINS service. If you need to have users with read-only access to the WINS database, add them to the WINS Users group.
- Don't move the WINS database files from their default location (%systemroot%\system32\Wins).

CHECKPOINT

✔ **Objective 3.01: Planning a DNS Strategy**   You should be able to plan a DNS namespace and, if necessary, subdivide your clients into departments, geographic location, or both. There should be two DNS servers for each set of clients. You can share information between servers by using zone transfers. Active Directory domain controllers automatically share the DNS information, but a domain controller must also be a DNS server to provide DNS resolving services. The placement of DNS servers is important because it may affect the security of your network and of the DNS service. When integrating with a third-party DNS server, it is generally easier to create a new subdomain within the main domain to hold AD DNS data, and then delegate the responsibility for the subdomain to the AD domain controller.

✔**Objective 3.02: Planning a WINS Strategy** WINS is an older service that resolves names for older versions of Windows such as Windows 98 and Windows NT. There are four types of WINS client: B-node, P-node, M-node, and H-node. H-node is the default type. WINS also provides lookup services to convert names into IP addresses, and you can share the responsibility of this process by using replication to exchange information between WINS servers. You can deploy WINS resolving services either through a dedicated WINS server, which clients must register with, the WINS built-in broadcast system, or the Lmhosts file.

REVIEW QUESTIONS

1. Your network consists of approximately 4,000 computers. You are using AD split into a number of organizational units across your company to logically separate departments. Up until now, you have used a separate DNS service to provide your name resolving, but you want to migrate this into an AD-integrated domain to make managing and updating the information easier. The current service uses a single domain name to hold the addresses of all your servers and printers and a set of generic names for DHCP clients. You want to move to dynamic updates for clients and static entries for the servers. How should you organize the DNS namespace when moving it to AD? (Choose one.)

   A. Import the DNS data directly into the primary domain and enable dynamic updates.

   B. Create new records for the servers within the appropriate OU and enable dynamic updates.

   C. Dump the existing DNS table and enable dynamic updates to build a new DNS table.

   D. Import the DNS data directly into the primary domain, delete the client records, and enable dynamic updates so that the tables can be re-created automatically.

2. You want to configure all the client machines within your network to use WINS server addresses of 192.168.1.2 and 192.168.1.34 and set the client node type to use M-node resolution. Which of the following services can be used to accomplish this? (Choose one.)

   A. DNS

   B. WINS

   C. Group policy

   D. DHCP

3. What is the default WINS node type for Windows XP clients when no WINS clients have been configured? (Choose one.)

   A. B-node

   B. P-node

   C. M-node

   D. H-node

4. Your network consists of two primary locations, London and Birmingham, connected via a low-speed link. You have servers located at both locations. The primary location is London and has a DNS domain of corp.com. The Birmingham location has a DNS domain of Birmingham.corp.com. You have two DNS servers at each location, each holding the local domain information. Users at each location need to resolve the names of servers at the other office. Which of the following solutions could you use? (Choose two; each answer is a complete solution.)

   A. Set up forwarding from Birmingham to London and delegation between London and Birmingham.

   B. Set up forwarding from London to Birmingham and delegation between Birmingham and London.

   C. Configure servers at London to delegate requests to Birmingham for the Birmingham subdomain and configure all clients to send requests to Birmingham.

   D. Configure servers at London to delegate requests to Birmingham for the Birmingham subdomain and configure all clients to send requests to London.

   E. Configure servers at both locations to act as secondary domain servers for the other domain.

5. You want to use an Lmhosts file to provide WINS name resolving information for the clients on your network. There are approximately 500 machines on your network at present. You are also in the process of going through a massive server reorganization that may result in the IP addresses and names changing a number of times over the next few months. You want to keep the Lmhosts file updated in the most efficient way, with the least amount of administrative effort. What solution should you use? (Choose one.)

   A. Use a shared Lmhosts file with localized Lmhosts files including the shared Lmhosts data.

B. Use File Replication Services to distribute a new Lmhosts file to clients when an update is necessary.

C. Copy the Lmhosts to the client computers each time an update occurs.

D. Create a logon script for the users that automatically copies the Lmhosts file to the client computer during logon.

6. You are using AD at your company with AD-integrated DNS zones. There are two domain controllers for your company. You have populated the zones with information and configured your clients to use the domain controllers as their DNS servers. However, when you try to access a server, you cannot access it by name. Access through IP address still works fine. What do you need to do to fix the configuration? (Choose one.)

A. Enable DNS on one of the domain controllers.

B. Enable DNS on all domain controllers.

C. Enable DNS on one server and configure the DNS service to replicate the zones from the other domain controller.

D. Configure your DHCP server with the appropriate DNS server records and set clients to obtain their IP address automatically.

E. Configure your DHCP server with the appropriate WINS server records and set clients to obtain their IP address automatically.

REVIEW ANSWERS

1. **B**   This allows all the other devices to register themselves with the server. Because they will already be part of the domain tree, they will automatically register themselves within the right OU and therefore DNS name.

2. **D**   Only DHCP can configure a client's WINS and node type information.

3. **A**   B-nodes resolve using the broadcast method first, followed by Lmhosts, and this mode is automatically selected when there is no WINS server to talk to at any stage.

4. **A E**   You cannot delegate up a domain, only down, so that eliminates B. C is impossible unless Birmingham forwards requests for London domains to London. D would increase the load on the WAN link for clients in Birmingham.

5. **A** All the other methods rely on copying the information, which is time consuming and prone to problems. If you copy the Lmhosts file once and then use #INCLUDE to incorporate the UNC shared copy, you need only update one file.

6. **B** A domain controller does not automatically operate as a DNS server unless it has been enabled to do so. Although A would work, the solution would fail if the primary domain controller was unavailable. D and E wouldn't work without enabling DNS on the servers.

P A R T

II

Network Infrastructure

Planning, Implementing, and Maintaining a Network Infrastructure

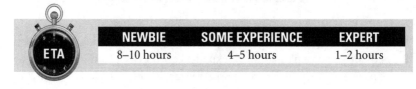

	NEWBIE	SOME EXPERIENCE	EXPERT
ETA	8–10 hours	4–5 hours	1–2 hours

Your network is the foundation on which your servers and clients—and the services they provide and use—rest on, so it's important to get the design and layout correct.

Planning a good network relies on a number of factors. First, you must get the physical layout right, which requires an understanding of the main components of your network so that you know where to place them physically within your network. Placed on top of that basic infrastructure are the servers that make up the core of your network services. The location of your servers will affect how they perform and how easily your users can access them and this will affect the performance of your network.

You can monitor that performance by using the various networking tools that help you monitor the network traffic. With these tools, you can compare the current network performance with known ideals and parameters. You can monitor your network performance over time so that you can determine if you need to upgrade your network infrastructure to handle the increased load.

It's inevitable that part of your infrastructure will involve the Internet at some point. Whether it's providing access to your servers to share information and resources with the general public over the Internet, or providing your users with Internet access, you must decide how you are going to route, protect, and provide access to what is a very public and potentially dangerous network.

Unfortunately, however well you plan, you are likely to end up with some problems that you will need to troubleshoot. The last part of this chapter will look at how to identify and resolve issues with your Internet connectivity, your TCP/IP addressing strategy, or your host name resolution system.

Objective 4.01 Plan and Modify a Network Topology

Planning your physical network layout is much like planning a city. Okay, perhaps you haven't had much experience with city planning, but maybe you've played SimCity! To be a successful mayor, you need to place your city resources—schools, hospitals, police—close to your residents for them to be useful. Each resource has a limited range; a school, for example, will only accept children from a few blocks away and won't accept a child from the other side of the city. It's too far to drive, and it saps local resources for the sake of a remote user. Connecting the residents and resources are roads, highways, bus routes, subways, and rail services, each providing different benefits such as speed of access and capacity.

Now, in a small city you might be able to get away with just one set of resources to handle the requirements of your residents. In a medium-sized city, a combination of localized resources for the suburbs and centralized resources for the city center make more sense. In a large city, you need not only localized and central resources, but also ways of physically separating traffic while providing high-speed links between them through rail and highways.

To be a successful network admin, the same rules apply. You need to create local areas where your users (residents) reside with servers (resources) and connectivity (networking hardware). In a small network, you can get by with a suite of servers and users on the same network, but by the time you get to a large network infrastructure, you're looking at high-speed interconnects between groups of users and localized and centralized servers providing information and services.

In this section, we'll discuss available network hardware and some networking layouts, as well as how to plan network capacity and introduce upgrades and changes into your infrastructure that will enhance your existing setup. Throughout, we'll be concentrating on the key points of planning your network structure.

Network Hardware

Before we look at the specifics of your network topology design, you should be familiar with the various types of network hardware that will be connecting and providing your network structure. In particular, you should understand the difference between a shared hub and a switch and be familiar with the theory, if not the practice, of virtual LANs. Windows Server 2003 also incorporates support for new types of technology including the wireless networking standard and xDSL internetwork connectivity.

Network Cable

The network cable you have will affect which hubs and what transmission speeds you can use. The majority of sites now use "structured cabling," that is, prelaid cables that connect to a patch panel, with network connections provided by patch cables placed between the network hubs and the patch panels.

Most cables used today are twisted pair, in which each pair of wires is twisted together with multiple pairs within the cable itself. The twisting prevents crosstalk between the two cables. There are two subtypes of twisted-pair cable, unshielded twisted pair (UTP) and shielded twisted pair (STP). UTP is the most common and can be used in most situations; STP is identical in all respects except that it has a layer of shielding around all the paired conductors and is therefore suitable for use in environments with high radio interference.

Fiber-optic cables are used in situations when cables are required to cover long distances. It was also used in high-speed cabling before Cat5 (discussed next) was certified for use with 100Mbps and 1000Mbps connections. (Initially, Cat5 was rated to only 100m, or 328ft, and fiber-optic cables can handle distances up to 2km or 1.24 miles, without a repeater.)

Local Lingo

Crosstalk When the signals on one cable interfere with (and influence) the signals on the other cable, they cause crosstalk. If present, crosstalk affects the performance and reliability of any cable. The twisting in twisted-pair cabling keeps the two cables close together for the entire length of the cable, which causes the electrical signals that would otherwise cause interference to cancel each other out.

Cables are also classified within a number of categories, the most common of these are as follows:

- **Category 3 (Cat3)** Rated for networks up to a maximum speed of 16Mbps. This is often used in older structured cabling installations and is compatible with 10Mbps Ethernet.
- **Category 4 (Cat4)** Used in Token Ring networks up to a maximum speed of 16Mbps.
- **Category 5 (Cat5)** Rated for networks up to a maximum speed of 1000Mbps. Cat5 cable is by far the most common and has been installed in most companies since around 1990. It can be used with Ethernet networks at 10Mbps, 100Mbps, and 1000Mbps.

Local Lingo

Repeater A component that amplifies the signal in a cable without otherwise processing the information. Think of it a bit like an advanced bucket chain—refilling the bucket when some gets spilled as the bucket is passed down the chain. Luckily, it's more reliable and it just amplifies and echoes the signal without affecting it in any way.

Shared Hubs

A standard network hub provides shared connectivity over the network. The connection is shared because all the traffic between the devices connected to the hub is repeated to each port. This is a cheap way of connecting machines, but it lowers the overall throughput and utilization of the network because it becomes very easy for the network to become saturated. For example, say you're transferring data from a client to a server. If you had 20 clients and one server, the data transfer would be repeated to all ports so each of the 20 clients would receive the data, but only one of them would actually accept the packets and process the information.

Local Lingo

Ethernet   A network standard that uses a system called Collision Sense Multiple Active/Collision Detection (CSMA/CD), which enables network devices to determine whether the network is able to accept the packet they want to broadcast. If the network is too busy, the device waits and then tries to send again later. The wait is in microseconds, but it's an effective way of reducing the network load without any central control. In a shared hub, this means that the effective bandwidth for each user is reduced—a 100MB hub with 20 users would reduce the overall throughput to just 5MB.

Network hubs are usually used to connect groups of clients to the main network backbone, but in most companies they are being replaced by network switches, which are about the same price (sometimes cheaper) and provide a number of advantages. Shared hubs are available in 10Mbps and 100Mbps (Fast Ethernet) speeds. They are also available in 1000Mbps (Gigabit) forms but are less popular than switched versions at this speed.

Switched Hubs

A network switch, or switched hub, is essentially a multiport bridge (see the section "Bridges and Routers" later in this chapter for more information on bridges). Unlike a shared hub where the data is retransmitted to all ports, in a switch the data is only transmitted to the network port that contains the receiving device. In a network with 20 clients and one server this would mean that a file transferred between a client and server would only involve the two ports that were supplied the network packets. In essence, the switch provides a completely separate path between each device during communication.

Because of this, switches are able to handle much higher levels of traffic, even when operating at the same quoted speed as a shared hub. As a further enhancement, network switches can operate at either half duplex or full duplex. At half-duplex speed, communication between two machines on the switch is only one way at any one time—that is, the client can send packets to the server, or the server can send packets to the client, but not both.

In full-duplex mode, packets can be transferred between the two devices at full speed simultaneously, effectively enabling a 100Mbps connection to run at rate of 200Mbps. This increases the throughput and enables machines to communicate with each other at much higher rates without additional hardware.

Network switches are used both as a client connection solution and to connect different network segments and servers to a central backbone. Switches are available in 10Mbps, 100Mbps and 1000Mbps (gigabit) formats.

> ### Local Lingo
>
> **Network segment**   A portion of a network on which all the traffic is shared through a shared hub or through shared-wire technologies such as coax (10Base-2 Ethernet).

Advanced Switches

Standard switches are multiport bridges, which means they selectively broadcast packets according to their Ethernet hardware address. They are also called layer 2 switches because the network card's hardware address is within the second layer of the OSI/ISO model. However, because the majority of the traffic on these networks is IP based, it makes sense to use IP as the basis for the routing and distribution of network packets. Layer 3 switches, therefore, improve on the Layer 2 model by allowing the switch to route and redirect packets according to their destination IP address, which allows the router to make more specific decisions about the best port over which to send the packet.

> ### Local Lingo
>
> **Seven-layer model**   The OSI/ISO seven-layer model for networking defines different layers for different aspects of the network, from the physical right up to the application level protocols. Interestingly, although the lower levels (one to three) are easily defined, protocols in the upper levels (four through seven) are not so easily pigeonholed into a specific layer.

Because the routing is handled in hardware, the overall throughput is very fast, easily matching the underlying transmission speed. Nonlayer 3 traffic is still forwarded, but its destination is determined by the layer 3 routing.

The benefit of the layer 3 switch is that it can be used to help route and redirect IP traffic at a network level without the specific use of routers. This makes a layer 3 switch a multiport router, but at a much more affordable price than the normal router-based solutions used with multiport networks.

Layer 3 switches are currently used on corporate backbones to route and separate traffic between large network groups and segments. They can also route foreign network traffic (such as branch offices and the Internet) without expensive routers or computer-based routing solutions. In addition, layer 3 switches help interconnect and support virtual LANs.

Virtual LANs

Virtual LANs (VLANs) build on the facilities offered by switches, and particularly layer 3 switches, to provide a virtual LAN within the confines of a large hardware network. For example, imagine a network with 20 nodes that you want to separate into two networks, completely isolating and localizing the network traffic but still allowing communication between the two networks.

You could do this by using switches and a router to separate the networks, or you could use one big switch that supported virtual LANs. Because the switch creates one-to-one communication channels between the devices, it's already acting as a router. With some additional software built into the switch, it can create logical networks made up of any number of devices connected to the switch. See Figure 4.1 for an example.

Each device within the virtual LAN can be part of the same broadcast domain, and the VLAN as a whole can have its traffic monitored and controlled just as if it were a stand-alone network. Other benefits include

- **More bandwidth**   Because the LANs are physically separate networks, you get all the benefits of a separate switch, including segmented broadcast and multicast traffic.

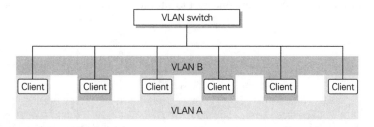

FIGURE 4.1   Virtual LANs in practice

- **Easier to manage**   The devices are connected to the same switch and you can reconfigure device membership on-the-fly, so devices can be moved to different VLANs as required.

- **Removes physical limitations**   In a complex network, it can be difficult to logically separate or combine networks that are otherwise physically separate. For example, an administration department would normally share a network, but what if they are in two different buildings? With a VLAN they can be logically organized, irrespective of their location.

- **Easier resource sharing**   Any device can be a member of more than one VLAN, so you can share a server over more than one network segment without having to use complex routing, metric, or hardware setups.

- **Performance management**   You can easily upgrade performance by separating clients into new VLANs without adding complexity or hardware to your network.

VLANs are still a relatively new technology, but they are gaining acceptance because of the benefits just listed. In particular, the ability to simply connect machines together in large corporate environments through one or more central hardware points while still being able to reconfigure and manage the network structure through software provides a significant advantage.

Firewalls

Just like the real-life equivalent, the idea of a firewall is to provide a complete break in network connectivity from one side to another with an intermediate device. The device can then make decisions about which packets to forward from one network to another according to various rules. See Figure 4.2 for an example.

Firewalls act as routers, but rather than blindly routing packets according to their destination address from one port to another, they route only those packets

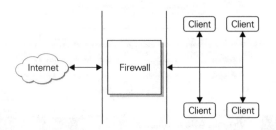

FIGURE 4.2   A firewall in action

that match the rules. Rules include checking the port number (TCP or UDP), for example, blocking all ports except port 80 (HTTP for Internet access) and redirecting certain ports, for example, redirecting any port 25 traffic (SMTP for e-mail transfer) to a specific host within the network (your mail server).

Typically, a firewall is placed on the border of your network between your private clients and either a public network connection (the Internet) or a gateway to another network within your organization (for example, between accounts and administration, or between branch offices and the central office).

Firewalls can also incorporate additional functionality such as proxy services, which force Internet traffic through a central host for security reasons (because it can be the only host that the firewall accepts Internet traffic through) and access speed. A proxy server can cache information from the Internet, reducing the amount of traffic transferred over the Internet connection and improving the overall user experience. Microsoft's Internet Security and Acceleration Server is an example of a firewall and proxy server; we'll be looking at it later in this chapter as a solution for Internet access.

One final element of the firewall is the demilitarized zone (DMZ). This can be a separate network segment attached to the firewall (as shown in Figure 4.3), a whole separate network on the public side of a firewall, or a separate zone located between two firewalls. DMZs enable you to provide public servers outside of your primary security firewall. In the case of a separate network segment, you can set up a dedicated network route between the public server segment and the public side of the firewall.

When using a separate network on the other side of the firewall (as shown in Figure 4.4), you lose the benefits of firewall protection for the public servers, but you also eliminate any potential lapses in your security infrastructure and settings in the event of a failure at your firewall.

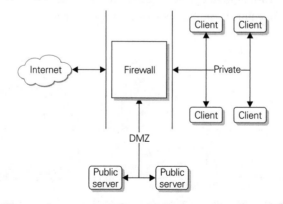

Using a separate network segment for public servers

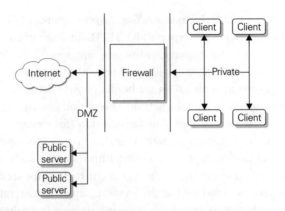

FIGURE 4.4   Using a public-side DMZ

The final solution presents the best of both worlds (as shown in Figure 4.5), but at a significant cost in terms of both administration and software/hardware costs. Using two firewalls allows you to protect your public servers and your private network and also protects you from break-ins that may occur from one of your public servers. However, two firewalls also makes it more complicated to manage the connections: you must route traffic between your private network and the Internet through both firewalls and make rules that are compatible with both connection points.

You must consider communication between your public servers and your private network if the role of your public servers is to support extranet or public interfaces to internal applications.

Bridges and Routers

A bridge enables you to connect two networks together at layer 2, that is, the underlying networking frame. Bridges are relatively dumb—they just broadcast traffic from one port to another port—but they do enable you to connect two

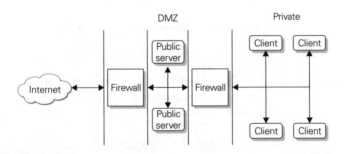

FIGURE 4.5   A true DMZ between your internal and public networks

separate networks together, even if they do not share the same transport medium. Using a bridge, for example, it's possible to connect Token Ring and Ethernet networks together. Even more popular at the moment is bonding Ethernet and wireless networks together to present a seamless network across both technologies.

Because a bridge works at layer 2, not layer 3, bridges forward all packets across the two networks. This is vital for systems like DHCP that do not use the TCP/IP standard to request or respond to IP address configuration details. A bridge, therefore, allows you to support DHCP across network segments (which is especially useful over wireless networks) without having to use DHCP relaying or proxying services. The downside to this is that because no decision is made about which traffic to broadcast, bridges can help spread, rather than segment, the load on the network.

Routers, on the other hand, connect two networks together at layer 3, the primary software protocol layer. For example, a router forwards IP packets across network interfaces. Routers are primarily used to route network traffic between one medium format and another, for example from Ethernet to a DSL or leased line connection to the Internet.

Routers can also be used to separate traffic within a LAN. Because they route IP, broadcast and multicast Ethernet traffic is not transferred, so a router can logically separate network segments while still allowing traffic to flow between the two sides.

Windows Server 2003 incorporates support for bridging between network types as well as routing between networks. We'll look at routing and its uses in more detail in Chapter 5.

Wireless Gateways

Suffering from a population explosion not unlike the Internet, wireless networking technology allows you to connect primarily notebook and PDA devices to your network without cables. This allows a user to walk around with a notebook and still access the corporate network.

To provide this connectivity, you need a wireless access point (WAP), which then communicates with the machines over a radio connection. Speeds at the time of writing include 11Mbps (for the 802.11b standard) and 54Mbps (802.11g and 802.11a), although the real performance depends on the conditions (for example, walls, electronic interference), the number of clients (generally, the more clients the lower the overall potential rate), and any additional network level security.

The security is a particularly thorny issue. In the rush to get such devices onto their networks, a number of companies have simply installed WAPs into their networks without thinking about the security. Of course, once you remove the requirement for a cable, it becomes very easy for anyone within broadcast reach of your WAP to connect to your network.

Local Lingo

War chalking   Walk around many streets in cities in the U.S., U.K., and other countries around the world, and you may notice odd markings on the wall next to some buildings. This is not some strange ritual or a new road sign design, it's war chalking, a way of marking buildings and the companies within them as having WAPs that are open to the public, albeit probably not officially.

Most WAPs include the ability to restrict access only to those people who

- **Know the wireless network ID (SSID)**   This is user defined and is impossible to break into without using brute force (that is, trying every combination) methods.
- **Match a given hardware address**   More useful in smaller networks than large-scale enterprise networks, this restricts access to only those wireless cards that match one of the hardware (Ethernet) addresses in WAP's lookup table.
- **Password access**   Some hardware allows you to require a password to connect to the network.

The other issue is one of packet sniffing—because your network traffic is being broadcast, it's possible for unscrupulous users to capture the packets and determine what your users are sending, including login and password details. You can restrict the chances of this by using encryption. The wireless networking standards include Wireless Equivalent Privacy (WEP) encryption using 40-bit, 64-bit (with the initialization vector), or, on more recent systems, 104-bit encryption, which is often misquoted as 128-bit (it's 128-bit with the initialization vector).

If you want to use wireless protocols and are concerned about security, consider adding IPSec security to your TCP/IP connections either instead of or (better) in addition to the WEP and other security features.

Exam Tip

Windows Server 2003 now includes support for wireless networking and even has group policy templates that can be used to set security, privacy, and preferred network settings. Although you probably won't be tested on these specifically, you may be asked to verify that the facilities exist.

Identify Network Protocols

The protocols you use on your network will affect to a greater or lesser extent the types of device and layout you end up using. Going back to the city design analogy, there is no point in building an extensive rail network if all of your users expect to drive their cars. The same is true in networking: if your users expect to use broadcast or multicast traffic, then separating the network with routers is going to prevent the users from working effectively.

Ultimately, it's unlikely that you'll use or need anything but TCP/IP, but you should be aware that the other protocols exist. Because TCP/IP is the likely candidate in nearly all situations, you get the benefits previously outlined above, such as layer 3 switching, which allows you to make reasonable decisions without worrying too much about the complexity of the other protocols in your network.

TCP/IP

TCP/IP is the now-ubiquitous protocol that provides communication between computers. The primary reason for this is the explosion of the Internet, which uses TCP/IP for communication, but it is also because TCP/IP is a relatively easy to manage and scalable protocol. It can be routed (that is, redirected and distributed) around a network easily, and, as you've seen with layer 3 switches, it also provides a hardware-level advantage because it's easy to distribute and control.

The default protocol for modern Windows machines and most other platforms is now TCP/IP; there are other protocols available, but most operating systems now provide a TCP/IP-compatible version. For example, Apple's AppleTalk Filing Protocol (AFP) has for some years supported a TCP/IP transport in addition to its original AppleTalk transport protocol.

It's unlikely that you'll install a network without TCP/IP—Active Directory and most Windows Server 2003 services actually require TCP/IP to operate—and it's likely that TCP/IP will be your only networking protocol.

NWLink (IPX/SPX)

Internetwork Packet Exchange/Sequenced Packet Exchange (IPX/SPX) is closely tied to Novell's NetWare network operating system, which provides file and printer sharing capabilities in much the same way as Windows server products. IPX/SPX was used as the primary communications protocol up until NetWare 5, when TCP/IP became the standard.

Exam Tip

IPX/SPX support has been removed from the 64-bit versions of Windows Server 2003.

AppleTalk

AppleTalk is currently a protocol and was formerly a hardware networking technology. AppleTalk is broadcast based, with devices that broadcast their name, service type, and other information to the network for other devices to pick up, identify, and communicate with. Surprisingly, it was routable but suffered from poor communication rates even when it moved to Ethernet-based networking under the name of EtherTalk.

Some of you are already familiar with AppleTalk as both a printer and file-sharing protocol under Windows NT. Between the release of Windows NT and Windows 2000, Apple redeveloped the AppleTalk Filing Protocol (AFP) for file sharing to use TCP/IP rather than AppleTalk/EtherTalk. This increased its performance and enabled you to use Apple drives across a network using existing hardware technology. With the release of Mac OS X, Apple has now all but dumped AppleTalk for anything but backward compatibility. Mac OS X and Mac OS 9 both support TCP/IP communication for file sharing and printer sharing, so it's unlikely that you'll need to know about this protocol, other than that it exists and can be used to allow older Macintosh computers to communicate with your Windows network.

DLC

The Direct Link Control (DLC) protocol is used to communicate with older Hewlett-Packard JetDirect network printers. Modern printers, including the JetDirect-based units, support TCP/IP as a communications protocol. When combined with Universal Plug and Play (UPnP), these printers offer identical and often significantly easier administration than DLC. DLC has been removed from Windows 2003.

Local Lingo

UPnP   A new feature of Windows Server 2003, Universal Plug and Play, allows many devices and clients to automatically discover what services are available. For example, when you connect to a file server, the UPnP system will automatically add other file shares to your Network Places folder. In the future, UPnP will probably allow devices other than computing devices (including your TV, hi-fi, and even your washing machine) to communicate and integrate with each other.

NetBEUI

NetBEUI is a broadcast-based, nonroutable protocol that was often used as a faster alternative to TCP/IP in small LAN environments. Because it was nonroutable, however, it was unusable in larger networks and eventually died when TCP/IP grew in response to the growth of the Internet. NetBIOS, which is part of the NetBEUI system, is still supported because NetBIOS is a session-level protocol and can therefore be supported over IP-based connections.

Exam Tip

It's unlikely you'll be asked a NetBEUI question, but if you are it will be along the lines of "A client using NetBEUI is unable to connect to ServerB running Windows Server 2003..." The answer will be the one that mentions installing TCP/IP.

Plan the Physical Placement of Network Resources

The resources on your network are basically anything that provides services or functionality. A server is an example of a resource, as is a printer, router, or network printing device. Putting these in the right place will affect the performance of your network, as well as who can access them and how they will be used.

Exam Tip

In this new exam, Microsoft expects you to be able to identify different components and to suggest where different components are placed. Although other technologies exist, the exam concentrates on Ethernet-based solutions, as these are the most prevalent.

Servers

There are a number of server solutions and situations that affect where you place a server within your network. Although there are no hard and fast rules, servers can be divided into the following groups and therefore locations:

- **Low-end servers**   These are designed to handle between 1 and 100 clients in a small office/home office environment. They are usually general-purpose workhorses that can provide file serving, printer spooling, and e-mail/Internet connectivity solutions all in the same box or can handle specific tasks within a larger department or business environment.

- **Mid-range servers** These are designed to provide the localized requirements for a single department within a larger, multidepartment company. Supporting between 1 and 400 users, they can be tailored for specific server needs, such as a file server or, depending on the exact number of users that need to be supported, they can be a general-purpose box. In small- to medium-sized enterprises, this could be a central server providing all the services for a company, but most companies at this level would have two servers for redundancy.

- **High-end servers** These are designed with major, single-use tasks in mind, such as supporting Microsoft Exchange Server or SQL Server in a dedicated capacity. They usually form part of a larger suite of servers to support the company's computing requirements.

Most servers fall within one of these areas. However, the exact layout will depend entirely on your network and company requirements. Some will use a big central file server for all users, others will use departmental servers, and others will use a mixture of the two. Also keep in mind that segmentation of a network allows you to improve and build on your network configuration without affecting the other areas of your network too much.

For example, if you look at a typical small office network, as shown in Figure 4.6, you can see that two servers provide file sharing, printer sharing, and other services to their clients using a switched hub to connect the machines together. A switched hub alleviates the background noise that would otherwise affect a shared hub–based network.

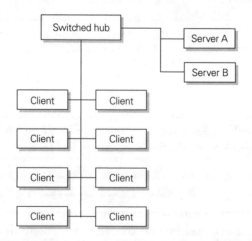

FIGURE 4.6 A small office network

In a medium-sized network, the problem is the sheer number of clients on the network and the traffic they generate. Figure 4.7 shows a sample layout with two separate client networks, both using switches, and a separate server network, also using a switch. Between these, providing a core network backbone for internetwork traffic to flow over is a layer 3 switch. A backbone handles core traffic between core network centers to flow over a fast connection. A layer 3 switch ensures that the networks will be kept logically separate while still allowing the core traffic to flow. For speed reasons, the backbone switch could be operating 1000Mbps with uplinks to the client switches at the same speed, while the clients could be operating at either 10 or 100Mbps.

Exam Tip

Microsoft now recommends that clients use a minimum of a 100Mbps network.

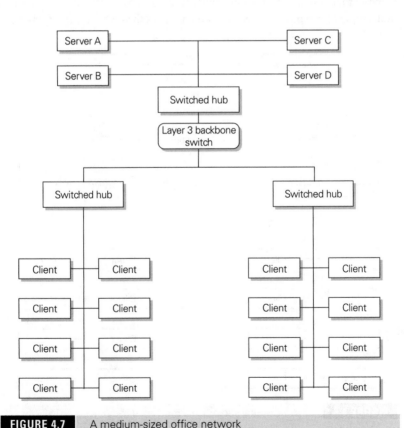

FIGURE 4.7   A medium-sized office network

As a modification of this plan, look at the network layout in Figure 4.8. The two client networks have their own file servers, as well as access to a central file server (file server C) and the main e-mail server. Because they are using switched hubs, the traffic is isolated between the two client networks and their communication with their departmental servers.

In a corporate network, as shown in Figure 4.9, there are other issues to contend with. Because all the servers are likely to be in the same domain, there will be a reasonable amount of traffic between the individual servers. It's possible you'll also have independent e-mail servers for each department in additional to a central e-mail server that distributes e-mail to the internal servers. For this reason, you need an internal server-only network to handle the server traffic, with independent links to the different departments. A VLAN switch can create the necessary departments logically as well as the separate server network and connectivity onto the main backbone. The backbone is created logically by the VLAN technology.

Note that you also have connectivity to the Internet through an ISA server and support for remote access and branch offices through a central firewall.

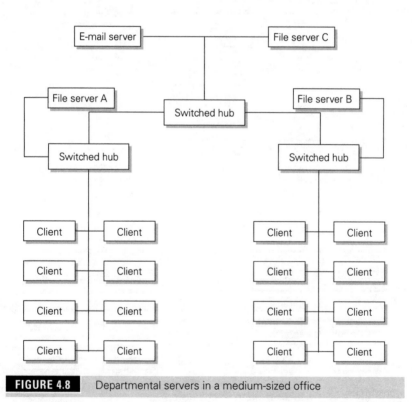

FIGURE 4.8   Departmental servers in a medium-sized office

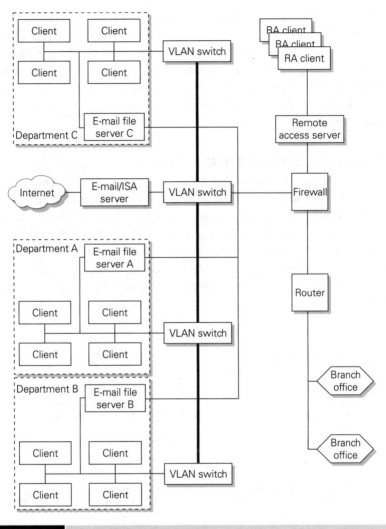

FIGURE 4.9   A corporate network

Printers

Printers are often a forgotten network element, but their placement can have a significant effect on your network performance. Locating your printers depends on how they are being used. If all printers are available to all users and are being used directly, they should be placed directly on your network along with your clients.

If, however, you are using printer spooling services under Windows Server 2003, then it's often better to completely separate the general network traffic from the client network traffic. This eliminates sending a 100KB print job to the server and having the server send it to the client, introducing a 200KB load on the network for a 100KB job. We've used the solution shown in Figure 4.10 to isolate the printers from the clients and gain a significant reduction in network bandwidth use.

Planning for Future Growth

Before becoming a full-time network administrator, one of this book's authors was advisor to a government organization that was in the process of moving into a new building and needed to have a network that would be able to cope with the new layout and the new requirements, all for about 110 staff plus the servers, printers, and other components. What the resident network admin put in, against this author's advice, was a network capable of supporting just 128 devices, exactly the right number required to support the then-current network usage.

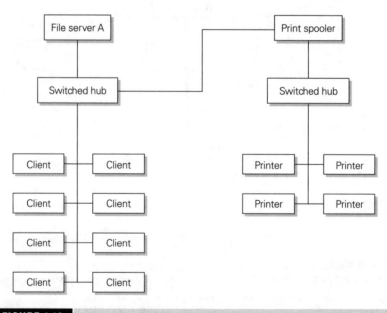

FIGURE 4.10   Using a separate printer network

However, between the time of the network specification and the day the staff moved in, the organization took on new staff and some new projects, and had some new devices to connect to the network. Moving was out of the question because the administrator hadn't left any room for any form of expansion. In fact, the particular hardware solution he'd used was unable to support any additional connections without replacing the entire system and purchasing a new one at an increased cost.

This aptly demonstrates a simple rule: whatever your current network requirements, never underestimate the ability to fill up the available slots with new equipment and users.

When planning your network, therefore, you should keep the following in mind:

- *Use scalable products and technologies.*   Don't tie yourself into a network solution that limits your ability to expand or that will restrict or reduce performance as the size of your network increases.
- *Be proactive.*   Use the network monitoring techniques to identify where your network bottlenecks are and help you choose where to expand or redesign your network next.
- *Don't ignore the warning signs.*   If users are complaining about occasional problems, investigate them. If you ignore them for too long, you'll alienate users, and it won't matter if you improve it later.
- *Slow-downs can be affected by other systems as well.*   Problems with file server performance or server application performance can be a problem with the server itself, rather than a network problem. Use System Monitor to determine problems within a machine against its network performance.
- *Test new applications or solutions in a separate environment.*   This ensures that they will not unduly affect your network performance when installed on the main network. If you think it will affect the performance, redesign the network and test the new design to ensure your plan works.

The bottom line is *always*, without fail, plan for future growth in your network design.

Upgrading Your Network

The usual reasons for upgrading your network are to increase or improve the network bandwidth or to expand or extend your network with new clients, servers, or features.

We'll start with the latter situation first. When extending your network, you need to consider the impact on your existing network. If extending is going to increase the number of clients or servers, then think about the impact on network bandwidth and performance. This is where having a central backbone has its advantages: you can simply connect another hub to the backbone without impacting existing clients. However, this will have an impact on the server and backbone performance.

If you don't already have a backbone, you should consider adding one to the existing infrastructure and separating your client and server components—in fact, the migration from small- to medium-sized networks, as shown in Figures 4.6 and 4.7, is a good example of how to extend your network beyond its current requirements.

When upgrading your network for performance reasons, it's important to know where the performance problem lies. First of all, identify whether the problem really is with the network as a whole, the network connectivity to a single server, or with the performance of the server.

You can do this by using the Network Monitor and System Monitor tools (which we'll be looking at in the next section), along with standard utilization performance and rates with different network types.

Don't forget the future growth potential in your network when planning an upgrade—if you are adding 15 devices, plan for 20; if you are adding a switch with 100Mbps connectivity, try to use one that has a 1000Mbps capability so that it can be bonded to a higher speed backbone if required.

Objective 4.02

Plan Network Traffic Monitoring

In the U.K., we have train-spotters who are the butt of jokes about their hobby, which is to observe trains and locomotive numbers. Although it may seem pointless to us, they perform an activity that we network administrators should be doing all the time: monitoring what's going past on the network. Luckily, we don't have to wear anoraks, sit on cold platforms, or carry around little notebooks—we can use the technology built into Windows Server 2003 and Windows XP clients to do the monitoring for us.

Measuring Performance

There are a number of factors that affect the performance of a network:

- **Bandwidth**   The availability of network speed (as opposed to the theoretical maximum).
- **Latency**   The time it takes for a packet to transfer from source to destination.
- **Throughput**   The actual rate of data transfer.
- **Capacity**   The practical maximum transmission rate.
- **Wire speed**   The theoretical maximum transmission rate according to the hardware. For example, the wire speed of Fast Ethernet is 100Mbps, but the actual capacity may only be 80Mbps due to the number of hosts, packet sizes, collisions, and other factors.
- **Utilization**   The percentage of time that the wire is occupied.
- **Actual data throughput**   The amount of usable data delivered to the transport protocol (TCP/IP).
- **Frame rate**   The number of frames sent per second.

Local Lingo

Collisions   With shared Ethernet, the CSMA/CD system prevents computers from broadcasting packets when network utilization is high. However, if two computers do send frames at the same time, the two frames collide and each computer must resend its frame. A high number of collisions usually indicates an over-capacity network.

Local Lingo

Frame   Ethernet transfers data in a number of frames. These are not that different from a TCP/IP datagram (packet), but the two should not be confused. Ethernet frames are transferred at layer 2 and are the lowest logical transmission format. TCP/IP packets are encapsulated in Ethernet frames during transmission. The frame size is variable, with the default size 1,500 bytes. Recent Ethernet devices are also capable of using "jumbo" frames up to 9,000 bytes in size.

All these factors contribute to the network performance, and it's possible to identify trends in the different factors. For example, in general

- As the number of nodes on a network increases, the throughput goes down because they each have to share the network connectivity.
- As the utilization of the network increases, the latency also increases.

It is possible, when armed with the right information, to be able to calculate the actual data throughput (ADT) for your network with the following formula:

ADT = (Utilization–Collisions) × efficiency × wirespeed

In the exam, you may be asked questions of the following form:

You have a 10Mbps shared network segment that is showing 25 percent utilization and 5 percent collisions. Assuming an average frame size of 1000 bytes, what is the actual data throughput of this network segment?

To calculate the answer, you need to know that every Ethernet frame has an overhead of 28 bytes, so the efficiency of the network is 962 bytes because that is the amount of useful data transferred in each frame. Using the ADT formula, the formula for the preceding question would be as follows:

ADT= (.25-.05) × 962 × 10 = 1.924 Mbps

Exam Tip

You will probably be given the formula for this equation during the exam, although it shouldn't be too difficult to remember.

The critical measurement component for your network is the network utilization. This gives the best overall impression about how busy your network is in real terms. Network utilization is generally on the rise in all organizations. This is primarily due to the number of computers now in use, but it also reflects changes in the way we transfer information. Modern networks don't just transfer relatively small amounts of document traffic, they also carry multimedia, Voice over IP (VoIP), and a larger quantity of Internet traffic. The majority of this is routed (that is, it uses TCP/IP) rather than broadcast based, which is best reflected in the increasing use of switches and layer 3 switching technologies in LAN environments.

You can apply some simple rules to the utilization and collisions on a network that will help you determine whether you need to upgrade or modify your network configuration. Table 4.1 shows the Microsoft-recommended Ethernet Utilization Guidelines, including maximum utilization rates and collision rates.

TABLE 4.1	Ethernet Utilization and Throughput Rates					
Network Type	Speed (Mbps)	Avg. Utilization Limit (%)	Raw Data Throughput Limit (Mbps)	Peak Utilization Limit (%)	Peak Data Throughput Limit (Mbps)	Peak Collision Rate (%)
Shared	10	30	3	80	8	20
Switched	10	85	8.5	90	9	N/A
Switched FDX	10	190	19	190	18	N/A
Shared	100	30	30	80	80	20
Switched	100	85	85	90	90	N/A
Switched FDX	100	190	190	190	190	N/A
Shared FDX	1000	60	600	120	1600	20
Switched FDX	1000	190	1900	190	1900	N/A

You can see from the table that you should not exceed an 80 percent utilization rate on shared 10Mbps Ethernet or more than 190 percent (because it's full duplex) on a 100Mbps switched network. Essentially, utilization rates over the peak data throughput limit listed in Table 4.1 indicate a saturated network that is due for either an upgrade or a new network layout to alleviate the problem.

To measure this information, you need to use one of the various networking tools. The two that come with Windows Server 2003 are System Monitor and Network Monitor. System Monitor monitors the network performance at a machine level, that is, you can use it to determine whether the network interface on the machine is saturated with data and whether this is related to a particular application. Network Monitor monitors only the network performance. There are other third-party tools available that may provide more useful information in certain circumstances, depending on your network infrastructure.

Monitoring Strategies

Whichever tool you choose, you should aim to record information over a suitable period. Testing network utilization over an hour at lunchtime is unlikely to give a realistic figure. Some of your users will be out enjoying lunch, while others will be browsing the Internet or reading their e-mail. True, some might even be working, but it's too short a period of time and the network is unlikely to be in used in a typical fashion.

By the same token, testing over a 24-hour period in a company that only normally operates over only a 12-hour period is unlikely to give useful figures either—the average utilization will appear to be a lot less than it is.

The following guide will help you make sensible decisions about when and where to gather your test information:

- Test over a period of at least four hours, preferably during a typical work period.
- Test during normal usage time and outside normal usage time to get an idea of the background traffic in relation to the active traffic.
- Test more than once over the period of a week or month to get average usage values. This prevents skewed results that might occur when there is particularly high usage because of a specific project or when there is unusually low usage due to holidays or company meetings.
- To prevent getting only localized usage statistics, test at different physical locations within your network, especially if you are using switches, routers, or bridges.

Also be aware of the source and destination of the traffic in question. For example, noting a network utilization of 60 percent is pointless unless you can also identify where the traffic is going to and coming from. For example, knowing that network utilization is particularly high when users communicate with a server tells you it might make sense to change the hub or switch type, or to use a faster interconnect between the server and the rest of the network.

Network Monitor (NetMon)

NetMon has been part of Windows server products since Windows NT. It captures and displays raw network data. The version bundled with Windows Server 2003 is limited to showing packets sent to the current machine, but an extended version, available with System Management Server (SMS), can work in promiscuous mode and monitor real-time traffic across your network.

Travel Advisory

On a switched segment, even with the SMS version of NetMon, you may not see all the network packets because the packets are never forwarded to your machine. Most modern switches allow you to forward all network traffic to one port for monitoring purposes.

The main benefit of NetMon is that it provides an almost running commentary of your network performance. You can see a sample of NetMon in action in Figure 4.11. The right-hand panel shows live network utilization figures, as well as live frames, bytes, broadcasts, and multicasts per second. The left-hand panel shows the statistics for the network connection, including frames and bytes transferred and running totals for the information transferred during a capture. The panel at the bottom of the window shows per-host statistics, allowing you to identify the host that is sending and receiving the most traffic.

Using NetMon

To use Network Monitor you must first install it with the Add/Remove Windows Components. You also need to be a member of the Administrators Group. Once installed, start Network Monitor; NetMon will not capture network packets (and therefore statistical information) until you tell it to start.

| Travel Advisory |

Network Monitor is a potential security risk as it can sniff the contents of packets and discover passwords and other sensitive information. To help prevent this, NetMon broadcasts its existence on the network using a special "bone" packet. This can be identified by other NetMon instances; you should periodically run NetMon to ensure that no unauthorized users are using NetMon on your network.

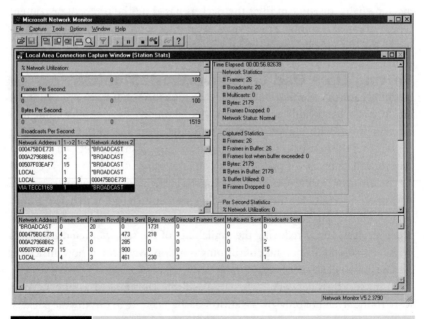

FIGURE 4.11   Network Monitor (NetMon) in action

Packets are captured into a buffer and then processed. When capturing packets, NetMon has two available modes:

- **Standard capture mode** Allows you to monitor the live capture statistics from the network. However, because the information has to be processed, the statistics can be a few seconds behind the actual traffic usage. On particularly busy networks, this mode can also cause NetMon to drop packets because it cannot cope with the network load. If this is the case, use dedicated capture mode.

- **Dedicated capture mode** Switches off the live statistic update but enables NetMon to capture more packets that you can then analyze at a later date.

If you want the best results and do not need live statistics then, obviously, dedicated capture mode is the better solution.

Filtering Data

It's easy to get swamped and drown in all the information that NetMon captures. To prevent this, you can set NetMon to filter the packets that you sniff from the network. The filter rules are quite extensive: you can choose to monitor the packets sent only to a specific machine or those flowing between specific machine pairs, or you can filter the packets based on the protocol or content type. You can also combine these rules to produce complex filters such as filtering all the IP traffic between a client and server.

Setting Up a Dedicated Network Monitor

Running Network Monitor puts a relatively high load on the server it's running on. In a low-bandwidth environment, that shouldn't be a problem, but in a larger network with higher network traffic the sheer amount of information passing over the network may cause NetMon to start losing packets—a sure sign that your machine is not up to the task.

You can avoid losing packets by upping the buffer used by NetMon to capture network traffic, but over the long term that probably isn't going to help if things get really busy. Remember also that if it's running on an existing server that runs other services, you're reducing the availability of the server to handle both its original tasks and the new task of running NetMon. We all know how difficult it is to be in two places at once!

In any very busy network, it's better to dedicate a machine to monitoring network traffic. That not only gives NetMon the best chance to capture the packets, it also ensures that NetMon does not adversely affect any other services you might be running on your machine.

If you want to use NetMon as a dedicated network monitoring tool, consider the following:

- You'll need a relatively fast machine with adequate RAM. In a small network, 256MB will be fine, in larger networks you may need to set a buffer size as high as 1GB to ensure that data is processed properly; that requires a machine with at least 1.5GB of RAM.

- If you want to save buffer information for later analysis, use a machine with a large hard drive.

- In a large network, use a dedicated machine for network analysis. In a small network, use one of your lesser-used servers to ensure that capturing network data does not unduly affect the performance of the server in question.

System Monitor

Whereas Network Monitor concentrates on the network performance as a whole, System Monitor can monitor the network performance of one or more servers within the network and compare the results to the application, memory, and other parameters of the machine in question. System Monitor allows you to correlate problems with the network performance of a server with the performance of the server itself.

For example, running a database application on a server is likely to stress the CPU and the RAM and could prevent the server from accepting network packets. This would cause a lot of lost packets, retransmissions, and ultimately what would look like a saturated network, even though the network was not actually busy.

You can also use System Monitor to look at the individual performance statistics of the network card—that is, the sent/received packet rate and the number of packets dropped at the network interface. Over the long term, System Monitor can also record information at set intervals and raise alarms in the event log when counters reach specific levels.

For example, the Current Bandwidth counter can be used to give an approximate value on the available bandwidth on the network. You can use this to create a baseline figure of your network bandwidth during normal hours and outside hours for a background figure.

Third-Party Solutions

There is an almost limitless supply of third-party alternatives available, both free and commercial. Some of the best are those that integrate with your network hardware infrastructure. Because they can connect to the hardware directly, they can often use built-in monitoring systems in the switches and hubs and allow you to monitor your network traffic flow. In a layer 3 switch or VLAN-capable switch, this can even be integrated so that you can modify the network structure dynamically based on the information you receive. Most network hardware vendors have solutions available.

 **Objective 4.03** # Internet Connectivity Strategy

You've probably seen numerous reports of failures and security breaches related to Microsoft servers. Often the problem is not a problem with the Microsoft software, however, but with a lack of security on the part of the people who manage the servers.

Your primary objective with your Internet connection strategy is therefore to ensure that your network is safe, and safety must go both ways. You need to protect your internal network from the public connection that is the Internet, which can mean specifically restricting access from the public side and/or restricting which sites people on the private (internal) side can access.

Before you decide on your strategy, you need to first determine your requirements:

- **Internal user access** Do your users need Internet access, and if so, do they need direct access to the Internet through a public IP address or indirect access through network address translation or a proxy service? If it's indirect access, either Internet Connection Sharing (ICS) or Network Address Translation (NAT) is the best solution. If it's direct connectivity, you can use NAT (up to a point) or Internet Security and Acceleration (ISA) Server.

- **External user access** Do you need to provide access to your internal network from the outside, for example, do you have public web servers or an extranet? For this you need a registered public IP address and the ability to route this IP address into your internal network.

- **VPN/IPSec** Do you need to provide a secure pathway for users or branch offices to connect to your head office via the Internet? If so, you'll need a public IP address and routing capability.

- **Firewall** Do you need to protect and/or restrict your visibility on the Internet? The answer should nearly always be a resounding yes. The easiest way to do this is to separate your allocated public IP addresses from the private IP addresses you use on your network. NAT can handle this for you to a point, but ISA server is better for larger, more complex installations.

- **Control** Do you need to control access to the Internet from your users, restricting who can access it, and which sites they can access and when? You can only achieve this with a proxying service, such as that offered by ISA Server.

Local Lingo

Extranet An intranet provides an information gateway to your internal services through a web server. An extranet is an intranet that is also available through a public interface. For example, you can use an extranet to provide secure access to some of your internal systems for your clients or business partners.

Most of the preceding information is summarized in Table 4.2.

Before we look at the specific strategies available, we need to first consider the physical method for connecting to the Internet, which can have an effect on which solution use.

TABLE 4.2 Summary of Internet Connection Requirements and Solutions

Requirement	ICS	NAT	ISA
Direct (IP-based) user access	No	No	Yes
Indirect user access	Yes	Yes	Yes
Public IP sharing	No	Yes	Yes
VPN/IPSec support	No	Yes	Yes
Protected public/private IPs	Yes (limited)	Yes (limited)	Yes
Access control	No	No	Yes

Exam Tip

Internet connectivity questions, barring those about troubleshooting, usually concentrate on ensuring the security of your network or the suitability of a particular strategy. For example, the requirement to restrict user access with authentication requires an ISA server. Make sure you understand the limits and suitability of the various options and you should be fine.

Internet Connection Options

We're all aware of the mind-boggling array of options available for the Internet access. In recent years, there has been an increase in xDSL and cable modems, which offer cheap, high-speed access but are limited in their suitability if you want to serve Internet data from your company.

The different connection methods also affect which connection strategy is available; this information is summarized in Table 4.3.

Dial-Up Access

Dial-up Internet access is really only suitable for end users or for branch offices. The problem with dial-up is both the slow speed and relatively high cost. Dial-up services are also on-demand services—they connect to the Internet only when you need a connection. This makes it generally impossible, and because of issues of speed, impractical to use it for hosting websites on your internal network to the public.

Dial-up access is usually provided by a server running ICS, as shown in Figure 4.12.

xDSL/Cable Modem

xDSL and cable modem access are rapidly replacing dial-up connectivity in situations where a modem was previously acceptable. Home users, SOHOs (small

TABLE 4.3   Connection Methods and Connection Strategies

Method	ICS	NAT	ISA
Dial-up	Yes	Yes	No (not easily)
xDSL	Yes (USB)	Yes	Yes
Cable modem	Yes	Yes	Yes
Leased line	No	Yes	Yes

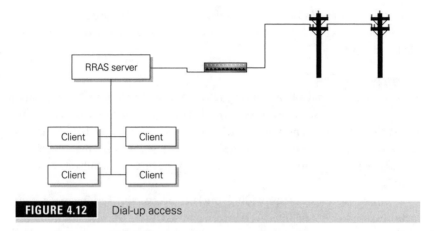

FIGURE 4.12 Dial-up access

offices/home offices), and even Small to Medium Enterprise (SME) environments can all make use of the various xDSL and cable modem options.

xDSL is available in two formats: Asynchronous Digital Subscriber Line (ADSL) and Synchronous Digital Subscriber Line (SDSL). ADSL provides different download and upload speeds. For example, an ADSL speed of 512/256Kbps means the download from the Internet is at 512Kbps and the upload to the Internet is at 256Kbps. ADSL is best used in situations where you want Internet access but don't expect to host your own Internet servers (Web, FTP, and so on). SDSL uses the same download and upload speeds and can be used both for basic Internet access and Internet serving. xDSL is available in speeds from 512Kbps up to 8Mbps; the maximum rate available to you depends on your distance from the local xDSL exchange.

Cable modems are offered by the various cable companies at speeds up to 2Mbps. Like ADSL, they offer different upload and download speeds and are not always suitable for providing Internet services.

Both xDSL and cable modems share their bandwidth among a number of users, so although the connection may be 512Kbps, you may be sharing the potential full bandwidth between 20 and 50 other users. If all 50 users download a large file at the same time, your actual performance could be only slightly above 1Kbps. This is another reason why these technologies are not always suitable for Internet server provision—you cannot guarantee the upload speed, which will ultimately affect your user's experience. The faster the connection, the less likely you are to feel the effects, but you still cannot guarantee 8Mbps of bandwidth.

There are two ways of connecting to the Internet using this technology. You can use a USB modem (xDSL or cable) attached to a suitable machine, which then shares its connection (using ICS, NAT, or ISA Server) just as standard

PSTN/ISDN modem does. Alternatively, you can use a dedicated DSL router, like the one shown in Figure 4.13. Access control can still be managed through NAT and ISA Server.

Leased Lines

Leased lines are available at varying rates, from 64Kbps up to 1.5Mbps and more. Generally, leased line access is handled by a dedicated router, just as with dedicated xDSL. (Looking at Figure 4.13, you can replace the xDSL router with a leased line router to see how this works.) Unlike ADSL, however, the connection speeds are the same both up and down and they are dedicated, full-rate connections.

If you're planning on providing Internet access and serving your own websites or other public Internet services, a leased line is the best solution.

You can still control and manage access to the leased line connection to the Internet by placing a Windows Server 2003 installation between the router and the rest of the network; you can also support NAT or ISA Server installations through this connection.

Branch Office to Internet

There are two ways to connect branch offices to the head office, either directly or through the Internet. The former method relies on dedicated access between branch offices and the head office. This can be done either through dedicated leased lines or through a dial-up service managed by a Windows Server 2003 operating a remote access service. The network diagram for this solution would look something like Figure 4.14.

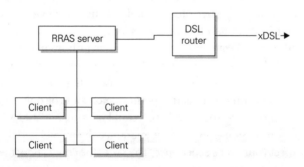

FIGURE 4.13   xDSL access through a dedicated router

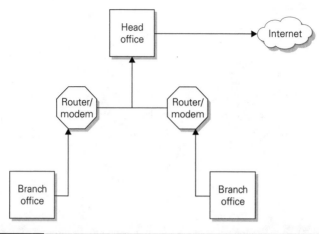

FIGURE 4.14 Internet access and branch office connectivity

The Internet connectivity would then be provided through the head office network and to the Internet. There are a few issues to consider with this method:

- Centralized Internet connectivity makes it much easier to control access and manage the Internet connection, bandwidth, and connectivity issues.
- You can normally get by with just one firewall.
- Bandwidth management on an office-by-office basis can be difficult, and it's possible that one remote office could tie up the bandwidth of the entire Internet connection.
- Typically, the costs of connecting branch offices to the main office will be higher than offices using their own connection, but this may be outweighed by the savings in firewall and management flexibility.

Internet to Branch Office

The logical opposite of the previous solution is to connect each of the branch offices directly to the Internet and then allow the branch offices to communicate with each other over the Internet. The network structure diagram will be much like Figure 4.15.

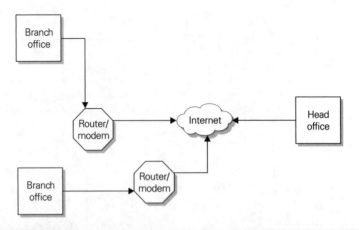

Branch office connectivity through the Internet

To secure such a connection, you'd need to use IPSec or VPN technology to provide a secure tunnel through which the machines can communicate. The main issues with this model are as follows:

- Lower connectivity costs, because it's generally cheaper to connect to a localized Internet Service Provider than directly to the head office.
- Distributed Internet connection strategy means that you'll need a Routing and Remote Access Service (RRAS) server to act as the IPSec/VPN router for the branch office network. You'll also need separate firewalls at each office.
- You'll have higher maintenance and administration costs to keep each site synchronized, especially with respect to firewall and office-to-office connectivity requirements.

Internet Gateway Connectivity

Planning your Internet connectivity is not just a case of lining up a connection with an ISP, plugging in a box, and letting things get on with themselves. The top of your priorities list must be the security of your network, closely followed by your actual connectivity requirements.

Your main concerns should be

- **Security**   Firewalls offer the best protection, but Network Address Translation (NAT) provides security by not automatically exposing internal IP addresses to the outside world. Microsoft's Internet Security and Acceleration (ISA) server is a firewall, NAT, and proxying solution.

- **Scalability and fault-tolerance**   If you are using an intermediate device or machine to support your Internet access, you must be able to recover from a failure and/or extend your capability if Internet access and usage begins to increase.

- **User access control**   You may wish to control user access to the Internet, either by requiring a user/password combination or restricting access based on a user's credentials.

- **Bandwidth control**   You may want to share the bandwidth of your connection and control how much data is sent and received over your connection. For example, if you have a large hosting requirement, you may want to allocate 80 percent of your bandwidth for incoming connections and restrict outgoing (user-based) bandwidth to 20 percent.

- **Time-of-day access**   Limiting access to the Internet at specific times enables you to control when your users use the connection. It's very popular, for example, to limit connectivity to break/lunch times, while restricting access at other times.

- **Extensibility and flexibility**   Your solution must be able to support the number of current users on your network and be able to cope with future increases.

- **Application connectivity**   Some application types, such as multimedia, videoconferencing, and Internet gaming, require fixed IP addressing and do not work through NAT.

Beyond your choices about the actual connection methods, three solutions exist for Internet connectivity: Internet Connection Sharing (ICS), Network Address Translation (NAT), or Internet Security and Acceleration (ISA) Server. We'll have a look at the benefits and pitfalls of all three systems.

Internet Connection Sharing

For a small office network, Internet Connection Sharing (ICS) is the easiest method of providing Internet connectivity for your organization. To use it, you need only have two network interfaces: the internal Ethernet interface to provide the connectivity from your clients, and another to provide connectivity to the Internet. Typically, this is a modem- or ISDN-based dial-up solution, but it can also be a cable modem, USB xDSL, or another network connection to a hardware-based router.

ICS can also be used with ISPs that allocate dynamic addresses to the ICS server, as with many low-cost dial-up, cable, and xDSL accounts. Because ICS does not support routing of external public addresses to your internal network, the inability to use a static, publicly configured IP address is not a limitation that is likely to cause problems.

Using ICS changes your Ethernet interface to use IP address 192.168.0.1, and clients must have addresses in the range 192.168.0.2–192.168.0.254. The easiest way to allocate these is through DHCP, but you can also set them up manually.

The only problem with ICS is that it assumes that you want to provide Internet access for your internal clients but that you don't want to provide Internet access to your network. Although this won't affect your ability to access websites, it does mean that you will need to use your ISP's e-mail server and facilities (unless you use a third-party solution). This is because there is no way to route incoming traffic such as SMTP or HTTP into your network. For that, you need to use either NAT or ISA Server.

However, Windows Server 2003 does now include a companion product, Internet Connection Firewall, that can protect and limit data on specific IP port numbers for both TCP and UDP traffic.

Network Address Translation

Network Address Translation (NAT) is a technology that enables one or more public IP addresses to be translated into private addresses. Although this can be done on a fixed IP-to-IP allocation, more typically it's used to share a small number of public IP addresses with a larger number of internal addresses. However, NAT is limited to a maximum of 253 internal addresses and is not suitable for sharing a larger number of public IP addresses.

Because NAT translates between the public IP addresses and your internal address, you get a reasonable level of protection. By default, NAT is configured to allow internal addresses to access the Internet. To allow public traffic into your network, you must specifically enable a filter that translates the public IP address into an internal IP address. For example, you might set up a filter that redirects port 80 (HTTP) traffic to your internal web server. This offers some security by not opening your network to the public, but it is not a complete alternative to a full firewall solution.

NAT in Windows Server 2003 is supported by the RRAS component. The solution is limited to supporting clients on a single subnet, so the maximum number of users you can support is 253 (once you've removed the network and broadcast addresses). The filtering is also very basic—you can only route through specific ports, but you can route external public ports onto internal private ports. For example, you could set up a route between port 80 on the public interface and port 11200 on the internal. You can see this demonstrated in the network diagram in Figure 4.16.

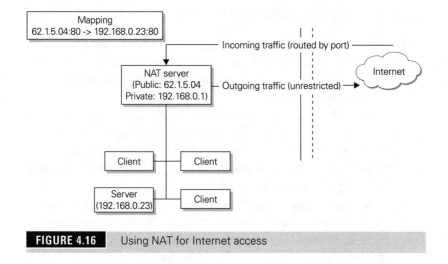

FIGURE 4.16   Using NAT for Internet access

You cannot make decisions based on the source or destination of the traffic from either the public or the private side. All users within your network that are within the NAT subnet have access. If you are using DHCP to set your client IP addresses, this will probably mean that all users on your network will be given Internet access. You cannot control access through authentication (either from the public or private side) or on an individual basis.

Internet Security and Acceleration Server

Microsoft's ISA Server addresses two main areas of concern when providing Internet access:

- **Security**   Provides extensive firewall and filtering capabilities for protecting traffic and authentication facilities for limiting internal use.
- **Acceleration**   Caches Internet data and acts as a proxy server, speeding up the Internet access for internal clients while reducing the load on your expensive Internet connection.

ISA Server is a separate, chargeable component that you can use in combination with Windows Server 2003 to support your Internet connectivity. Unlike NAT, ISA Server can be deployed in an environment with multiple subnets, as it works much like a file or printer spooling service—that is, as an application-level solution for connecting to the Internet.

ISA Server also has a number of other abilities:

- **Filtering**   As a full-blown firewall solution, ISA Server can make complex decisions about filtering and routing packets from the Internet to your internal network. For example, you can limit connectivity to SMTP traffic only from your ISP.

- **Scalable**   ISA Server can be installed either as a stand-alone solution or as an array. In array formation, multiple ISA Servers provide the same core set of services across your network while sharing the load and providing redundancy, in much the same way as network load balancing technology does for incoming web connections.

- **Authentication and control**   Connectivity to the Internet from the internal network can be controlled from an individual point of view and at more granular levels such as by members of specific groups, times, and even the websites individuals access.

- **Routing and distributed access**   ISA Server can act as a routing solution even when used within a routed network. Unlike NAT, which has to route specific ports from public addresses to private ones on the same subnet, ISA Server can route traffic from any IP address to any other, either at an IP address or port level. For example, a larger internal LAN with routing controls or a branch office solution can both be routed through to the Internet using ISA Server.

- **Fixed IP routing**   If your clients or servers require fixed IP addresses (for example, VPN connectivity, video streaming, videoconferencing, gaming servers), ISA Server can handle the routing. You also can use the filtering abilities of ISA Server to control access even though you are routing public IP traffic straight into your internal network.

- **Proxy server**   With a proxy server, all web requests coming from your clients are routed through a single machine. This protects your internal network by only exposing your proxy server's IP address. It also caches information to speed up client access and provides content filtering limiting access to specific websites or content.

Travel Advisory

To allow your clients to use the proxy server, you need to configure the client's Internet connection properties. In most cases, the easiest way to do this is to set the clients to use automatic proxy server configuration—this will try to load the config from the gateway machine (which will also be your ISA Server).

ISA Server sits between your network and your Internet connection of any method, and it provides both incoming connection security and outgoing connection security. In a single ISA Server solution, the network diagram looks like Figure 4.17. Note that ISA Server now notionally sits over the firewall as it connects to both the internal (private) and public networks.

In a larger network environment, one ISA Server is unlikely to be able to handle the load. However, ISA Server is scalable, and you can place a number of ISA Server computers into a group. They will share security and filtering systems while sharing the load on the actual connections.

Objective 4.04 Troubleshoot Internet Connectivity

Occasionally, something slips up in your Internet connection that you need to check. The primary problems are usually IP or DHCP allocation problems, which are covered later in this chapter. Other problems can be more esoteric. For example, when looking up an address by its name, you might find that the wrong address is returned. We'll look at Internet-specific problems in this section and at more general IP connectivity problems later in this chapter.

Network Address Translation (NAT) Issues

Troubleshooting NAT generally comes down to troubleshooting basic TCP/IP connectivity. DHCP issues arise if you've configured NAT to automatically distribute IP addresses over DHCP, in which case you should check out the "DHCP Server Address Assignment Issues" section later in this chapter.

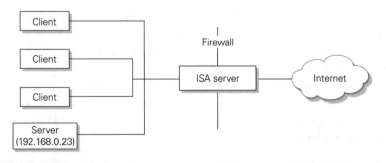

FIGURE 4.17   Internet access with ISA Server

Whether you are using static or DHCP addressing, you should also make sure that you can connect to the NAT server and that your IP address, gateway, and DNS server settings are correct. Tips on checking these can be found later in this chapter.

Finally, issues within NAT mappings—that is, an inability to connect to a web server, even though it's been published through NAT—can be checked by checking the NAT mappings. You can do this through the Routing and Remote Access Server (RRAS) manager.

Name Resolution Cache Information Issues

The DNS client service keeps a record of DNS lookups in a cache so that it does not have to continually resend requests to the DNS server. The problem is that occasionally the information in the cache can stick around for too long and updates and changes to the DNS, or sites that used multiple IP addresses assigned to the same name, do not get updated. This ultimately leads to clients receiving the wrong, or dubious, information from the server.

The ipconfig command can list the current DNS cache by using the /displaydns option. The output can be quite lengthy and won't always show you any useful information. If you think the issue is with the DNS cache, use the /flushdns command-line option to flush the client's DNS cache, which will cause DNS queries to once again contact a DNS server for resolution.

Client Configuration Issues

Despite being developed to survive a nuclear war, the Internet is not quite as resilient as the media or the owners of numerous websites would have you believe. We lost track a long time ago of the number of times we've been unable to communicate with a website for no reason other than some transient failure between our computers and our ISP or our ISP and the rest of the Internet.

Always check another website before you assume something more fundamental is wrong, and make sure that you check that general Internet connectivity is working by using ping or tracert to reach a remote network. It could quite easily be a problem beyond your or your ISP's control.

If you are using Internet Connection Sharing (ICS), make sure the clients are using DHCP to get their addresses, that the DHCP address they are given is within the 192.168.x.x range, and that their default gateway and DNS address information points to the ICS gateway on your network.

There are usually three areas of client Internet connectivity issues that are directly related to the individual client configuration:

- *Check that the gateway address is correct.* The gateway address is sent all packets that aren't otherwise intended for the local network, which includes the Internet.
- *Check that the client's DNS resolves addresses properly.* If you are getting "host cannot be found" errors, it means that the DNS is not resolving properly. If you are using a local DNS resolver, you might also want to check that the server is correctly configured to pass on DNS requests to your ISP's DNS servers.
- *Check the client's proxy server address, if you are using one.* You can find these in the Internet Options control panel.

If the clients use automatic addressing, check that your DHCP options are set correctly on the server; it could be the DHCP server is broadcasting the wrong information, DNS and gateway addresses in particular.

Finally, it's worth checking that TCP/IP filtering has not been enabled on the clients. Not all sites use the standard port 80 address, and it's possible that the client is blocking the port that the remote server is using.

Objective 4.05 Troubleshoot TCP/IP Addressing

TCP/IP addressing problems are like phone numbers. Imagine that you have a phone number and that everybody in your circle of friends and family has it. If you change your phone number, then everybody else needs to know what it is in order for them to talk to you on the phone. Getting the addressing right is therefore vital to enabling everybody to talk to each other.

Once you understand the basics of TCP/IP addressing, finding and identifying faults should become relatively easy.

Client Computer Configuration Issues

The ipconfig tool, used without any options, will give you your current IP address settings, irrespective of how they have been set:

```
C:\>ipconfig
```

```
Windows IP Configuration

Ethernet adapter Local Area Connection:

        Connection-specific DNS Suffix  . : windows.mcslp.pri
        IP Address. . . . . . . . . . . : 192.168.1.180
        Subnet Mask . . . . . . . . . . : 255.255.255.0
        Default Gateway . . . . . . . . : 192.168.1.1
```

Common TCP/IP addressing problems are

- **The IP address**   It must be within the scope of your subnet or one of your subnets, and it must be unique. You will get a warning on both machines if you choose an IP address that is not unique.
- **The netmask**   It must match the mask for your subnet or subnets. If set incorrectly, the client might not know whether a machine it's trying to talk to is on the local network or another network.
- **The gateway address**   IP packets that the client has determined do not fit into the current network (by using the IP address/netmask combination) are sent to this IP address for routing. If set incorrectly, it can cause packets to be routed incorrectly or not to be routed at all.

There are a few other tests you can do to check the configuration and stability of a client's network configuration:

- **Ping 127.0.0.1**   This is the localhost address and should always work if the TCP/IP stack is installed correctly, even if the IP address settings are not correct. If this test fails, there's a fundamental issue in your TCP/IP drivers: they are not installed correctly, or they are corrupt. Either way, they need to be reinstalled.
- **Ping local address**   This will check that the IP address for the client has been bound to the card properly. Do this in combination with ipconfig to ensure that you are checking the right address. If the test fails, then the network card is probably faulty. Reinstall the drivers for the card or replace the card.
- **Ping default gateway**   This should verify the connectivity to another device on the network. If it fails, check the cabling and physical connectivity to the card.

- **Ping remote IP address** This should verify that the routing is working correctly and should verify that both the gateway IP address and the netmask are correct. If it fails (particularly with "destination host unreachable"), verify the default gateway and netmask settings are correct and check the WAN for connectivity problems.

Exam Tip

Make sure you know the effects of the various tests, either way. It's possible you'll be asked to identify where a failure is within the configuration based on the result of a ping to one of these areas.

Questions on the exam in this area tend to center around the issue of getting the address/netmask/gateway correct. For example, a popular question type is "Your client has an IP address of 192.168.1.180, a netmask of 255.255.255.0, and a default gateway address of 192.168.2.1. What should you change?" In this case, the problem is that the default gateway is not reachable because it's on a different subnet from the client (based on the IP and netmask).

Other questions will give you a network diagram with various servers and routers and ask you to determine which machines can talk to which, or determine whether a specific machine is able to talk to another. For example, look at the information in Figure 4.18. You can ping ServerA from the other servers, and you can ping the Router0 from ServerA, but ServerA is unable to connect to the servers on network B. Which setting is preventing ServerA from communicating with the outside world?

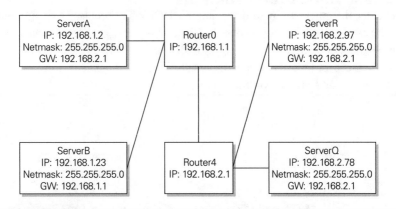

FIGURE 4.18 A sample network as used in a typical question

> **Exam Tip**
>
> Diagrams like the one in Figure 4.18 are pretty common, and it's quite possible to have 4 or 5 of these in a given exam. The trick is to ignore the items that don't matter—the fact that the other servers are working means you can eliminate them from the diagram before you even start to look elsewhere. Mentally, this can be quite difficult, so it might help to use the paper you're given in the exam to draw your own version of the diagram—albeit without the detail—so that you can see which areas need to be concentrated on.

The key is to check the individual network settings. All the servers and Router0 are within the 192.168.1.0 network with a netmask of 255.255.255.0. If you can ping the router, there is nothing wrong with the network card, physical connectivity, or the installed software. However, if you check the default gateway, you can see that ServerA is trying to talk to a router on the wrong subnet using the wrong IP address. The effect will only be felt by ServerA when it tries to communicate out.

DHCP Server Address Assignment Issues

DHCP is pretty reliable as long as your clients can talk to the server and the server can talk back to the clients. You need to be particularly careful if your clients are beyond the scope of your local network—for example, if they're on the other side of a router or part of a different subnet—when the communication between the clients and server can cause problems.

Client Allocation Problems

Usually, the quickest way to determine a DHCP client problem is to find out what address has been allocated to the client. This gives a good indication of the problem, if one exists. The easiest way to determine the IP address allocation is to use the ipconfig command with the /all option on your client. You can see a sample output from the command here:

```
C:\> ipconfig /all

Windows IP Configuration

        Host Name . . . . . . . . . . . . : DXPXP5
        Primary Dns Suffix  . . . . . . . : windows.mcslp.pri
        Node Type . . . . . . . . . . . . : Hybrid
        IP Routing Enabled. . . . . . . . : No
        WINS Proxy Enabled. . . . . . . . : No
        DNS Suffix Search List. . . . . . : windows.mcslp.pri
                                            mcslp.pri
```

```
Ethernet adapter Local Area Connection:

        Connection-specific DNS Suffix  . : windows.mcslp.pri
        Description . . . . . . . . . . . : AMD PCNET Family PCI
Ethernet Adapter
        Physical Address. . . . . . . . . : 00-0C-29-F7-70-6D
        Dhcp Enabled. . . . . . . . . . . : Yes
        Autoconfiguration Enabled . . . . : Yes
        IP Address. . . . . . . . . . . . : 192.168.1.180
        Subnet Mask . . . . . . . . . . . : 255.255.255.0
        Default Gateway . . . . . . . . . : 192.168.1.1
        DHCP Server . . . . . . . . . . . : 192.168.1.138
        DNS Servers . . . . . . . . . . . : 192.168.1.138
                                            192.168.1.135
        Primary WINS Server . . . . . . . : 192.168.1.138
        Lease Obtained. . . . . . . . . . : 20 June 2003 11:22:39
        Lease Expires . . . . . . . . . . : 28 June 2003 11:22:39
```

First, check that DHCP is actually enabled on the client; it's on by default, but it's possible that someone played with the settings.

Next, use the output of ipconfig to check that the DHCP server address is the one for your DHCP server. If it isn't, find out which device is distributing DHCP addresses. Either the wrong server is giving out the addresses or a server is giving out addresses that map to an existing DHCP or static IP address range that it shouldn't be using.

Next, check the IP address that's allocated to the client. You can usually determine where the problem lies according to the address:

- If the client has an address that lies within one of the scopes, then DHCP is probably working. However, keep in mind that the server may have been misconfigured with the wrong IP address range (scope).

- If an address is within the Automatic Private IP Addressing (APIPA) scope, the DHCP client has auto-configured itself an address because it can't contact a DHCP server. APIPA addresses lie within the IP address range 169.254.0.1 through 169.254.255.254 with a class B netmask of 255.255.0.0. There are four possible reasons for this problem:

  - The server is unavailable, either because it crashed, it's down for maintenance, or the DHCP service failed to start properly.

  - The DHCP server ran out of IP addresses. (It's a good idea to have between 5 and 25 more IP addresses than you expect to need within your scope.)

  - The DHCP is the other side of a routed or otherwise separate physical network connection.

- The DHCP server has not been authorized in Active Directory—remember, you must authorize DHCP servers in AD before the DHCP is enabled.
- If the IP address is 0.0.0.0, it indicates a more general problem with the TCP/IP stack of the client. This is usually a good sign, as it means the problem is not with your server but with the client. Try restarting the client or updating/reinstalling the network card drivers.

You can renew the IP configuration from a DHCP server by using the ipconfig /renew command.

DHCP Database Corruption

The DHCP database is located within the %systemroot%\System32\DHCP directory, with a backup copy located in the %systemroot%\System32\DHCP\ backup directory. You can change these directories using the Advanced property settings of the properties from within of the DHCP manager. If you have more than one physical disk available, you might want to place the backup copy on one of the additional disks.

The DHCP service will automatically try to recover from the backup copy in the event of any problem. If the system can't recover from this information, you might have to recover a copy of the files from an external backup. If this fails, you'll have to re-create the scope and mappings by hand.

Checking the Logs

The DHCP logs are located in the Windows\System32\DHCP directory by default, along with the databases. The logs are automatically generated, and new logs are created each day. At the top of each log is a handy Event ID reference to help you track any problems, as well as standard events such as assigning or renewing IP address leases to clients.

Objective 4.07

Troubleshoot Host Name Resolution

DNS is the system that resolves Internet names into the IP addresses that are actually used by the Internet, and the reason we need DNS is that humans aren't very good with names.

In the exam, you're bound to get some questions related to name resolution, whether that's through DNS or WINS. Yep, I said WINS. Even though it's a relatively underused and under-promoted tool for name resolving, WINS is still used by many companies, especially if they have pre-Windows 2000/XP clients. Most of time, the questions will actually be related to DNS in some way, because Windows Server 2003 will try and resolve WINS requests through DNS if the initial WINS fails or if the WINS name you are looking for is outside your immediate subnet. If the question tells you that you can reach a machine via IP address but not by name, then it's a WINS or DNS problem and the question will usually tell you which is and isn't configured.

Most of the time these problems are fairly insignificant—you're not going to need to completely reinstall the operating system or do anything complex. In our experience, 99 percent of all name resolution issues are because of mistyping. We'd be rich if we had a dollar for every DNS server address that was mistyped or every name/IP address configuration that was misregistered.

Generally, finding and identifying the problem is that easy, too. You'll probably notice the issue as soon as you look at the configuration; if you don't, you'll notice it when you run nslookup or something similar. To help you along though, we're going to look at three main areas: DNS issues, WINS issues, and client configuration issues.

DNS Service Issues

The DNS service is not self managing, but with a combination of Active Directory integration, DHCP registration, and the self registration provided by clients, it's possible to pretty much fit and forget a DNS installation from the server side. That doesn't mean you're not going to run into problems. It just means that you'll need to take a bit more care when it comes to resolving the problem.

It most cases, the problem is either directly with the client not picking up the information correctly or with a client or server not registering the information correctly in the first place.

Database corruption can occur on a DNS server, but it's less likely to occur if the DNS service is integrated with Active Directory, especially if the AD is replicated around to additional servers. If it does become corrupted, you'll need to recover the entire active directory. If you are using standard zones—that is, not linked to AD—then these are stored within the %systemroot%\system32\DNS directory. You can back up these files or re-create them or recover them from a backup.

One way to find possible DNS issues is to use nslookup. We'll also look at some of the specific problematic areas in WINS and DNS at the client and server level.

Using nslookup

The easiest way to check your DNS setup and configuration is to use the nslookup command. You can use this either directly through the command line or through an internal shell built into the nslookup command.

At the simplest level, you can use nslookup with the name of a machine to get its IP address:

```
C:\>nslookup polarbear
Server:  bear.windows.mcslp.pri
Address:  192.168.1.138

Name:     polarbear.windows.mcslp.pri
Address:  192.168.1.126
```

Notice that it gives you the IP address of the DNS server that the response came from—if this address is wrong, then you've got a problem with your DNS configuration or DHCP configuration for this machine.

You can also use nslookup with an FQDN:

```
C:\>nslookup www.microsoft.com
Server:  bear.windows.mcslp.pri
Address:  192.168.1.138

Non-authoritative answer:
Name:     www.microsoft.akadns.net
Addresses:  207.46.134.190, 207.46.134.222, 207.46.249.27
            207.46.249.190, 207.46.134.155
Aliases:  www.microsoft.com
```

And also with IP addresses to lookup a name:

```
C:\>nslookup 192.168.1.180
Server:  bear.windows.mcslp.pri
Address:  192.168.1.138

Name:     dxpxp5.windows.mcslp.pri
Address:  192.168.1.180
```

If you get an error message from any of these requests, use Table 4.4 to get an indication of what the problem might be.

TABLE 4.4	Error Messages and What They Could Mean from nslookup

Error Message	Description
Timed out	The server did not respond to a request after a given number of seconds and retries. You can change these values by using the set command with the timeout and retry values. This could indicate that the server is running slowly, has too many or too complex a domain name service, or if the request is for a remote host name—that is, on the Internet—it may indicate a communication or server problem with your ISP or its domain name servers.
No response from server	No DNS name server is running on the server computer. Check that the DNS service is running on the server in question, and also check that the DNS server address is correct.
No records	The DNS name server does not have resource records of the current query type for the computer, although the computer name is valid. For example, you could be looking up host info or mail exchanger (MX) information, but although the host exists, no HINFO or MX records are in the tables.
Nonexistent domain	The computer or DNS domain name do not exist. If you asked for a host name resolution rather than using an FQDN—for example, you asked for "bear" rather than "bear.windows.mcslp.pri," your DNS suffix is set incorrectly in your Advanced DNS preferences.
Connection refused or network is unreachable	A connection to the DNS server could not be made. If you are connecting to a local server, double check that the service is running and that you don't have any filtering switched on that would filter out the requests.
Server failure	An internal inconsistency made it impossible for the server to return a correct address. This can indicate a corrupt DNS database or a bad connection

TABLE 4.4	Error Messages and What They Could Mean from nslookup *(continued)*
Error Message	**Description**
Refused	The DNS name server refused to service the request. For security reasons, some servers will refuse to answer certain request types (for example, the ls subcommand, which lists all the hosts in a domain), either unconditionally or to certain hosts or domains.
Format error	The DNS server received a badly formatted request packet.

From the command line, you can also set various nslookup options, such as the type of record to look up or the timeout value to use. For example, to look up mail-exchanger (MX) records instead of address (A) records, use this:

```
C:\>nslookup -type=mx mcslp.pri
Server:  bear.windows.mcslp.pri
Address:  192.168.1.138

Non-authoritative answer:
mcslp.pri       MX preference = 1, mail exchanger = mail.mcslp.pri
```

The nslookup tool also has a built-in shell that allows you to perform lookups that can be particularly useful if you are testing more than one host or type for a given domain or if you want to perform a test on an alternative server or address type. To start the shell, just run nslookup without any arguments. The commands available within the nslookup shell are listed in Table 4.5.

TABLE 4.5	Subcommands of the nslookup Tool
Subcommand	**Description**
exit	Exits the nslookup shell.
finger	"Fingers" a remote user, which can be used to determine if a user is logged on to a remote machine.
help	Displays the built-in help.
ls	Lists all of the hosts with the current type (default is address (A) records) in the given domain. This can fail.
lserver	Changes the server that DNS lookup requests are sent to, using the initial (default) server to resolve a given name into an IP address. You can alternatively specify the IP address.

TABLE 4.5	Subcommands of the nslookup Tool *(continued)*

Subcommand	Description
root	Sets the current default server to the root.
server	Changes the server that DNS lookup requests are sent to, using the current server to resolve a given name into an IP address. You can alternatively specify the IP address.
set	Sets various options that affect what information is returned and how addresses are looked up.
set all	Prints the current option list settings.
set class	Sets the query class.
set [no]d2	[Unsets]Sets exhaustive debug information to be displayed.
set [no]debug	[Unsets]Sets debug information to be displayed.
set [no]defname	[Unsets]Sets the default domain name to be appended to each query.
set domain	Sets the default domain.
set [no]ignore	[Unsets]Sets ignore on packet truncation errors.
set port	Sets the port number to use for contacting the DNS server (default is 53).
set querytype	Same as set type.
set [no]recurse	[Unsets]Sets recursive name lookups. When switched on, forces the server to ask other servers whether they know the address (this is the default behavior).
set retry	Sets the number of retries that the server will attempt before giving up.
set root	Sets the root server.
set [no]search	[Unsets]Uses the domain search list (which you set through set srchlist).
set srchlist	Sets the list of domains to append when looking up a name.
set timeout	Sets the timeout value for requests.
set type	Sets the type of record to search for.
set [no]vc	[Unsets]Sets the virtual circuit when sending a request to the server.
view	Sorts and page views a file (usually used with the redirected output of the ls command).

Forward Resolution

Problems in forward resolution, that is, name to IP address, are usually related to one of the following:

- **Bad manual entry**   You've typed in the entry incorrectly into the DNS database.
- **Bad client registration**   If your clients and servers are registering their own addresses into the database, make sure they are registering them with the right server and with the right domain suffix, especially if you have multiple domains.
- **Bad DHCP registration**   If your DHCP is registering your IP address/ name when the request comes from the client, make sure the settings are correct.
- **Bad domain suffix**   On the client's (if using static address) or in the DHCP server preferences, ensure you've set the correct DNS suffix so that registration and lookups occur correctly.

Reverse Resolution

Reverse resolution, that is, IP address to name, are less common but can create all kinds of problems with mail servers and websites that require reverse lookups to verify that the address is a valid (not spoofed) address. Manual entry is pretty rare because a reverse lookup entry should have been automatically created for you when you created the forward lookup. Problems can usually be traced back to

- **Bad client registration**   Check the static IP address and/or DHCP address that was assigned to the server if the client also registers with the DNS server itself. If it picks up the wrong DHCP address or has the wrong IP address configured, it's possible that it's registering the wrong one back.
- **Bad domain suffix**   If using client-based registration, check that the domain suffix for the client is configured correctly.

Dynamic Updates

DNS, DHCP, and WINS all work closely with each other. The DHCP service, for example, can be made to update the DNS with the host name and IP address and a reverse pointer record when the client requests an IP address from the server.

Static clients and servers can register their name/IP address combination when they start up by using the registration system, which is configurable through the TCP/IP properties dialog.

If you are using the DNS service and want to be able to connect to specific clients or servers by name, you will need to ensure that clients are registering their IP addresses properly. This requires that the DNS server is configured to accept dynamic updates and that the clients and servers are registering their addresses properly.

WINS Service Issues

WINS, like DHCP, is pretty self sufficient: give it the basics of your WINS requirements, start the server, and it'll be pretty reliable. However, occasionally you get problems with a few of the systems.

The main problem that can occur with WINS is some form of database corruption. If you want some insurance and you have more than one server, set them up as multiple WINS servers in a replication group. That way a corruption in one database can be handled by one server while another server takes the load.

Travel Advisory

WINS requests do not roll over—that is, a failure in a server doesn't automatically trigger the client to ask the next server in the list. If the server fails, the WINS client just accepts that it can't resolve. However, in recent operating systems (Windows 2000, Windows XP, and Windows Server 2003), DNS will be used in place of WINS if the DNS service is able to resolve the name.

If a database does become corrupted, stop the service, delete the WINS database files, and restart the service. The WINS database will be re-created as clients reregister. You can find the WINS database in the \Windows\System32\wins directory. Unlike DHCP, it's not backed up automatically by default, but you can configure it to be backed up automatically during a server shutdown: just set the location of the backup copy in the General properties for the server. You can also manually force a backup to this location by right-clicking the server in WINS Manager and choosing Backup.

To restore the information backed up this way, delete all the WINS files, open WINS Manager, right-click and choose Restore Database, and choose the location of the WINS backup folder. Remember, however, that this information will be automatically re-created if you kill the database files and restart the service. It will take some time for the database to be re-created this way, but it is probably easier to deal with if time is a critical factor because killing and restarting can take time, too.

If you are using WINS replication services and the database is not being replicated properly, there are two areas to investigate:

- *Check that all the replication servers have the same time.* The WINS service records an expiration date on each entry in the database, and this information is used to determine whether the information should be replicated. If the times are different on two replication servers, the replication won't occur. You can synchronize the time either by using the built-in domain controller–based time synchronization service or by using the Internet time service. If the WINS service crosses subnets and/or time zones in a multilocation/branch office installation, use the Internet time service on all the WINS servers.

- *Check the extinction timeout value applied to each record against the replication periods.* If the timeout is less than the replication settings, the record could time out before the replication takes place.

Client Computer Configuration Issues

The best way to avoid problems at the client end is to use DHCP to distribute all of the client configuration information. However, if you are using static addressing or have more complex requirements, such as multiple DNS suffixes, and have therefore used the advanced DNS and WINS settings within the TCP/IP properties, you will need to individually check some of these areas to determine the location of the problem. The advanced DNS settings are shown in Figure 4.19.

In particular, you should check the following when resolving DNS issues:

- The DNS server addresses are correct and each server exists and is reachable. If the servers are beyond your local subnet, ensure the gateway address is configured so that the servers can be reached.

- When using the Append Primary and Connection Specific DNS Suffixes option, make sure that you enter the correct DNS suffix for the domain. This should be your FQDN, not the shorter NT-style domain name.

- When using the Append These DNS Suffixes (In Order) option, make sure the suffixes are valid. If they are outside your Active Directory scope (for example, on a parent domain), make sure they match the FDQN for the domain.

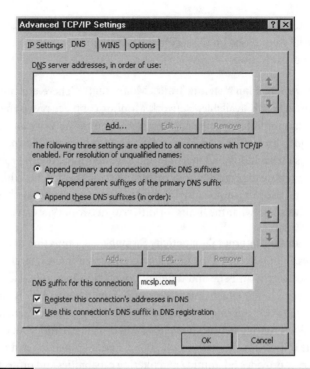

If you've updated/fixed DHCP information, you'll need to use ipconfig /renew to update the DHCP configuration information. If this doesn't work and the client is Windows XP, 2000, or Windows Server 2003, try disabling the network connection and re-enabling it, as this flushes all the information. Unfortunately, on earlier operating systems, you'll need to reboot.

Also, be aware that the DNS client on client computers caches information, just as the servers do, so use ipconfig /flushdns to flush the DNS cache if the name lookups are failing or returning bad information.

✔ **Objective 4.01: Plan and Modify Network Topology**   You should be able to identify network components and choose the best component based on your network requirements. For example, you should know the difference between a shared hub and a switch and the potential performance benefits that you can gain from using the switch. You should also be able to plan a network layout based on the server and client requirements and the departmental organization.

✔**Objective 4.02: Plan Network Traffic Monitoring**　There are two network monitoring tools available. Network Monitor captures raw frames and allows you to monitor specific network frames on the network and get overall bandwidth and utilization results. System Monitor provides performance statistics for an individual machine and can identify network problems and how they relate to problems with performance on the system. Whichever solution you use, you should also be able to determine the network utilization and understand what the limits for different network types are.

✔**Objective 4.03: Internet Connectivity Strategy**　Connecting to the Internet requires you to decide the physical connectivity and gateway strategy. In both cases, security is an issue and different connection methods lead to (and in some cases, limit) which gateway strategy you can use. ICS is suitable for smaller networks but cannot share public addresses with the internal network. NAT allows routing between the public and private networks but can accommodate only 253 hosts on the same subnet and is limited in what it can filter. ISA Server provides full routing and filtering capabilities and protects the network from external intruders.

✔**Objective 4.04: Troubleshoot Internet Connectivity**　You must first identify where the problem lies. You can do this by checking how Internet connectivity is provided. Different Internet connectivity solutions will lead to different potential problems. For example, a problem with your IP address when using ICS or NAT could have something to do with the DHCP system assignment. Other problems may stem from a badly configured IP address or default gateway or the DNS system resolving Internet names. There may also be problems outside your control, such as down or unavailable sites.

✔**Objective 4.05: Troubleshoot TCP/IP Addressing**　TCP/IP address problems generally boil down to a failure in the IP address and subnet on each machine. If the address is allocated dynamically through DHCP through the client, then it may be unable to communicate with the DHCP server. To resolve this, the most useful tool is typically ipconfig, which will display the allocated IP address of a machine.

✔**Objective 4.06: Troubleshoot Host Name Resolution** Resolution occurs either through DNS or WINS. A DNS fault is usually related to a problem with the DNS addresses on the client or with the DNS service on the server. It may also be a cache problem that can be resolved by clearing the name cache with ipconfig.

REVIEW QUESTIONS

1. Your company has 200 clients using four servers connected to each other on a network using shared hubs. All your machines have 10Mbps network cards. You used NetMon to monitor your network and determined that the network is at about 60 percent utilization and that the majority of traffic is being handled by the two primary file servers in your network as they exchange files with the clients. What would be the quickest and easiest way to improve performance? (Choose one.)

   A. Replace the 10Mbps network cards with 100Mbps cards

   B. Replace the shared hub with a switched hub

   C. Move the servers to a switched hub

   D. Move the clients to a switched hub

2. Users within your office use notebook computers to connect to the servers and the Internet. You have placed wireless access points (WAPs) around your office, and you must now choose where to place them physically within your network. The WAPs do not support either encrypted connections or restricted access. Where should you place your WAPs within your network while ensuring the maximum security for your network? (Choose a location from the network diagram shown in the following illustration.)

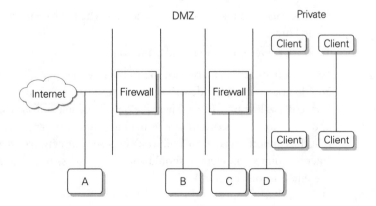

3. Your current network layout looks like the one shown in the following illustration. All the networks use 100Mbps Ethernet. Server A and Server B are file servers used by the clients attached to the switched Hubs C and D. Clients on Hub E do not need to access Server B, and vice versa. After monitoring the network performance on shared Hub C, you notice that utilization of these two servers is high. There are spare ports on all hubs. How would you improve performance on your network? (Choose two; each answer is a complete solution.)

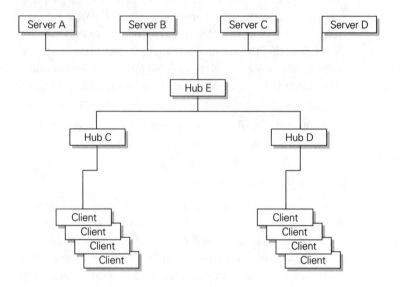

A. Replace Hub E with a switched hub.

B. Move Server A to Hub C and Server B to Hub D.

C. Replace Hubs C and D with shared hubs.

D. Place Server A and Server B on a new switched hub connected to Hub E.

E. Place Server A to Hub D and Server B to Hub C.

4. Your company requires a connection to the Internet to send e-mail. You do not want to provide web access to your users, and you want to keep costs as low as possible. There are only 20 people in your company and you initially expect only light e-mail use. You also want to ensure that the connection is secure and won't expose your network. Which Internet connection method should you use? (Choose two, each answer presents a whole solution.)

    A. ADSL connection with Internet Connection Sharing (ICS)

    B. Leased-line access using Network Address Translation (NAT)

    C. Dial-up connection using Internet Security and Acceleration (ISA) Server

    D. Dial-up connection with Internet Connection Sharing (ICS)

5. Branch offices at your company are directly attached to your network through a series of leased lines and routers. There are a total of about 250 clients spread over the various offices. Different offices use a different Class C network address from the private 192.168.*x.x* range. You want to provide Internet access to your users but do not need to share any of your servers over the Internet. You also want to maintain a high level of security. What method should you use for connecting your users to the Internet? (Choose one.)

    A. Use manual routes within Routing and Remote Access Service (RRAS).

    B. Use Internet Connection Sharing (ICS) and the Internet Connection Firewall (ICF).

    C. Use Network Address Translation (NAT).

    D. Use Internet Security and Acceleration (ISA) Server.

6. You are about to install a permanent connection to the Internet and you want to install a web server to share your company's website. Your Internet Service Provider has provided you with a number of fixed IP addresses, and you connect to the Internet through a dedicated router connected to a leased line. You need to set this up while ensuring the maximum security for your internal network and the web server to prevent malicious attacks. In particular, you want to protect your internal network from malicious attacks that may come from your web server. What solution should you use to provide the best security? (Choose one.)

    A. Use Internet Connection Sharing (ICS) and the Internet Connection Firewall (ICF) to provide Internet connectivity, with the web server connected to your internal network.

    B. Use Network Address Translation (NAT) to connect to the Internet and configure a port redirection from port 80 to your web server, which is connected to your internal network.

    C. Use Internet Security and Acceleration (ISA) Server to connect to the Internet and then use another ISA Server to create a DMZ and place the web server within the DMZ.

    D. Use NAT to connect to the Internet, placing your web server on the same network as your Internet router.

7. One of your computers cannot resolve names either for sites on the Internet or the machines within your network. You are using DHCP to allocate addresses and DNS server information to all of your 200 computers. Other computers within the network are unaffected. You run ipconfig and it tells you that the IP address allocated to this machine is 169.254.0.23. What should you try first to resolve the problem? (Choose one.)

    A. Configure a static IP address for this machine within the DHCP scope.

    B. Configure a manual DNS server.

    C. Renew the DHCP lease with ipconfig /renew.

    D. Flush the DNS cache with ipconfig /flushdns.

8. Your network is laid out like the network shown in the following illustration. ClientA is unable to connect to the Internet but can communicate with the other servers and clients on the network. What should you change to enable Internet access on this machine? (Choose one.)

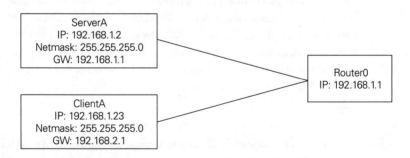

    A. Change the default gateway address of the client.

    B. Change the subnet mask on the client.

    C. Change the IP address of the client.

    D. Change the IP address of the default gateway.

    E. Change the subnet mask of the default gateway.

REVIEW ANSWERS

1. **B**   Replacing the shared hub with a switched hub will improve performance because it will stop general traffic and affect the utilization right across the network. C and D will not alleviate the situation, because the communication between the clients and servers in both cases will still have to go through one port. A is not a quick solution to the problem!

2. **B**   Without security in your access points, you must assume that each WAP is a potential security breach, so it must be placed outside of your network on the other side of a firewall. However, you shouldn't put them outside the DMZ as that would require you to open up the ports on the outer firewall to enable users to access your internal network.

3. **A B**   Changing to a switched network will improve the overall performance of the network. Moving the servers from the shared hub to the relevant hub for their users will reduce the utilization on the shared hub. Both solutions will ensure dedicated paths to the two servers from each client network.

4. **A D**   Dial-up and ADSL connections are relatively cheap. With ICS, which is built into Windows Server 2003, you can protect the network from outside attacks. A leased line is overkill, and ISA Server is not required.

5. **D**   Only ISA Server can handle routed networks with centralized Internet access.

6. **C**   The only way to protect a server from the outside and a network from the server is to use two separate firewalls.

7. **C**   The 169.254.0.23 address is an APIPA address, which means that the client wasn't able to connect to the DHCP server. This could be a transient problem, so trying to get the DHCP address again is the easiest way to try and fix the problem. Setting manual addresses or flushing the cache won't fix the problem if your other machines are using valid IP addresses.

8. **A**   If you can connect to local machines but not the Internet, the gateway address is the problem. Changing the configuration of the gateway will break all the other machines in the network.

Planning Routing and Remote Access

	NEWBIE	SOME EXPERIENCE	EXPERT
ETA	6+ hours	3+ hours	1 hour

We don't know about you, but if we get disconnected from my e-mail and Internet access for a while, we start to get the jitters. If we don't have a computer of any kind when we go away on holiday (and this rarely happens), then it takes us a few days to get over the initial shock of no longer having a keyboard. Usually by the end of the first week, we're fine. By the end of the second week we're ready to go live on a farm in the middle of nowhere and swear never to use technology ever again.

Now the truth is, we don't need to be connected all the time. All we need is a regular fix of access, and we're not the only ones who feel this way. It's inevitable that in a company there will be some people who are permanently out of the office, go on regular business trips, or work from home some days of the week. In these situations, they need some way of connecting back to the office.

It's not just e-mail they need access to. They might need to copy a file from one of the shared drives or access the corporate database system, or perhaps they need to access the Internet through your proxy and security system to protect them and their machines from viewing sites and downloading files outsiders shouldn't have access to.

There's more to remote access than simply plugging a modem and letting people dial in. Thinking about those lucky people who work from home for a second, what if they have a DSL connection? They're not going to want to dial in using a 56Kbps modem when they have a 512Kbps or faster DSL connection.

And how about your remote offices? What if your office in Thame and your office in Edinburgh want to be able to share files and information or access that corporate database again? You don't want to force users within the organization to dial up individually to access the information. Quite aside from the cost, imagine the administration overhead, not to mention the potential security problems of having dozens, even hundreds of modems attached to all your clients. If they are both connected to the Internet, you could use that, but what about the security of such a connection? You don't want all and sundry to snoop on your network packets and discover the company secrets—including passwords and banking information—and I'm sure Ethel doesn't want Bill to know what happened at Fred's house on Friday night either.

Whatever method you choose, it's going to take some planning to get your remote access right, and that's what this chapter is all about. When planning for remote access, your top three priorities should be security, security, and security. The reason we repeated ourselves? The moment you open your networks to the outside world, especially over a public service like the Internet, security becomes a problem, and the less you do to secure your systems, the more likely there will be a problem.

In this chapter, we're going to look at how to plan your Routing and Remote Access Services with not only accessibility and practicality in mind, but also with that all-important security touch. We'll start by taking a close look at routing within a typical network environment and how we can integrate Windows Server 2003 into an existing routing environment. We'll then move on to planning for remote access for your users so that they can dial into your network. For branch offices connected to your main network over the Internet, you need some way of securely connecting the machines. We'll look at the primary solutions, VPNs and IPSec networks. Finally, we'll cover the methods available for troubleshooting your routing connections.

 **Plan a Routing Strategy**

Routing is the action of forwarding packets between networks. In order to plan a routing strategy, you need to know what routing is, the significance of the process, and how it works. Once you know that, you can turn your attention to converting some networks to use a routed solution and ways you can use routing to help alleviate network problems.

Exam Tip

In the exam, you'll be expected to demonstrate your knowledge and understanding of routing, particularly how to plan your routing requirements to meet the needs of some sample networks and situations.

Routing Fundamentals

If you want to know how to get from one location to another, you use a map or a piece of software like MapQuest, AutoRoute, or Route 66 to determine the best path to take. Network routing essentially works in the same way, but unlike AutoRoute or your own brain, you don't need to determine the route for an individual packet as you would a route for a single car journey. Instead you need to provide recommended routes along which many packets should travel, as if you were providing directions to a massive party for all the guests.

Okay, I guess that makes it a bit more like SimCity, but that's still not a bad analogy. Different cities have to be connected together, but in general a single city has a maximum size, after which the sheer number of people, vehicles, and housing makes the city unpleasant to live in. We connect cities together using motorways and interstates—big roads designed to take lots of cars, but which are designed only to carry the intercity traffic, leaving the local roads to carry the local traffic.

The same is true of networks. As networks grow and the number of machines they support increase, it becomes impossible, even with faster and faster networking hardware, to continue putting all machines into one big physical network. Instead, you split the networks into different networks, or subnets. For example, in a graphic design company you might have two networks, one for the graphics side and one for the administrative.

However, the two networks still need to talk to each other and still need to communicate with central resources like the e-mail server and proxy server for connecting to the Internet. Using a router (our equivalent of an interstate ramp), you can connect the two networks—cities—without the local traffic affecting the communication. That makes the local traffic affect only local machines while still allowing you to communicate between the two networks.

The actual connection between the two networks—the interstate—can be of any type, including standard LAN solutions or dial-up (Public Service Telephone Network [PSTN] and Integrated Services Digital Network [ISDN]), digital subscriber line (DSL), frame relay, and other services.

The router is a switch (a *packet switch* is another term for a router) that processes packets and switches between different network interfaces. When deciding where to switch, the router looks at each network packet, otherwise known as a *datagram*. Each datagram identifies the source of the packet and the destination, and the router uses its *routing table* to identify where to send the packet next and over which interface and connection type. A router doesn't, however, choose a destination along the entire route. A router knows only about its local routes, that is, those interfaces built into the router and the network subnets configured on them. Once the router has forwarded the packet, that's it—the router does not change the datagram contents or make any further decisions or provide any further input.

Local Lingo

Packets   Usually when we say a packet, we mean a TCP/IP packet. TCP/IP consists of a source IP address, a destination IP address, and the data itself.

Routers also make decisions about which route is best through the use of a *metric*, which applies a cost to a given route so that it can make decisions about which route is the best. The lower the metric, the cheaper the cost (and typically, the higher the transfer rate), so the higher the priority when the router makes a decision. Going back to the city analogy, an interstate has its lowest metric when it provides the fastest, most efficient connection between cities. Standard highways would have a higher cost, as they provide a less efficient connection, albeit still a valid one.

Translating this to networks, a router might be configured to use a high-speed frame relay connection with a metric of one, but it may also have a backup ISDN connection available configured with a metric of 20. Because of the metrics, the high-speed connection will be used in preference to the ISDN, because the ISDN is more expensive. When the frame relay fails, the ISDN automatically kicks in.

When networks are connected in this way, they are known as internetworks, probably the best known of which is that small, insignificant entity you never hear about called the Internet. Incidentally, the larger the network, the larger the number of interconnections and therefore the more routes a network packet has to travel over. For example, connecting the U.K. to a machine in the U.S. could take 10, 15, or even 30 *hops*, and each hop is one connection between two routers. Metrics are used all the way to make decisions about how to route the packets. It's quite possible to follow different routes at different times as the various connections come and go.

On transatlantic connections, the lowest metrics apply to the fiber optics that go under the ocean, and the most expensive (and slowest) apply to satellite communications. Going to such low-speed backups is unusual but not unheard of, as they had to when, in November 2000, a dredger mistakenly snapped just such a cable between Perth and Singapore.

Travel Assistance
See The Southern Warbirds Chronicle (www.southernwarbirds.com/ news/november2000.html) for a good description of what happened and the effects.

At its core, routing forwards packets and makes decisions about the forwarding process so that packets can be sent to the right destination. Routers route packets between networks. They can be dedicated devices such as those from Cisco or 3Com, or you can support routing services on a variety of machines, providing they have more than one network adapter (including dial-up devices) using special routing software. Any machine, including those running Windows Server 2003, Windows 2000, or Windows NT, can offer a full routing service. Windows 98, Windows 2000 Professional, and Windows XP all provide basic routing functionality when using the Internet Connection Sharing (ICS) system. In addition, most other platforms, including Unix, Mac OS, and Mac OS X, can provide routing services.

Travel Advisory

It's important not to confuse a router and a bridge. Whereas a router makes decisions about specific protocols and packets on a network and where to distribute them, a bridge is an echo device—packets it receives on one network are anonymously copied to the other. Bridges are useful if you want to join two networks together that use multiple networking protocols, for example TCP/IP, IPX/SPX, and AppleTalk, or when you want to connect to different networking systems, say Ethernet and Token Ring, together.

Routing and the Routing Tables

The routing table is an internal device built into any router that maps destination network addresses with the IP address of the next router in the chain. From a client perspective, each client has its own IP address and subnet mask. It uses a combination of these to determine whether the machine it wants to connect to is on the local subnet. If it isn't, then it sends the packet to the default gateway.

Exam Tip

You'll need to know the significance and effects of IP addressing and subnet masks to be able to make decisions and choices on routing strategy.

The default gateway is always some kind of router, and it examines its routing table to find out where to send the packet next. You can see this in action in Figure 5.1.

Now let's assume that Client wants to communicate with Server. It can't do it directly because they are on different subnets. So Client sends its packet to Router A. Router A looks at the packet, spots the destination IP address, and looks up the network in its routing table and identifies that the quickest (lowest metric) route to the destination IP is by sending the packet directly to Router C

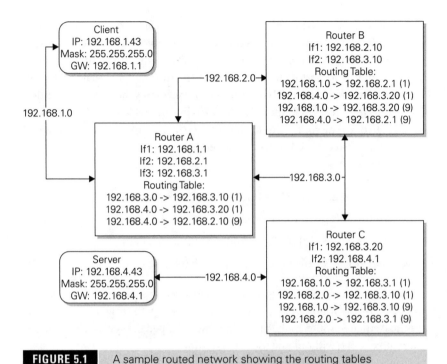

FIGURE 5.1 A sample routed network showing the routing tables

on IP address 192.168.3.20. Router C then forwards the packet to Server. To summarize, you get a route like this:

1. Client (192.168.1.43) → Router A (192.168.1.1)
2. Router A (192.168.3.1) → Router C (192.168.3.20)
3. Router C (192.168.4.1) → Server (192.168.4.43)

You can see the significance of the metric here—at Router A it chose the most efficient route, directly to Router C, because the link was working. If the link between Router A and Router C is severed, Client needs to find an alternative. Let's try it.

Exam Tip

Questions and scenarios like this are common in the exams, so make sure you can identify subnets and default routes, and follow sample routing tables to reach one destination from another.

Client wants to talk to Server but can't communicate directly, so it sends the packet to Router A. Router A looks up its routing and chooses to communicate directly with Router C because that's the cheapest route. But wait—the link is down. Router A looks for the next entry in the routing table that reaches the 192.168.4.0 network. Router B is more expensive, but it's the next best solution. It forwards the packet to Router B, which then looks at its table for the best route to the network. The route with the lowest metric will talk directly to Router C. The packet is sent on and Router C then sends it on to Server. To summarize, we get this route:

1. Client (192.168.1.43) → Router A (192.168.1.1)
2. Router A (192.168.2.1) → Router B (192.168.2.10)
3. Router B (192.168.3.10) → Router C (192.168.3.20)
4. Router C (192.168.4.1) → Server (192.168.4.43)

The significance of routing and the metric value should be apparent: the metric helps the routing system determine the best path by giving hints about the most efficient route. In the preceding case, it helped the system determine an alternative route, without any user intervention.

The same basic principles are used in routing to determine routes when things are working correctly as well as when something goes wrong. If a router determines that a route is too busy (that is, oversaturated) or is down (due to a failure), the metric system also comes into play because the router depends on it to automatically suggest an alternative route.

Updating Routing Tables

There are two different ways of keeping your routing tables up to date: manually and automatically. The manual method requires that you enter and update the tables by typing in the addresses and working out the best routes and metrics on your own. Although such highly interactive routed services are not uncommon (they are sometimes used in ISPs and large private networks where the metric really does relate to cost and there are rules that have to be micromanaged), they are obviously very high maintenance.

Manual routes also don't scale well. It would be an impossible task to manually update the tens or hundreds of routers used even in a relatively small ISP. In theory it works fine, until you have to change a route, at which point you find that it takes two or three days to go through and modify each router. In a highly competitive market, especially if the reconfiguration is due to a major connectivity failure, that two or three days can be the difference between being a market leader and needing to file for Chapter 11 (bankruptcy).

Small networks, say with only one or two routers or subnets, can handle manual routing. For anything larger or more complex, you need a more efficient method—that's where dynamic routing fits in.

Most companies will use some form of dynamic routing. These take the complications of the static routing system away by allowing the routers to both determine their own routes and to distribute their own routing capabilities over the networks to other devices; for example, if network 192.168.1.0 from Figure 5.1 was reallocated and became 192.168.45.0.

To update the configuration manually, you'd have to update Routers A, B, and C before you could get the network back and available to all of the subnets. Using dynamic routing, you'd update the IP address for Router A's interface to the network, and it would then broadcast the changes on the other two interfaces. Router B and C would pick this up and modify their own tables—the whole process could take less than a minute to propagate through the network.

There are two primary dynamic routing solutions, Routing Information Protocol (RIP) and Open Shortest Path First (OSPF). We'll discuss these in detail later in this chapter. For now, it's important just to know that these options exist.

When to Use Routing

Routing is not just a case of forwarding packets around for the sake of connecting up to the Internet, although that's probably its currently most popular and prevalent use. There are also some specific areas across all types of networking situation where a router can either be useful or essential.

The primary uses of a router are

- To isolate a network to localize network traffic (think back to the city analogy) or for security reasons.
- To provide connectivity between private and public networks, for example between your LAN and the Internet. This is also called border routing—that is, providing connectivity between the border of your network and some other public or private network.

Windows Server 2003 is capable of handling these situations, and we'll be discussing each of them. We'll also look at some other solutions and situations that Windows Server 2003 can handle.

Between Different Network Technologies

If you use a mixture of networking technologies in your network, you will need a router to route between the two networks. You may be thinking, "But I use Ethernet," but routers apply wherever there is a change of medium, including

- Dial-up (ISDN or PSTN)
- WAN routes (including over standard leased lines, frame relay, T1, T3, and others)
- ATM
- Frame relay
- Ethernet
- Token Ring
- Fiber Distributed Data Interface (FDDI)
- Serial (technically the way Serial Line Interface Protocol [SLIP] and Point to Point Protocol [PPP] work with dial-up connectivity)
- Parallel (not popular, but can be used with desktop operating systems to share Internet connections)
- USB
- FireWire (Some companies already use IP services over FireWire, which is four or eight times faster than 100Mbps Ethernet and cheaper to implement than Gigabit Ethernet.)

Routers provide more functionality in these situations than a bridge because a router can route packets for specific protocols and make decisions about where the packets should go, rather than just blindly duplicating packets on the two networks.

Within a LAN

You can use routers within a LAN environment when you need to localize individual network usage while still providing centralized services and access. For example, you can use routing to keep network traffic localized to different departments. This cuts down on the effects of heavy-use environments such as design and digital video from lower use environments like sales and administration. Using a router, you can connect the departments together so that departmental servers can still share directory information. You can see a sample of how this works in Figure 5.2.

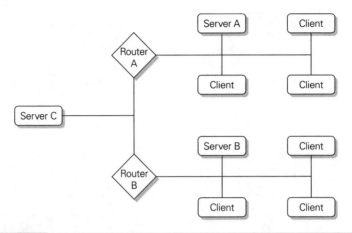

FIGURE 5.2   Routing between LAN segments

The same basic system of networking can also be used for security reasons. It's unlikely that you'll want the accounting department to be left wide open on the same network as the rest of your organization because it presents a potential security risk. Using the same diagram, if the two routers were configured suitably, there's no way the two networks could talk to each other while still talking to Server C.

Within a WAN

The WAN is probably the most obvious use of a router. You should already be familiar with the use of a router to provide connectivity to the Internet. These same principles apply when routing between two offices using some form of WAN connection. You can see a sample of this in Figure 5.3.

In a multioffice configuration, you can use routers with appropriate routes and metrics to provide connectivity between all offices, even if each office is not directly connected to the other, as shown in Figure 5.4.

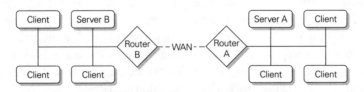

FIGURE 5.3   Using routers to connect networks over a WAN

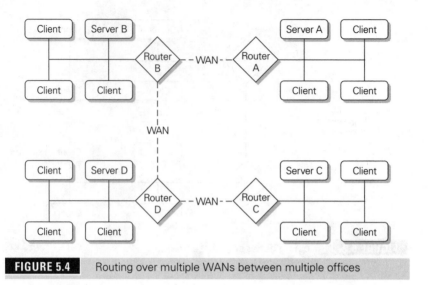

FIGURE 5.4   Routing over multiple WANs between multiple offices

You can also use routers to create private networks over public connections such as the Internet using Virtual Private Network (VPN) technology. This works just like standard routing, forwarding a packet to a remote destination, but you just do it over a public network. For security reasons, however, the router encapsulates the original packets in encrypted format for forwarding—the remote end then decrypts and extracts the original packet and forwards it on the internal network.

Identify Routing Protocols to Use in a Specified Environment

Updating lots of manual routes is a thankless and frankly boring task, so dynamic routing is obviously the way to go. Choosing which routing protocol is the right one depends entirely on the size of your network and the other devices within the network that need to accept and provide routing information.

As we mentioned earlier in the chapter, there are two routing protocols, RIP and OSPF, and both have their advantages and disadvantages and the ideal or proposed solutions. Both provide more than a way of simply propagating routing tables. The purpose of dynamic routing is also to allow individual routers to make decisions about where to send a packet according to both the metric for the connection and the speed of the connection available.

> ### Travel Advisory
>
> It is possible to support multiple protocols, but you must set a priority for each protocol. You can configure individual interfaces to support specific protocols, so you can have a router that maps between a mixed platform network and a Windows-only network using RIP and OSPF accordingly.

Understanding RIP

The Routing Information Protocol (RIP) is relatively simple in its operation. Essentially, each router broadcasts its routing table to other routers connected to its interface using the UDP protocol. Other routers examine the table and merge the information with their own tables in order to build up the various routes. You can change the routing table in one router, and its updated routes will get propagated to the others in the network. The information exchanged includes the metric information, so routers can take the metric into account as they update their own tables.

> ### Travel Assistance
>
> You can read more about RIP in RFC1058.

Version 2 of RIP improved on the original specification by adding a few extra facilities, including

- **Simple authentication system** This prevents routers from updating their own tables based on bogus information from another router. Without authentication, it's possible for a router to effectively update all of the routers connected to the network, whether or not the routing information is valid. In the early Internet years, use of RIP v1 caused a number of problems, including invalid tables from routers in other ISPs updating competitors' routing records.
- **Route tag** This enables the router to identify routes as coming either from internal or external sources. This helps the routing protocol to determine whether the route was manually entered into the router tables or learned from other routers, and it can help it work out the validity or significance of the routes and how they should be used.
- **Subnet mask** This is vital for sharing subnet routing information, particularly where the subnet is less than a Class C network.

Windows Server 2003 supports RIP v1 and v2 and can exchange routing information using either format.

Advantages of RIP   The major advantage of RIP is its simplicity:

- It's easy to use and update the information, and it's automatic and transparent enough that you shouldn't ever need to be concerned with its operation.
- It's compatible with most network environments, including those using Unix-based routers and older networking equipment.

Disadvantages of RIP   RIP's strength is also its weakness: the simplicity of RIP is its limiting factor. It was designed and introduced years before large-scale routing installations such as the Internet existed and therefore it has distinct limitations:

- Because of the distribution mechanism, it can take some time for the routing tables to propagate. Also, because of the way it propagates from router to router through the various network interfaces, it's possible for some routers to be arbitrarily excluded from the network or for packets to be bounced between routers until all the necessary routes have been updated.
- In the default configuration, routing information is broadcast every 30 seconds by each router. In large routing environments, the amount of information distributed becomes excessive and can lead to degradation of the very links the routers are designed to manage. Increasing the time between updates makes the overall update time even longer. Striking a happy medium between over saturation of the information and reliable and effective updates is difficult.
- RIP is incapable of distinguishing between efficiency and speed. It allows you to provide metrics according to the relative cost of the connection, but RIP itself does not measure the quality of a connection. Instead, it bases its decisions on whether the network is up or not—if a 100Mbit link is operating at only 50 percent efficiency, RIP still treats this as a working connection.
- Can handle metrics only up to a value of 15, making it difficult to implement large scale routing plans.

That said, RIP fits in perfectly with small-scale networks involving fewer than 10 routers with relatively simple routing needs. As the number of routers and the routes that need to be supported increases, however, RIP becomes less practical.

Understanding OSPF

Open Shortest Path First (OSPF) was designed to address many of the shortcomings of the RIP v1 specification. Unlike RIP, which exchanges routing tables consisting of network addresses and metrics, OSPF exchanges information about the state of its links. As the information is broadcast, each router that receives the update then updates its own routing configuration. This information is held in a topology database, which is identical on each router in the group and defines the layout and connectivity of the network. Using the topology and state information, each router can determine its own fastest route from itself to a destination.

If you think back to the road and city analogy I used earlier in this chapter, you can get a better idea of how it works. Imagine you have a road network like the one shown in Figure 5.5.

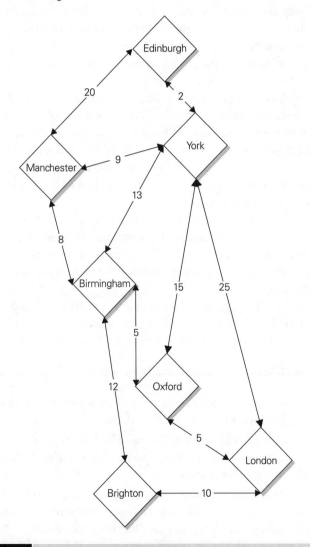

| FIGURE 5.5 | A multirouter road network |

The diagram is essentially the topology that each router holds in its configuration. Using the topology and the metrics information, each router can work out the best route from one point to another, in just the same way those route-finding applications calculate the fastest or shortest route from one city to another.

Now imagine that the main route between London and Oxford dies. In AutoRoute, you can tell it to avoid a given route and provide an alternative solution, and this is essentially what OSPF does—when the link fails, it broadcasts the link failure to the other routers. They can then eliminate the route from their topology map and recalculate the most efficient alternative for a given packet destination. When using RIP, all that would happen would be that the Birmingham router would have to choose an alternative route—without careful consideration, that could lead to packets being bounced between two routers as they argue over the best destination.

For example, when routing packets from Manchester to London, the most efficient route is Manchester, York, Oxford, London—a total of 29 miles. With the Oxford router out of action as a valid route because the London link is severed, RIP might forward the packet to Birmingham (the shortest), which would probably bounce it back (because it's not a valid route, and also because the Oxford part of the connection is down), or if we're lucky send it to Brighton, which would then send it on to London.

With OSPF, the next most efficient route calculated would be Manchester, Birmingham, Brighton, London. Rather than forcing Oxford to cope directly with the failure, you can spread the load to other routers in the network and calculate more efficient routes from any point in the network that avoid the link with the problem.

The actual exchange of information and topologies is handled automatically—you configure each router by telling it its adjacent routers, and they work together to build the topology that is then used to calculate routes.

Advantages of OSPF   The main advantages of OSPF are

- It's much better suited to larger network environments because it makes holistic, rather than localized decisions.
- The quantity of information exchanged is much lower, and the information is relevant only to a specific link, reducing the background chatter between the routers.
- It can make decisions about the quality as well as the availability of the link, so it routes only packets that it knows will be transmitted, even if the overall quality and speed of the link have degraded.

- It can assign a metric to a type of service as well as the interface. For example, secure Internet traffic for a bank can be given higher priority than standard public Internet traffic. This allows OSPF routers to shunt Internet traffic on to slower, lower capacity links while maintaining the quality of the bank's VPN.

- Once installed, it's far more autonomous and able to cope with changes to the network configuration.

Disadvantages of OSPF   Here it's the complexity of the system that causes the problems. In OSPF the main disadvantage is that it's complex to set up and manage. If you can get over that problem, the benefits far outweigh the problems.

Sample Routing Environments

To make a reasonable decision about a routing protocol (beyond the obvious advantages and disadvantages we've already discussed), you need to look at some sample environments and suggest the most appropriate protocol to configure on your Windows Server 2003 system.

> ## Exam Tip
>
> In the exam you may be asked to choose a protocol based on a scenario description. Be familiar with each and the situations to which they are best suited.

- **Small office/home office (SOHO)**   It's unlikely that you would have more than one router in the network anyway. If a Windows-based router is in use, it's probably running Routing and Remote Access or Internet Connection Sharing to share the connection. A routing protocol is not required.

- **Small office**   Use either a static route or RIP if more than one router is in the network.

- **Medium office**   Routers will probably be employed to separate networking traffic between departments. RIP is the easiest solution for up to 10 routers; it also retains compatibility with other platforms.

- **Large/corporate network**   With a higher number of routers, especially those offering WAN links to branch offices and the Internet and for control within a LAN situation, OSPF is the ideal solution. Where required, interfaces can be configured with RIP for compatibility.

- **Heterogeneous network** RIP is the most supported routing protocol so it's the most likely solution for routing in this situation.

- **Branch office network** As with a small office, a static route is the most likely solution here, which would be designed to route packets directly to the corporate network.

- **Branch office using VPN** For the same reasons, no routing protocol should be required.

Plan Routing for IP Multicast Traffic

There's nothing like sitting down to a good movie. One of our favorite elements of the Internet is the ability to download previews, trailers, and short movies over it. The downloading takes a long time, but it's a good example of a point-to-point technology. Communication of this form is handled by Unicast routing. Up to now that is what we've been discussing: routing technology designed to route packets with a single destination IP address.

Watching live streams of information, however, is a multipoint technology. When you open a live stream, you are not opening a single connection to streaming server, you are capturing multicast packets traveling over the Internet. If you had a single connection, it would very quickly saturate the network with information as more and more people tried to watch the stream at the same time. For example, have 1,000 people open a 56Kbps stream at once and you'll have 56Mbit headache on your hands.

Instead, streaming technology uses multicast routing, which broadcasts single packets on a multicast address, and players like Windows Media Player capture the multicast packets and then display the information. The same 56Kbps stream can now be watched by many hundreds or even thousands of people without requiring any additional bandwidth.

Windows Server 2003 incorporates multicast traffic-handling abilities and can forward and route multicast traffic. In general, the same basic principles apply when planning for IP multicast traffic as planning for standard IP traffic: you must determine where the traffic is coming from and where it is going to.

Multicast Forwarding

Multicast forwarding is handled by the Internet Group Management Protocol (IGMP), which is an option with the Routing and Remote Access Service (RRAS) component of Windows Server 2003.

When working in IGMP router mode, RRAS sets the network adaptor into multicast-promiscuous mode so that packets can be accepted and processed by RRAS. To use, you must supply a multicast forwarding table, which defines which multicast traffic should be forwarded to which destination interface.

> ### Local Lingo
>
> **Promiscuous mode**   Normally network adaptors accept only traffic sent to them. Promiscuous mode sets the network adaptor to accept traffic not directly sent to the adaptor. In multicast-promiscuous mode, the network adaptor is set to accept multicast packets from the network.

Multicast Routing

As a rule, Windows Server 2003 doesn't support multicast routing, but you can use the IGMP routing protocol with IGMP router mode and IGMP proxy mode to forward packets between a source and a destination (as outlined in the preceding "Multicast Forwarding" section).

In a single-router environment, where one router connects all computers to a multicast source, you can use RRAS to forward the IGMP packets. You do this by enabling IGMP routing on all the interfaces.

If you are connecting to the Internet and are able to connect to the multicast backbone on the Internet, you must use IGMP in proxy mode to accept multicast packets from the Internet; the packets are then routed/forwarded to the rest of the internal network.

| Objective 5.02 | # Security for Remote Access Users |

I can't stress this particular point too highly: remote access is a weak point in your network in terms of security. Take a look at the diagram in Figure 5.6. What's wrong?

Well, there's a firewall in the system to protect you from attacks from the Internet, but the remote access server is on the "safe" side of the firewall. What happens if someone successfully manages to dial into your server and access your corporate network? That firewall has become useless as a method of protecting your network because it's effectively been blown right open by your remote access approach.

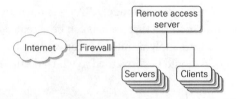

FIGURE 5.6   Your network has a fatal error

The immediate inclination here is to place the Remote Access Service (RAS) device outside the firewall, but this can create more problems than it solves. For a start, if you want the user to have anything more than restricted access to the inside of your network, you need to start opening up your firewall to alternative protocols. Even if you restrict connections only to those originating from the RAS device, the original threat remains—once the user has connected, they're in.

To secure your network, you therefore need to think about who and why anyone needs to access your network resources remotely. If there is a valid reason for a user requiring remote access, you need to look deeper at the RAS capabilities in Windows Server 2003.

Simple as it may seem, the most fundamental part of the security process is to restrict the users who can connect to your network. You can do this by enabling or disabling dial-in capability in the user's properties within the Security and Accounts Manager or Active Directory.

If you give a user access, you need to use the facilities of the remote access service, which enable you to control when and how users can log in, and also to enable secure authentication methods and secure communications once the remote access service has been established.

Exam Tip

You may be asked to determine how secure a remote access policy is, or how you can restrict access to improve the security of your network. Generally it's going to be a combination of the remote access policy and the security/authentication settings. For example, you might need to secure access only at certain times or to specific classes or groups of users.

Plan Remote Access Policies

Remote access policies provide an additional layer of security beyond the standard authentication and authorization system to give you more control over who connects to your network and what they can do once they have connected. Settings include restricting access to certain times and allowing calls only from certain phone numbers, as well as specific settings applying to the connection such as security settings, authentication protocols, and IP address settings.

The policies are split into three sections:

- **Conditions** Control individual client access times and sources.
- **Permissions** A toggle between granting and denying access, based on the conditions.
- **Profile** Sets connection-level preferences, including security and authentication, for the connection.

Remote Access Conditions

When a user connects, they are granted access only if their profile within Active Directory allows them remote access and only if they are accepted by the different policies within the RRAS system. Policies are numbered and processed in a top-down fashion. Each condition within a policy needs to be matched only once, however, even though a policy can contain multiple conditions. You can see an example of the main policy window in Figure 5.7.

Exam Tip

Note that policies are only processed if the user has been granted permission to dial in in the first place. If the user's dial-in permission is set to Deny Access, the user is disconnected before the various policies are processed.

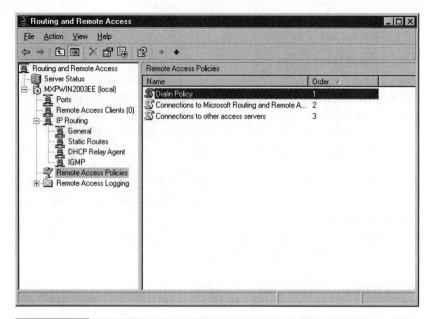

FIGURE 5.7   Setting remote access policies

The various conditions available for configuration are shown in Table 5.1.

TABLE 5.1   Conditions for a Remote Access Policy

Condition	Description
Authentication-Type	The authentication scheme used to verify the user
Called-Station-ID	The phone number dialed by the user
Calling-Station-ID	The phone number from where the call originated
Client-Friendly-Name	The friendly name for the RADIUS client (Internet Authentication Service [IAS] only)
Client-IP-Address	The IP address of the RADIUS client (IAS only).
Client-Vendor	The manufacturer of the RADIUS proxy or Network Access Server's (NAS) manufacturer (IAS only)
Day-and-Time-Restriction	The time periods and days during which a user is allowed to connect

TABLE 5.1   Conditions for a Remote Access Policy *(continued)*

Condition	Description
Framed-Protocol	The communication protocol used by the client
NAS-Identifier	The string that identifies the NAS that originated the request (IAS only)
NAS-IP-Address	The IP address of the NAS where the request originated (IAS only)
NAS-Port-Type	The type of physical port used by the NAS originating the request (IAS only)
Service-Type	The type of service requested by the user
Tunnel-Type	The tunneling protocols used
Windows-Groups	The groups to which a user belongs

Once you've set the conditions, you must specify whether this grants access, which is the role of the remote access permissions. We'll cover how to do that next.

Remote Access Permissions

When remote access processes the individual conditions, you can then apply a grant or deny access action according to whether the permissions were matched. For example, you can create a policy that has a condition to restrict access to a period between 9 A.M. and 6 P.M. each day. If you then set the permission to grant access during this period if the condition is matched, users will only be able to connect during this time.

If you set the condition so that access is denied if the condition is matched, access will be restricted to after 6 P.M. but before 9 A.M. each day.

Remote Access Profile

The last stage of the puzzle is the remote access profile. This sets preferences and settings for the connection according to whether the condition was matched. Because profiles are attached to policies, you can use them to set specific options depending on how a user connects. For example, you can create a profile that enables encrypted communication if a user has connected using their mobile phone (as identified by the policy) and another profile that uses nonsecure communication when the user connects from their ISDN line.

Profile settings are configured through the window shown in Figure 5.8. The window is split into six tabs, Dial-in Constraints, IP, Multilink, Authentication, Encryption, and Advanced. We'll cover authentication and encryption in just a moment; the others we'll cover now.

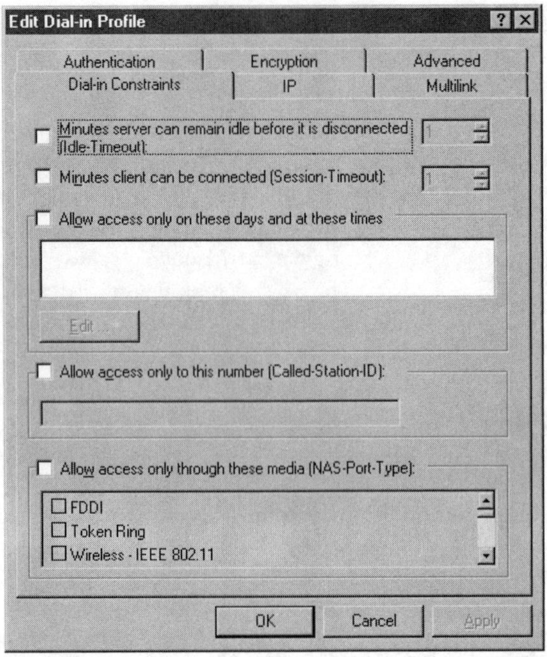

FIGURE 5.8   Remote access profile settings

Dial-in Constraints   The dial-in constraints control the dial-in properties of the connection, including timeouts and media types. The full list includes

- **Idle Disconnect Time**   Sets the amount of time after which a connection will be disconnected if it remains idle
- **Session Timeout**   The maximum period that a user can be connected
- **Day/Time Restrictions**   Establishes a schedule when access is permitted
- **Dial-in Number**   Forces the user to dial in from a specific number (typically used in demand-dial network to network communications, rather than remote user connections)
- **Media Type**   Limits the connectivity to specific media types, for example, ISDN and PSTN

IP   The IP tab configures IP address assignment policy for the connection. You have four choices:

- Server must supply an IP address.
- Client may request an IP address.
- Server settings define policy (that is, if the server uses DHCP, then DHCP is used to assign the client an address).
- Use a defined static IP address.

You can also use this page to set input and output filters on IP traffic. For example, you can restrict a dial-in connection to port 25 so that it can be used only to exchange e-mail.

Multilink   The Multilink tab enables you to bond more than one connection together to achieve higher connection rates. This is most useful on links that support the use of additional communication channels; ISDN is a good example. Multilink protocol supports a defined number of simultaneous links and, with the addition of Bandwidth Allocation Protocol (BAP), enables you to dynamically increase and decrease the number of simultaneous links according to the transfer load on the connection.

With the multilink settings, you can default to the global settings, restrict to just a single connection, or support multilink up to a specified number of ports. With BAP, you must also specify the utilization and time period when a port will be dropped. With the default settings, for example, a utilization of less than 50 percent for two minutes will trigger the reduction of one port for the connection.

Note that multilink/BAP must be enabled on both the server and the client for it to work, and BAP settings are ignored unless the multilink settings allow multiport access.

Advanced   The Advanced tab enables you to set a number of protocol-, device-, and manufacturer-specific settings. There are too many to list here, but you should review them just so that you're familiar with what's available to you.

Exam Tip

It's unlikely you'll be asked to cover any of the settings in this section. The settings are manufacturer device specific, rather than generic Microsoft settings—but you should know that such settings exist.

Analyze Protocol Security Requirements

For added security during your remote access connection, you can encrypt the link between the server and the client. This will protect you from packet snoopers checking out your network and communication packets for passwords and other sensitive information. A number of different protocols exist for this encryption, but you need to be able to identify which solution will suit your requirements. There are four encryption levels:

- **No Encryption**   Doesn't require any form of encryption during communication; you should use this for connections from clients that do not support link encryption.
- **Basic Encryption**   The least secure after No Encryption, this requires the client to support 40-bit Microsoft Point-to-Point (MPPE) encryption or IPSec 56-bit DES encryption.
- **Strong Encryption**   Enables 56bit MPPE or IPSec 56-bit DES encryption.
- **Strongest Encryption**   Enables IPSec Triple DES or MPPE 128-bit encryption.

If you select all settings, the server will attempt to negotiate a connection at the highest level selected and proceed further down until a valid encryption combination is supported by both ends. If none of the available options work, the connection is dropped. If you select only one option, if the client fails to negotiate the connection, the connection is dropped.

Plan Authentication Methods for Remote Access Clients

It's important not to confuse authentication and authorization and to know the difference between them. Authentication is the ability to identify a dial-in user as valid, much the same as a passport verifies your identity to the authorities when you travel. Authorization validates a user's credentials as being allowed to log in to a server, much the same as a boarding pass validates your ability to get on the plane.

Either one is not enough: you can't get through security without a valid boarding pass and passport, and much the same is true with the authentication systems built into Windows Server 2003. Here, the system is two stages:

- **Authentication**   This occurs at the remote access server when the user logs in. The purpose of authentication is to provide a basic mechanism for controlling access—that is, a simple login/password.
- **Authorization**   This occurs after authentication at a domain controller, and it verifies that the user who logged in is authorized.

There are two aspects to consider, the *authentication provider*—that is, the database or server that will validate an authentication request—and the *authentication method*—the protocol that exchanges information between the client and the server during the logon process.

Authentication Provider

When a user logs in remotely, you need to check that their credentials are valid. After all, just because a passenger is carrying a passport doesn't automatically mean they're allowed to travel—you need to verify that the passport they're carrying is theirs and that the photo that you just laughed at really does look like the person traveling.

The authentication provider is just like passport control, checking to make sure that the credentials supplied by the client are valid. Client computers don't have passports, so rather than relying on the client to essentially self-validate themselves, they need to check the information in a database.

There are two solutions available in Windows Server 2003:

- **Windows Authentication**   This validates the user against either the local user database or the Active Directory database.
- **Remote Authentication Dial-In User Service (RADIUS)**   This sends the request to a RADIUS server that can either be a Windows server running the Internet Authentication Service or another server or device running an alternative operating system.

Travel Advisory

RADIUS is commonly used to provide authentication within an ISP or other large dial-in service as it's a networkable service that is also cross-platform capable and supported by dedicated dial-in hardware.

Authentication Methods

Logging into a machine requires that the client supply a user name and password to the remote access server. Because the client is sharing login and password information, it's important to be able to secure or encrypt the request as it's transferred to prevent unscrupulous users from gaining access to your network. Unfortunately, not all clients and systems support the various methods.

Table 5.2 summarizes the various authentication methods and when and where they are most suitable.

TABLE 5.2	Authentication Protocols in Windows Server 2003
Method	**Description**
EAP	Extensible Authentication Protocol, a catch-all solution that supports a number of subauthentication types integrated into the EAP infrastructure. Clients must support the same subtype as the server is configured to use for the authentication to work.
EAP MD5 Challenge	Uses challenge/response format, encrypting the questions and responses with Message Digest 5 (MD5). Similar to CHAP.
EAP TLS	Used in certificate-based security environments, usually with the use of a separate smartcard that provides the correct key when a challenge code is supplied.
EAP RADIUS	Not strictly an authentication type, this is the act of passing valid authentication information from an EAP session to a RADIUS server.
MS-CHAP	The first version of Microsoft Challenge Handshake Authentication Protocol. Encrypts the user's password during transport, but the password can be captured and decoded using brute-force methods. Use with older Windows clients.
MS-CHAP v2	Version 2 of MS-CHAP improves on the original by using different keys for sending and receiving, making it technically much more secure than the other solutions. Use with newer Windows clients (Windows 2000, XP).
CHAP	A standard protocol that uses encryption but is compatible with non-Windows clients.
PAP	The Password Authentication Protocol is the least secure option because it does not encrypt or otherwise challenge the client during authentication. Can be used with all clients.
SPAP	The Shiva PAP is specific to Shiva (a remote access hardware manufacturer) devices. Like PAP, passwords are not secure.
Unauthenticated	Lets users connect without any challenge. This should only be used to provide registration services, where the initial connection is used to register the user and provide a real login/password combination.

Travel Advisory

EAP-TLS is only supported on a remote access server running Windows 2000 or Windows Server 2003, which is part of a mixed or native mode domain. It cannot be used on a stand-alone server.

Local Lingo

Challenge/response This is the term given to systems that ask a question and expect an answer beyond the standard user/password combination. Often used with smartcards or other technology where you enter a code and get a corresponding ID back—because the challenge code is random, and the response code is keyed to a specific card, challenge/response systems are typically very secure. Some challenge/response systems are automatic, with the server and client handling the process.

Implement Secure Access Between Private Networks

Objective 5.03

If you have more than one office, the communication between the two is important. Some offices can get by just by using e-mail over the Internet. For larger companies or situations where users need to exchange more than e-mail and the odd enclosure, however, you need to provide some form of connectivity between the two offices.

You can do this in two ways, you can use either a dedicated link such as a leased line or frame relay connection, or you can use the Internet. Direct connections are relatively secure because it's hard to intercept information being transferred over what is a private connection directly between two sites. In most cases, this type of connectivity can be supported through the dial-in and routing solutions already discussed in this chapter, and the security can be handled either by using encryption over the communication links or through the use of IPSec, which is discussed in the next section, "Create and Implement an IPSec Policy."

The problem with dial-up connections or even direct links is that they require more intense management and can become expensive. Linking 10 offices together requires at least 9 dedicated links, or more if you want to avoid too many long routes. Today, most sites are connected to the Internet, often relatively cheaply, so if you can communicate with each other over the Internet, why not use it to support connectivity between different locations?

The primary reason not to is one of security. The moment you start to distribute network packets from your company onto the public Internet, your packets are available for scrutiny. At the simplest level, this could involve a security breach in the form of clear-text passwords being exchanged between clients and servers. Further up, the security concerns are people snooping into company secrets and even intercepting e-mails and data as it crosses over the network.

The solution is to encapsulate and encrypt your site-to-site communication within a protocol that can then be distributed over the public Internet, such as a virtual private network (VPN). A VPN is virtual because it exists only in the realms of the two machines communicating with each other; it's private because it's been made secure through use of encryption technology; it's a network because it enables two or more networks to communicate with each other.

Windows Server 2003 supports two different tunneling protocols, Layer 2 Tunneling Protocol (L2TP) and Point-to-Point Tunneling Protocol (PPTP). Both solutions rely on the underlying Point-to-Point Protocol (PPP) to communicate with devices when communicating to the Internet. Both are secure because each end encrypts and encapsulates each packet—the contents of the packet can only be read by the destination when they have been decrypted.

PPTP works only over IP networks. It does not compress the encapsulated packet or provide any form of authentication to validate the source of the packet. It uses the MPPE encryption discussed earlier in this chapter.

L2TP can work over a number of networks natively, including IP, frame relay, ATM, and X.25. The TCP/IP headers can be compressed, and it uses IPSec for encryption, which not only offers more secure encryption but can also validate its source and destination. The only downsides to L2TP are that it will not work through a NAT Internet connection, and it is supported only by machines that support IPSec, including Windows 2000 and Windows Server 2003, and many dedicated devices, but excluding Windows NT and many low-end devices.

Exam Tip

L2TP is not supported by NAT connections unless you are using Windows Server 2003 at both ends. You cannot use L2TP between a Windows Server 2003 and any previous version of Windows if you are using an NAT solution for connectivity.

To set up a VPN connection, your server must have two network adapters, one connected to the internal network and the other connected to the Internet. Alternatively, you can use a separate hardware router in combination with an RRAS server, providing the router forwards packets directly to the RRAS server at each end. The server then routes packets between the two adapters, encapsulating them in the process. To set up your VPN service, do the following:

1. Configure the connection to the Internet.
2. Configure the connection to the intranet.
3. Configure the remote access server as a corporate intranet router.
4. Configure the VPN server.
5. Configure firewall packet filters.
6. Configure remote access policies.

Steps 1 and 2 should have been completed as part of your initial setup. Step 3 requires configuring the appropriate static or dynamic routes to direct packets designed for your remote VPN network through your VPN server and Internet connection.

Step 4 involves running the VPN Wizard, accessible through the Configure Your Server Wizard located in the Administrative Tools folder. Select the Routing and Remote Access role and click Next.

When you go through the Routing and Remote Access Setup Wizard, you will be asked to select what type of RRAS server you are creating (as shown in Figure 5.9). Select Virtual Private Network (VPN) access and NAT, click Next, and then click VPN and continue through the rest of the wizard. You will need to select the network interface connected to the Internet and specify whether you want to use DHCP or static addressing.

When you set up VPN, a number of VPN miniports are created for you automatically; there should be either 5 or 128 ports for each of L2TP and PPTP, depending on the settings you chose during the wizard.

To complete the setup, you must configure any appropriate firewall settings (Step 5) to allow VPN connections and tunneled packets through the firewall.

Finally, Step 6 requires you to set remote access policies that use the network interface for the Internet on your VPN server and set the various users and groups and other VPN and encryption settings as required through the rest of the profile. We covered these settings earlier.

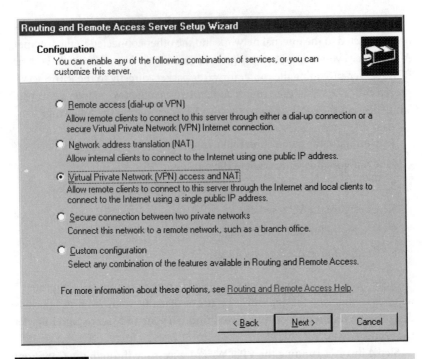

FIGURE 5.9 Creating a RRAS server

Create and Implement an IPSec Policy

IPSec policies can be used to further secure network connections between private networks and between public routed networks using a VPN connection. For more information on IPSec policies, including creating and applying them, see Chapter 6.

Tunnel mode within the IPSec standard allows for an IPSec tunnel to be created. Just like the tunnel used to route VPN traffic, an IPSec tunnel can be used to exchange traffic between two machines either on a private network, such as between two routing servers, or over a public network, such as the Internet. However, unlike VPN connections, which can be used to share network traffic between two sites, an IPSec tunnel secures only the two machines configured as the start and end points.

To create a local IPSec policy in tunnel mode between two servers, Server A with an IP address of 192.168.1.10 and Server B with an IP address of 192.168.1.100, follow these steps:

1. On Server A, click Start | Programs | Administrative Tools and select Local Security Policy.

2. Select IP Security Policies On Local Computer and then double-click Secure Server (Request Security) to open the properties.

3. Select the rule All IP Traffic and click the Edit button.

4. Select the Tunnel Settings tab and select The Tunnel Endpoint Is Specified By This IP Address, and enter the IP address **192.168.1.100**.

5. Repeat the preceding steps for Server B using an IP address of 192.168.1.10.

That's it! The two machines will now communicate with each other using encrypted communications.

Troubleshoot TCP/IP Routing

Even with the best planning and intentions, you can never be 100 percent sure that your system will work correctly, so it's important to be able to test the various options to ensure that the system works. In this section, we're going to have a look at some of the key command-line tools that you can use to monitor your server's routing and connectivity.

Checking a Machine's Accessibility

The easiest way to determine if a machine can be communicated to is to use the ping command. It pings a machine, which means it sends a packet to a remote machine using the ICMP protocol and waits for a response. To use it, just supply the name of a server you want to contact, or use its IP address:

```
C:\>ping polarbear

Pinging polarbear.mcslp.pri [192.168.1.126] with 32 bytes of data:

Reply from 192.168.1.126: bytes=32 time<1ms TTL=128
Reply from 192.168.1.126: bytes=32 time<1ms TTL=128
Reply from 192.168.1.126: bytes=32 time<1ms TTL=128
Reply from 192.168.1.126: bytes=32 time<1ms TTL=128

Ping statistics for 192.168.1.126:
    Packets: Sent = 4, Received = 4, Lost = 0 (0% loss),
Approximate round trip times in milli-seconds:
    Minimum = 0ms, Maximum = 0ms, Average = 0ms
```

Travel Advisory

"Ping" is an acronym, short for Packet InterNet Groper. Although many believe that this was an acronym that was expanded after the term was coined, its origination is the submariner term, where a ping is used by the sonar system to send and receive a response and find the time, and therefore the distance to a target. Luckily, its use in computing is not quite as dramatic as that in *The Hunt for Red October*!

The name will be resolved (or an error will be returned if it can't be resolved) through the normal channels, and the packet will be sent. The command provides three useful pieces of information: the accessibility of the machine, the time it takes for a packet to reach the machine and be responded to, and a rough guide to the quality of the link.

If the command returns anything other than the reply information, it's a good indication that there is some kind of problem, and the error message should help you identify the problem. For example:

- **Request timed out**   This means that the request could never be sent to the host, although the host name, IP address, and potential route to reach the machine were perfectly valid. Usually this is just an indication that the machine was down, and therefore the request packet couldn't be sent.

Travel Advisory

Some sites switch off ping responses because ping is sometimes used by hackers and crackers to support Denial of Service (DoS) attacks that flood a network device with packets that it has to respond to. It's therefore possible that the machine is just not answering, rather than unavailable. There is no easy way to check, but if a route goes through a device that doesn't respond, or if you can ping the destination, it's probably working fine. Of course, on your own routers and networks, you'll know whether access has been removed.

- **Host unreachable**   This indicates a routing problem. The error is usually combined with the name/IP address of the device that reported the error. For example, it could be a router on your network that is being forwarded the packet but doesn't have a rule that tells it where to send the packet. You can use this information to fix or report the error.
- **Packet loss**   Any loss of packets indicates a problem with the quality of the link: either the link is over capacity and the routers are having to drop packets, or the link is unreliable (for example, analog modem links).

One other useful piece of information is that the -t command-line option tells ping to continually send packets and measure responses until you terminate the command (with CONTROL-C). You can use this over time to monitor the link quality or, sometimes more helpfully, to report the accessibility of a machine while you try and fix/trace the problem—the moment the machine suddenly responds, you know it's working again.

Checking Routes and Paths

When you take a trip somewhere, do you always check that your destination is there before you start? Probably not, but do you check the traffic and the roads you're going to take on the way? I hope so. I mean, you *can* phone Disneyworld before you leave to make sure it's still there, but what you really want to know is whether the roads that get you there are going to make it a 2-hour journey or a 17-hour journey.

The same is true of networks. Although determining availability is useful, often it's the path or route to the device or machine that causes more problems. You can ping a server and get a 230ms response time, but is that higher or lower than it should be? If it's higher, *why* is it higher?

Travel Advisory
Many people think the tools here are only useful for checking Internet sites. Although we'll use Internet sites to demonstrate their facilities, they are in fact general tools for determining availability and routes and have just as much relevance in a local, routed network as they do in the scope of the Internet.

What you need to do is check the routes and make sure that information is being routed around properly, and there are a few tools available for that within Windows Server 2003.

Using tracert

You determine the route packets take between two machines by using the tracert (traceroute) command. The result is similar to ping, but instead of showing the response time for one machine, it shows you the response time for all the devices the packet has traveled through to make it to its destination. To use, supply the name or IP address of the machine you are trying to reach. For example, here's the entire trace from our office network to our hosting service:

```
C:\>tracert www.mcslp.com
```

```
Tracing route to www.mcslp.com [66.33.213.64]
over a maximum of 30 hops:

  1     <1 ms     <1 ms     <1 ms    192.168.1.1
  2     22 ms     22 ms     22 ms    gauss-ds11.wh.zen.net.uk [62.3.83.2]
  3     23 ms     24 ms     23 ms    chrysippus-ve-131.wh.zen.net.uk [62.3.83.78]
  4     23 ms     24 ms     23 ms    deleuze-ge-0-2-0.hq.zen.net.uk [62.3.80.81]
  5     30 ms     30 ms     30 ms    suarez-so-0-0-0.te.zen.net.uk [62.3.80.62]
  6     31 ms     31 ms     30 ms    ge9-0.mpr2.lhr1.uk.mfnx.net [195.66.226.76]
  7     31 ms     31 ms     30 ms    so-4-1-0.cr2.lhr3.uk.mfnx.net [208.185.156.2]
  8    102 ms    104 ms    103 ms    so-7-0-0.cr2.lga1.us.above.net [64.125.31.182]
...
 21    191 ms    191 ms    191 ms    g50.ba01.b001202-2.lax01.atlas.cogentco.com
[66.28.67.250]
 22    176 ms    177 ms    178 ms    gw-co.sd.dreamhost.com [66.250.7.246]
 23    178 ms    178 ms    177 ms    basic-argon.gimli.dreamhost.com [66.33.213.64]

Trace complete.
```

Each line shows a different device that the packet has been routed through on its way to its destination, including three individual ping times and the host name and IP address of each device. You can see from this that there are big jumps between Steps 7 and 8, for example. A slowdown like this indicates one of two things: either it's a slower link—for example a 512Kbps line instead of a 2Mbps line—or there's network saturation on that part of the link. In this case, you can see from the U.K. and U.S. denomination that it is just the difference due to a slower link over the Atlantic.

Because we're essentially using the same system as ping, it's subject to the same errors and issues. You can get routing problems highlighted by a tracert, just as with ping, with some modification. For example, request timeouts still indicate an inability to communicate with the device, but it's possible to have timeouts along a route while still effectively determining the route it used.

There are a few additional traps to look out for that ping doesn't already identify:

- **Repeated/bounced packets** Sometimes you get repeated devices/IP addresses in the route, or the route seems to bounce between two or more addresses. Usually this indicates a problem with the routing of the two devices—they're each pointing to each other expecting the device to route—but it can also indicate that the two devices have been configured not to forward ICMP packets.

- **Different/unexpected routes** Depending on your network configuration, you may find that tracing a route to a host does not take the same route each time. This could be perfectly valid if your routing metrics are the same. But check the settings carefully; if your metrics were designed to be identical, then it will almost certainly point to incorrect metric settings. Check your general routing configuration at the same time, because it could also be a case of routes pointing to the wrong devices and having the packets end up getting distributed around your network rather than taking the more obvious direct route.

Using pathping

Although tracert is useful, it doesn't provide a particularly well-rounded view of the response times. It only tests the response time for each device on the route three times. To get a better view over a longer period, use pathping. This works like a combination of tracert and ping, not only determining the route the packets take, but also running ping on each device a number of times over a longer period to get a better idea of the response times. Here's a slightly truncated version of a trace to the BBC website, this time using pathping:

```
C:\>pathping www.bbc.co.uk

Tracing route to www.bbc.net.uk [212.58.224.114]
over a maximum of 30 hops:
  0  bear.windows.mcslp.pri [192.168.1.138]
  1  192.168.1.1
  2  gauss-dsl1.wh.zen.net.uk [62.3.83.2]
  3  chrysippus-ve-131.wh.zen.net.uk [62.3.83.78]
  4  deleuze-ge-0-2-0.hq.zen.net.uk [62.3.80.81]
  5  suarez-so-0-0-0.te.zen.net.uk [62.3.80.62]
  6  rt-linx-a.thdo.bbc.co.uk [195.66.224.103]
  7  www14.thdo.bbc.co.uk [212.58.224.114]

Computing statistics for 175 seconds...
              Source to Here   This Node/Link
Hop  RTT     Lost/Sent = Pct  Lost/Sent = Pct  Address
  0                                             bear.windows.mcslp.pri
[192.168.1.138]
                                0/ 100 =  0%   |
  1    0ms   0/ 100 =   0%     0/ 100 =  0%   192.168.1.1
                                0/ 100 =  0%   |
  2   22ms   0/ 100 =   0%     0/ 100 =  0%   gauss-dsl1.wh.zen.net.uk
[62.3.83.2]
                                0/ 100 =  0%   |
  3   24ms   0/ 100 =   0%     0/ 100 =  0%
chrysippus-ve-131.wh.zen.net.uk [62.3.83.78]
                                0/ 100 =  0%   |
  4   25ms   0/ 100 =   0%     0/ 100 =  0%
deleuze-ge-0-2-0.hq.zen.net.uk [62.3.80.81]
                                0/ 100 =  0%   |
  5   32ms   0/ 100 =   0%     0/ 100 =  0%
suarez-so-0-0-0.te.zen.net.uk [62.3.80.62]
                                0/ 100 =  0%   |
  6   31ms   0/ 100 =   0%     0/ 100 =  0%   rt-linx-a.thdo.bbc.co.uk
[195.66.224.103]
                                0/ 100 =  0%   |
```

```
  7   31ms     0/ 100 =  0%     0/ 100 =  0%  www14.thdo.bbc.co.uk
[212.58.224.114]
```

Trace complete.

You can see from this that we have a healthy link, with no packet loss and rel-atively quick times. You can, however, still use this information to determine at what part of a particular route there is a problem. For example, if your ping test shows a loss of packets, pathping will help you identify which part of the route is causing the problem.

Using route

If you identify a potential weak link or other problem in the route your packets are taking, and it's a Windows server, you need to examine the routes that are configured on the machine. You already know that routes are configured in two ways, either manually—such as the route applied when you configure the de-fault gateway on a machine—or dynamically, through one of the routing proto-cols.

You can determine the current routing table using the route command and the print subcommand. For example:

```
C:\>route print

IPv4 Route Table
===========================================================================
Interface List
0x1 ......................... MS TCP Loopback interface
0x10003 ...00 04 75 bd e7 31 ...... 3Com EtherLink XL 10/100 PCI For
Complete PC Management NIC (3C905C-TX)
===========================================================================
===========================================================================
Active Routes:
Network Destination        Netmask          Gateway       Interface  Metric
        0.0.0.0          0.0.0.0      192.168.1.1    192.168.1.138     20
      127.0.0.0        255.0.0.0        127.0.0.1        127.0.0.1      1
    192.168.1.0    255.255.255.0    192.168.1.138    192.168.1.138     20
  192.168.1.138  255.255.255.255        127.0.0.1        127.0.0.1     20
  192.168.1.255  255.255.255.255    192.168.1.138    192.168.1.138     20
      224.0.0.0        240.0.0.0    192.168.1.138    192.168.1.138     20
255.255.255.255  255.255.255.255    192.168.1.138    192.168.1.138      1
Default Gateway:       192.168.1.1
===========================================================================
Persistent Routes:
  None
```

You can see that the output includes the destination network/IP address, ap-propriate netmask, gateway IP address, the interface IP address, and the metric.

The Active Routes section shows you the routes currently in use and in the table. In the list you generally find the following.

- **Default Gateway (AKA 0.0.0.0)**   The destination all packets are sent to if they are not within the current network/netmask.

- **127.0.0.1** The local loopback address.

- **224.0.0.0** The IP multicast address

- **255.255.255.255** The IP broadcast address; all computers on the network segment pick up packets sent to this IP.

- *x.x.x*.**255** The network broadcast address; packets sent to this IP are picked up by all machines in the *x.x.x* subnet—that is, 192.168.1.255 broadcasts to all computers with a 192.168.1 prefix.

- *x.x.x*.**0** The network address.

- **Local computers** Occasionally, you'll find local computers—that is, within the same network/netmask as the host—in the list.

- **Remote computers** Occasionally, you might find remote computers—that is, those beyond your own subnet—in the list.

- **Persistent routes** These are routes you have manually added to the table, either using the route command or the RRAS tool, that you have marked as persistent across a reboot.

Other command-line options useful within route are listed in Table 5.3.

The Net "Shell"

You can monitor and configure many elements of your network configuration through the netsh command, which provides a command-line driven interface to the networking components. The system goes through a series of contexts, which are layered so that you can go up and down through the layers to access different aspects of your setup.

TABLE 5.3	Additional Options to the route Command
Option	**Description**
-f	Clears the routing table of all gateway entries
-p	When used with ADD, marks a route as persistent over reboots
ADD	Adds a route to the table; you must specify the detail in the form \<destination> mask \<netmask> \<gwip> metric \<metric> if \<interfaceID>
DELETE	Deletes a route matching the destination address supplied
CHANGE	Changes an existing route (uses the same format as ADD)

Travel Assistance

Check the online and inline documentation for more information on using netsh's extensive features.

CHECKPOINT

✔**Objective 5.01: Plan a Routing Strategy**   Planning a routing strategy relies on knowing your network layout and topology and making decisions about which routes and connections should be used according to their relative speed and/or cost. There are two main routing protocols, RIP and OSPF. RIP maintains compatibility with older routing and networking equipment but does not scale well in large networks. OSPF is more efficient and useful in large routing situations where complex but efficient routes must be calculated according to the route availability. However, OSPF is not as widely supported as RIP and can be complex to set up and manage. Multicast traffic is used for broadcast services such as live video. Routing multicast traffic uses the IGMP protocol and can be supported either in forwarding mode, which simply redistributes multicast traffic, or in routing and proxy mode, which can be used to provide multicast services on a network through a multicast proxy server.

✔**Objective 5.02: Plan Security for Remote Access User**   Remote access is a weak point in the network, and you must provide methods for securing access to your remote access server by controlling who, when, and under what conditions a user can connect. The simplest solution is to block access on a user-by-user basis. More complex system rules and settings can be controlled by using remote access policies. Remote Access Policies use a combination of conditions and profiles to control access to the server according to group membership, dial-in location, and even dial-in method. The profile then applies conditions to the connection, which includes limiting access to specific times, adding encryption, and requiring specific authentication methods. Remote access connections can be encrypted to prevent other people snooping on the contents. Windows Server 2003 supports four levels of encryption, from no encryption up to the strongest encryption using the DES and MPPE encryption systems. DES is used for L2TP connections, and MPPE is used for PPTP and dial-up connections. Authentication methods enforce ways of transferring authentication and login information to your remote access server. Windows Server 2003 includes support for PAP, SPAP, CHAP, MS-CHAP v1, and EAP authentication protocols. EAP-TLS is the strongest.

✔️**Objective 5.03: Implement Secure Access Between Private Networks**
Secure access between private networks involves using either direct connections and encrypted communication or encryption and encapsulation with a VPN over the public Internet. By using the VPN functionality combined with remote access policies, you can both encapsulate and safely encrypt and control access to your VPN network. IPSec policies allow direct connections between sites to be further secured by setting additional security, authentication, and packet filtering. Within a VPN connection, this is handled by IPSec running in tunneling mode. To enable tunneling, you use the Local Security Settings or the IPSec snap-in to the MMC and set up the tunnel endpoint on each machine.

✔️**Objective 5.04: Troubleshoot TCP/IP Routing**   A number of tools exist to monitor your network connections. Ping can be used to test the accessibility of a machine, and through the use of pathping, tracert, and route, it's possible to isolate and identify the location of the problem.

REVIEW QUESTIONS

1. Your company is spread over a wide area using a number of branch offices. Most of the offices are connected together using Windows Server 2003–based routers and dedicated frame relay connections. One of the offices uses a Unix-based router. You want to automate the routing process so that offices will automatically use an alternative route when a connection goes down. Which system should you use? (Choose one.)

   A. RIP
   B. OSPF
   C. Static routes
   D. DHCP

2. As part of your remote access plan, you want to limit access to the network only during normal working hours, between 8 A.M. and 6 P.M. How should you configure this option? (Choose one.)

   A. Set up a script to enable and disable the remote access service at specified times.

   B. Change the user dial-in properties.

   C. Create a remote access policy.

   D. Create a remote access profile.

3. You want to force all remote users to use certificates to authenticate with your remote access server. Which of the following will you configure?

   A. EAP-TLS

   B. MS-CHAP v1

   C. MS-CHAP v2

   D. IPSec

4. You are concerned about the unencrypted communication between your remote users and your server, and you want to force encryption. You want to enable MPPE 56-bit encryption as a default but also allow only 40-bit encryption to retain compatibility with some older equipment. Which of the following encryption settings should you select? (Choose all that apply.)

   A. No encryption

   B. Basic encryption

   C. Strong encryption

   D. Strongest encryption

5. Which utility will allow you to see all the hops that a packet takes on its way to its final destination?

   A. ping

   B. nslookup

   C. tracert

   D. Network Monitor

6. You are having connectivity problems to one of your branch offices. You suspect the problem is with a malfunctioning router, but you need some figures to back up your claims. You use ping to check the availability of a server at the remote office and get a long response time. When you run tracert, the times are much lower and within normal limits. You want to determine where the problem lies within your routing setup over a period of time without adversely affecting your overall network performance. What should you do? (Choose one.)

A. Periodically use ping to test the connectivity and collate the results.

B. Periodically run tracert and collate the results.

C. Use pathping to test the connectivity.

D. Use System Monitor to monitor your server's network performance.

REVIEW ANSWERS

1. **A**   OSPF might be supported, but cannot be guaranteed. Static routes are not an option because you want to automate the update process. DHCP does not provide any form of routing help.

2. **C**   Profiles can also specify times but are only valid once a user has connected to the network. Setting up a script would work, but it might lock out administrators who want to be able to connect at any time.

3. **A**   Only EAP-TLS supports certificate-based authentication.

4. **B C**   Strong encryption enables 56-bit MPPE and Basic enables 40-bit MPPE. You must select both to allow the server to negotiate. No Encryption must be unselected, otherwise nonencrypted connections would be allowed.

5. **C**   The ping utility only tells you whether a machine can be reached and how long it takes. The nslookup utility resolves names or IP addresses.

6. **C**   Although you could achieve the result using ping and/or tracert, it would be difficult and probably inconclusive. System Monitor only monitors network packets on a particular interface, not performance over a distance.

Planning Network
Security

	NEWBIE	SOME EXPERIENCE	EXPERT
ETA	6+ hours	3+ hours	1 hour

237

Just when you thought it wasn't possible to have anything spread faster than the .com rash of the late 90s, it is happening all over again. This time, however, it's not the World Wide Web making all the waves; it's the notion of network security that has taken the computing world by storm. The word "security" is arguably the most popular word spoken when it comes to networked environments. From the end-user desktop to client/server applications to web environments, security is now the number one priority for any network administrator. This isn't to say that administrators haven't always had an eye out for security issues, but now it's imperative to the network that they do so. Now it's not just the information technology department pushing for security, but upper management as well. Lucky for us administrators, Microsoft is building its operating systems and accompanying server products in a way that makes it easier to secure our systems.

Objective 6.01

Plan for Network Protocol Security

One of the authors can remember back some years ago spending summer days as part of a secret club in a tree house with his friends. Aside from their number-one rule of "NO GIRLS ALLOWED," he and his friends went to great lengths and spent countless hours trying to come up with ways to ensure that their club was just that, *theirs*. From passwords, special codes, secret handshakes, and knocks, to sometimes even their own language, they spared no expense in ensuring the secrecy of the club. Aside from his being a bit bigger, not much has changed till now, as he spends a great deal of time working with network administrators teaching and implementing security measures to implement integrity and confidentiality within information systems. Of course, the cereal box decoder rings, pig Latin, and code names have all been replaced by things like Kerberos, biometric devices, IPSec, certificates, and more. But the guiding conception behind it all remains the same: keep my information from falling into the hands of someone inappropriate.

Planning your network security is an intricate and time-consuming process that requires the input of everyone from upper management down to the newest intern. No matter how many systems and mechanisms get put into place to safeguard your resources, inevitably it will always come down to the education and effort of the end users. The corporate security policy should be built by group effort in a manner that allows people to complete their jobs efficiently yet still adhere to the security needs of the organization.

Your corporate security policy *will not* be a static document. Your security policy will be very dynamic in nature. The process, as shown in Figure 6.1, will be ongoing as you continue to grow, as you most likely will find a recurring pattern of security planning, security implementation, and reevaluation.

Document Required Ports and Protocols

Do you have a network diagram? Is it a current network diagram? Have you documented your server configurations? Do you know which servers provide what services? All of these are important questions to answer before you can begin implementing any type of security policy. Documentation of your network resources and services should be done. By documenting the resources and services on your network, you will find it easier to construct a security policy that

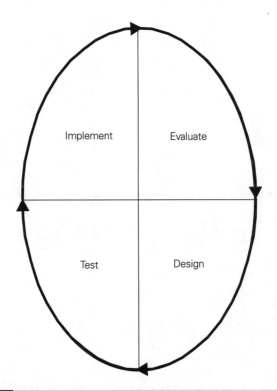

FIGURE 6.1   The security policy process is an ongoing process that includes planning, implementing, and reevaluating.

won't disturb the production environment. An important part of this documentation is the identification of the ports and protocols in use by a given system.

Let's look at an example of a typical company's demilitarized zone that has a
web server and a file server as shown in Figure 6.2. The main function of a web
server is just that, to provide web services to clients issuing requests. The server
could be giving static .html pages, dynamic .asp pages, some entertaining
Macromedia Flash content, or maybe even some streaming video. The file
server is there simply to allow the download of files. Why, then, should we leave
the web server or file server open for requests to other services? The answer is
that we shouldn't. The separation of services across your network should allow
you to isolate specific services for specific systems. Thus in the case of our web
server and file server, there wouldn't be a reason to leave open any unnecessary
ports, leaving the system vulnerable to attack.

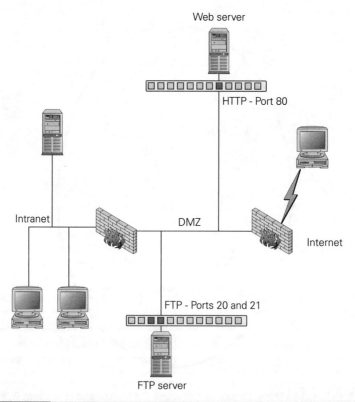

FIGURE 6.2 A web server locked down to only provide HTTP information
through port 80

The web service option on a system is just one of many services available on a system. There are literally hundreds of services available through thousands of ports on a system, many of these ports being prime targets for attacks from external hosts. Documenting the ports and protocols needed by a system helps eliminate the possibility of attack through an unused port or protocol. Some of the more common ports and protocols and their uses are shown in Table 6.1.

Okay, maybe you know all about the ports and protocols, so you ask "Why do I need to document?" Well, the reality is, you don't. Documentation is not done for functionality but more for the purpose of demonstrating due diligence. By documenting, you are showing that you have taken the time to understand the purpose of a particular system and can comfortably move forward to implement a security procedure. Documenting your network has its benefits, including

- **Easier and more efficient troubleshooting**   Problems can be solved much faster when you have a tangible resource to use for finding the locations of different network resources and services.

TABLE 6.1   Common Ports and Protocols and Their Uses

Port	Protocol	Use
80	HTTP—Hypertext Transfer Protocol	Responding to web page requests
443	HTTPS (SSL)—Secure Socket Layer or Secure HTTP	Secure web pages
20/21	FTP—File Transfer Protocol	File transfer
88	Kerberos	Authentication in a Windows 2003 Domain
25	SMTP—Simple Mail Transfer Protocol	E-mail services
53	DNS—Domain Name Service	Domain name resolution
1701	L2TP—Layer 2 Tunneling protocol	Virtual private network tunneling
1723	PPTP—Point-to-Point Tunneling Protocol	Virtual private network tunneling
500	IPSec—Internet Protocol Security	Secure IP communication between systems
3389	RDP—Remote Desktop Protocol	Remote desktop communication
1433	SQL—Structured Query Language	SQL Server communication

- **Less possibility of information loss during transition periods**   When employees leave the company or even transfer within the company, having documentation makes it easier to follow up on the work they completed.

- **Easier implementation of the policy of separation of services**   Having documentation makes it much easier to apply the separation of duties and allow individuals to do nothing more than the jobs they are expected to do. (You don't want your SQL Server administrator messing with your Microsoft Exchange services!)

- **Saving time**   The value of documentation is never better displayed than when you are in a time crunch. Detailed documentation will always save you the time it takes to find someone who knows or to troubleshoot by trial and error.

- **Saving money**   Without documentation, an administrator may inadvertently shut down a needed service and cost your company millions of dollars.

If documentation has all of these benefits, then why doesn't everyone do it? Perhaps most administrators consider it job security if their only documentation is a mental note! In reality, most networks go undocumented because documentation is not a mandatory practice and does not have a direct impact on daily network performance. In fact, many administrators will say that documentation takes time and they just don't have enough of that already. All in all, documentation is not a truly essential part of your network operation; however, as you can see, it certainly has its bonuses. Plus, it's a nice gesture to all the administrators who will follow in your footsteps. Remember, do unto others!

Plan an IPSec Policy

Internet Protocol security (IPSec) is an industry-standard protocol created to provide data protection between computer systems. IPSec is used to provide data integrity and data confidentiality. *Data integrity* refers to the assurance that information originated from the expected source and has not been modified en route to its destination. *Data confidentiality* refers to the assurance that information has not been read, in transit to the intended recipient, by unauthorized individuals. The configuration of IPSec on your network is referred to as the *IPSec policy*. Devising an effective IPSec policy is no walk in the park. Implementing IPSec piles additional overhead into the transmission of each packet and thus has a direct impact on network communication efficiency. Imagine walking down the street and bumping into someone you know, but before you can talk to them, you have to make a phone call to verify their correct identity and then you have to scan the immediate surroundings to be sure no one is listening to you. Only once you have completed the authentication and secured the communication environment can you begin to talk to them. This is the same process that IPSec follows when systems communicate on your network. Of course, you could easily implement IPSec by forcing all systems in your domain to communicate securely, but is that really warranted? A successful IPSec policy is one that can blend communication efficiency with communication security. Finding the correct blend requires

- Classifying data according to their needs for security
- Constructing security policies that meet the needs of your organization
- Evaluating security risks and vulnerabilities
- Providing the proper security mechanisms
- Educating end users on proper use of the security mechanisms

The right mix of security controls will certainly be swayed by what functions a system serves. For example, the security settings for a system will be different depending on whether it is a database server, domain controller, file server, web server, DNS server, or network access server. Identifying the types of traffic and locations of secure information will most certainly be your first step in planning an IPSec policy.

As a general rule, you will find that your systems will fall into three general categories with respect to security:

- **Basic security or minimal security**   Systems without the inherent need for secure communication. These systems do not require the configuration of an IPSec policy.
- **Standard security**   Systems that store sensitive information but should not be configured so securely that regular communication is adversely affected. These systems are good candidates for the default IPSec policies of Client (Respond Only) or Server (Request Security). (You'll learn more about these soon.)
- **High security**   Systems that contain highly confidential data and are prime targets for data theft or hacking. These systems are ripe for implementing the Secure Server (Require Security) IPSec policy.

Once your data has been classified and tagged with the appropriate security levels, Microsoft has made the implementation of an IPSec policy rather easy. Since data encryption at the domain level is rarely justifiable, the preferred method is to group servers of similar security levels together into organization units (OUs) and use Group Policy to push down the appropriate IPSec policy.

Let's look at an example. Say your company has a handful of file servers that hold confidential data that is crucial to the success of the company and if compromised could lead to the company's demise (like maybe the Coca Cola recipe or the code behind a popular operating system). In your company, only a dozen or so computers utilize this information. You want to be able to ensure secure communication with the file servers; however, you do not want to affect the client's communication with other servers beyond the confidential servers. Situations like this, where security is a primary concern for only a handful of systems, are best solved by using Organizational Units and Group Policy. Our solution here is to place all secure file servers into an Organizational Unit named Secure Servers and implement a Group Policy Object that propagates the Secure Server IPSec policy to all servers within the OU. This policy will force all communication to and from these servers to utilize the highest level of data encryption. For the clients, since we don't want to affect everyday communication with other servers, we don't want to implement the same Secure Server IPSec policy that requires security; instead, we use the Client IPSec policy that gives the system the ability to respond to an IPSec request but will never initiate secure communication.

So what exactly does it mean to establish an IPSec policy? An IPSec policy is made of three main components:

- **Authentication methods**   Kerberos v5, certificates, preshared key
- **Filter list**   A list of the different types of traffic that require or don't require IPSec
- **Filter action**   The resulting action Permit, Block, or Negotiate Security for traffic that meets the criteria defined on the filter list

The authentication methods for IPSec as shown in Figure 6.3 are provided to give administrative control over the stringency of authentication between two systems using IPSec. Multiple methods can be preconfigured in order of preference and are dependent on the environment in which you are utilizing IPSec. For example, in a Windows Server 2003 domain environment the option for Kerberos v5 is available, but in a nondomain environment, that option is not available. Along the same lines, if you don't have a certificate implementation or have not purchased certificates from a commercial vendor, then the certificate authentication method is not possible.

When choosing between the different authentication mechanisms, you should avoid using the preshared key like the plague. The preshared key is the

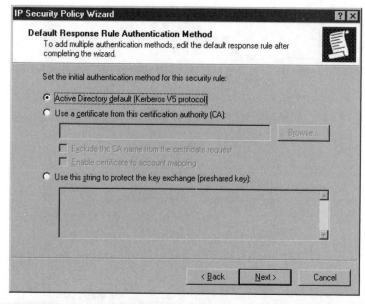

FIGURE 6.3 Authentication methods available in an IPSec policy as shown in the IP Security Policy Wizard

weakest of the three mechanisms, as it is a static value, is plainly seen in the window, and was, after all, created by a human as opposed to being dynamically created by a "smart" computer.

The filter list allows an administrator to select specific types of traffic to follow or not follow the IPSec policy. For example, as an administrator, you may not want to force all of your name resolution requests to be encrypted using IPSec, and thus you add port 53 to the filter list and allow the traffic to flow unencrypted. Figure 6.4 shows an example of an IPSec filter set up to allow unencrypted DNS name resolution traffic.

The filter actions set in IPSec as shown in Figure 6.5 determine what happens to the traffic as it enters the machine with the IPSec policy. The permit and block options, by no surprise, simply allow or deny traffic. However, the Negotiate Security option is where the real meat of IPSec comes in to play. When you dig a little deeper into this option, you find that this is where you can determine just how secure you want the data to be: you can decide to maintain just data integrity by using a setting called Authentication Header (AH), or you can choose integrity and confidentiality by using the Encapsulating Security Payload (ESP) option. In addition to choosing AH versus ESP, you can customize the algorithms that perform these functions. Stay tuned for more detail on all of IPSec in the later section "Configure Security for Data Transmissions."

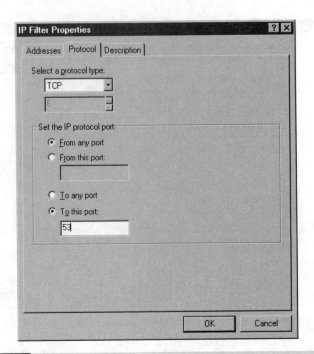

An IPSec filter created to allow DNS name resolution traffic to flow without needing the encryption provided by the IPSec policy

Your IPSec policy planning should include

- What communications require IPSec (server to server, remote access, and so on)?
- What level of IPSec is appropriate?
- What traffic should follow the IPSec policy?
- What are the vulnerabilities and threats covered?
- How will the policy be applied?
- Who will manage the policy?
- Who will monitor the policy?

Answering these questions will help fill in your IPSec policy, and revisiting these questions on a regular basis will help you continue to provide a secure network environment.

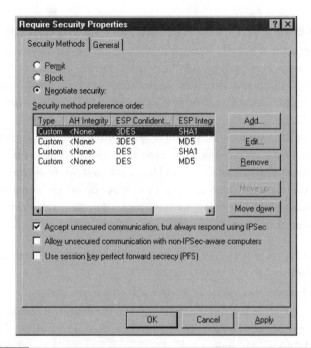

FIGURE 6.5   Filter actions used in IPSec determine how traffic that meets the filter list criteria should be handled.

Objective 6.02

Plan Secure Network Administration Methods

A nd now for the most pressing question of the day: Do you want to administer you network from a lounge chair on a tropical beach? Well, fellow admin, the idea is not that far-fetched. The technologies are already here. Take, for example, the most recent handheld computers manufactured by companies such as HP (Compaq), Dell, and Sony. Each of these devices is compatible with Microsoft's Pocket PC operating system, which includes the terminal services client. So maybe the 240 × 320 screen is a little challenging, but at least the opportunity is there, and with the growing popularity of the TabletPC, the screen limitation is no more. Pay close attention, friend; on your next job interview, you just may be able to negotiate into your contract a clause that lets you stay home and manage the network in your pajamas!

Create a Plan for Remote Assistance

It is important that before we go any further, we define the differences between remote assistance and remote administration. *Remote assistance,* as the name implies, is the ability to assist a user in need of help. *Remote administration* is the ability to remotely access a system as if you were sitting directly in front of it, regardless of a user's needs.

With remote assistance, the person needing help is referred to as the "novice" and the person assisting is called the "expert." The ideal scenario for implementation of remote assistance involves a Help Desk staff. Allowing the Help Desk staff to remotely assist users reduces the number of PC visits that need to be made. Planning a remote assistance implementation means ensuring that all of the following criteria are met:

- The expert and the novice users are both operating a system running Windows XP or Windows Server 2003.
- The expert and novice are connected to the same network.
- The novice must have the ability to send the expert an "invitation" for remote assistance using Microsoft Outlook, Outlook Express, or Windows Messenger.

These criteria are the bare necessities for implementing remote assistance. Assuredly, you will find that additional steps, such as opening port 3389 for the RDP-TCP protocol, must be taken to allow this service, especially when you begin to look at networks that traverse different geographic areas and are perhaps separated by firewalls or other devices. Tables 6.2 and 6.3 provide a summary of what types of invitations are allowed through the different mediums you find between interconnected networks.

As an administrator, of course, you will have final control over remote assistance. You certainly don't want users allowing just anyone to accept an invitation for remote assistance, especially someone from outside the trusted network. Your

TABLE 6.2	Summary of Remote Assistance Connection Possibilities Using Windows Messenger to Deliver the Invitation File		
Level of Expertise	Windows XP Internet Connection Sharing (ICS)	Non–Universal Plug and Play Network Address Translation (NAT) Device	UPnP NAT Device
Novice	Yes	Yes	Yes
Expert	Yes	Yes	Yes
Both novice and expert	Yes	No	Yes

TABLE 6.3	Summary of Remote Assistance Connection Possibilities Using E-Mail to Deliver the Invitation File		
Level of Expertise	Windows XP Internet Connection Sharing (ICS)	Non–Universal Plug and Play Network Address Translation (NAT) Device	UPnP NAT Device
Novice	Yes	No	Yes
Expert	Yes	Yes	Yes
Both novice and expert	Yes	No	Yes

control of the remote assistance application can come in any of the following forms:

- At the individual computer, you can disable the remote assistance feature.

- Through Group Policy, you can prevent a user from sending a remote assistance invitation or reduce the remote administration to read-only assistance only.

- At the firewall, you can deny traffic through port 3389, which is used by the Remote Desktop Protocol used by remote assistance.

Plan Remote Administration Using Terminal Services

Now that you have been motivated to stay at home and run the network or, better yet, hit the beach and manage the network, it is time to plan exactly how you will do this. Perhaps the first and most important step in the process is to lay out a plan documenting the network connectivity, the wide area network infrastructure. Remote administration sounds like a wonderful idea, but if your WAN infrastructure doesn't support efficient communication with your internal network, the remote administration/assistance process can actually cross the line to becoming a headache.

Once it has been determined that the WAN infrastructure will support remote administration, the next step is to identify the individuals who will have this privilege. Obviously, with increased remote administration comes an increased possibility of remote hacking, and therefore adequate documentation and security planning should be part of your due diligence. Once these users are identified, they can be managed and organized using Global groups through Active Directory Users and Computers.

Remote desktop administration is the new term for what used to be referred to as Terminal Services in Administration mode. The principal function remains the same, in that we can access a system from a remote system using thin-client software often called the Terminal Services Client, and now seen on the Windows XP operating system as the Remote Desktop Connection. Remote desktop administration thus allows access to a system as if you were sitting down right in front of it, when in fact you could be in a different location on the LAN or even a distant location across the WAN or dial-up. The remote desktop administration feature is not meant for a large multiadministrator environment where simultaneous access is required, as it allows for only two concurrent connections from the administrator group to start a terminal session, while one logon is enabled at the console. It would not be healthy for two administrators to terminal into a system and attempt to make opposing changes, so to successfully implement remote administration requires cooperation from all administrators.

Planning an effective remote administration policy requires taking into consideration all of the following points:

- *How should the server handle disconnected sessions?* Since the remote administration mode is limited to just two connections, leaving a disconnected session open could effectively lock other administrators out of the system until that remaining connection is closed. The downside to this is that if an administrator is performing a time-consuming function and gets involuntarily disconnected, the time-consuming function will cease and the administrator will have to restart the job.

- *How will remote administration tasks be managed by a group of administrators?* Having three administrators, two remote administrators and one at the console, logged in and performing tasks at the same time can cause a serious degradation in server performance, not to mention increase the chances of administrators performing competing jobs on the server.

- *How will your remote administration policy handle administrative functions that require a reboot?* Without being physically present, you could be opening yourself to a problem even as rudimentary as a rogue floppy disk being left in the machine and thus preventing the system from correctly restarting.

- *How will you secure off your remote administration?* Since remote desktop administration allows users to perform any job they would normally perform while sitting right in front of the system, security is of utmost importance. For starters, the system you are remotely monitoring should be located behind a firewall to ensure that you can filter out illegitimate traffic. In addition, you should be sure that all remote administration users are configured with strong passwords. As for encryption, the Remote Desktop Protocol (RDP) has the inherent ability to use up to 128-bit encryption; however, you may want to consider an IPSec policy, depending upon the security requirements.

Travel Advisory

By default, RDP does not have any encryption. However, since RDP does not perform a data transfer, an unauthorized user sniffing the line would see only the keyboard, video, and mouse information going from thin client to server.

Thanks to Microsoft and its push for remote administration, our dream of managing the network from a sun-filled tropical location is really not that far-fetched. Of course, then you'll have to constantly worry about getting sand in the laptop, or inadvertently swallowing that little drink umbrella stuck in your margarita. Cheers!

Objective 6.03   Configure Network Protocol Security

Perhaps somewhere in this great world, there is an all-Windows network, most likely a small network environment; but in most large network implementations, there is no escaping the intermingling of operating systems. Microsoft has a done quite a job getting people to deploy their products, but until the day arrives when they hold 100 percent of the market share, we will continue to have to work in heterogeneous environments. For some time, we will have to resolve issues with communication to Novell, Macintosh, and Unix systems.

Configure Protocol Security in Heterogeneous Client Computer Environment

When it comes to protocol security in a heterogeneous network environment, it is tough to pick a single solution. In an all-IP network, we could rely on the encryption services of IPSec and feel comfortable with the level of security in place. When you add Novell and NWLink, Microsoft's implementation of IPX/SPX, even configuring communication, let alone security, is an administrative burden.

> **Travel Advisory**
>
> Though the latest versions of Novell all utilize the TCP/IP protocol, the older versions still require the IPX/SPX protocol. In addition, the Microsoft services for communication with Novell still require the NWLink protocol as well.

As an administrative rule of thumb, you should always try to limit the available protocols on your network. If you don't have Novell clients, there is more than likely no reason to allow the NWLink protocol. Excess protocols open doors for attacks that otherwise would not be available.

If you must have additional protocols due to multiple operating system types, then the binding order of the protocols should at least be set with the most common protocol listed at the top. When a system attempts communication, it begins with the protocol listed first in the binding order. As Figure 6.6 shows, this system would attempt communication by first trying the NWLink protocol. This would be fine if the system you were communicating with could respond with the same protocol. However, in a primarily Windows environment where TCP/IP is the core communication protocol, this would actually

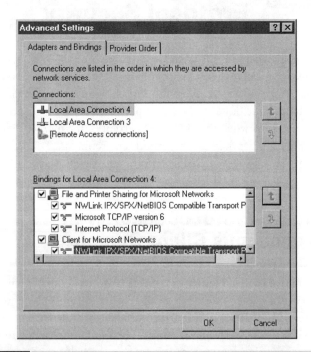

FIGURE 6.6   Inefficient network binding order configured with a less commonly used protocol at the top of the list

cause a delay in communication. The bindings for your network adapters can be configured off the Advanced settings option from the Advanced menu on the Network Connections option of Control Panel. Figure 6.7 shows a corrected binding order replacing NWLink at the top of the list with TCP/IP.

Configuring network protocol security in mixed operating system environments boils down to creating proper documentation regarding which segments of the network require the protocols and which specific ports on those participating systems should be available for use.

If your environment is not so heterogeneous as to include operating systems from other vendors but only different operating systems from Microsoft, you still have a few concerns. First and foremost, any client or server in your network that is not running Windows 2000, Windows XP, or Windows Server 2003 will not be affected by your Group Policy implementation, as only these operating systems know what to do with such policies. Your down-level clients, the Windows 98 or Windows NT clients, can be secured using system policies. Since these clients cannot understand the processing of Group Policy, they will not be able to follow any IPSec policies you may implement, thus not permitting secure data communication. As of around June 2002, Microsoft released an L2TP/IPSec VPN client for down-level systems; however, this doesn't affect their

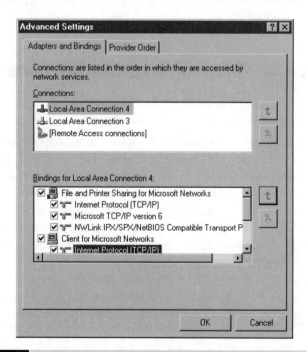

FIGURE 6.7   A more efficient binding order reflecting the most commonly used network protocol at the top of the list

shortcomings for directly connected LAN communications. Legacy systems still lack the functionality to take part in the security management and system administration delivered through Group Policy.

Configure Protocol Security Using IPSec Policies

A bit earlier, we discussed planning IPSec policies and how you should follow a documented plan outlining port and protocol use. Now we will take a look at configuring the IPSec policies. Let's start by reviewing the three important settings to configure in an IPSec policy:

- **Authentication** Kerberos v5, certificates, preshared key
- **Filter list** The ports and protocols that fall under or out of the IPSec policy
- **Filter action** The result of falling under the IPSec policy

Depending upon how broadly your IPSec policy is being implemented, you can configure IPSec on a local machine or on groups of machines by placing them into an Organizational Unit and configuring a Group Policy Object for all the systems in the OU.

Objective 6.04   Plan Wireless Network Security

If the word security has become the latest buzz in the networking industry, then the word wireless can't be too far behind. The recent rise of the wireless network has introduced many new security exposures that network administrators must face in a given day. It used to be that all we had to worry about were disgruntled employees and Internet attackers, but wireless hacking adds a whole new dimension to the game. Planning your wireless network implementation involves understanding the authentication and encryption used by the wireless access point (WAP).

This chapter discusses a few of the steps you can take to configure security for your wireless local area network (WLAN) in addition to some of the more advanced technologies that are helping to make wireless networks more secure.

WEP Security

Wireless networks using any of the 802.11 standards, a, b, or g, have a predefined encryption algorithm known as Wired Equivalent Privacy (WEP) to provide data confidentiality. Although the design of WEP was well intended, it has fallen under heavy scrutiny. WEP has been found to be a rather easy encryption algorithm to break, despite its ability to encrypt with an RC4 stream cipher using a 40-bit or 104-bit key. This is a tremendous vulnerability for wireless networks in environments that put a heavy emphasis on data security. Windows XP and Windows Server 2003 support the 802.1x authentication mechanism, which is subject to stronger encryption algorithms and certificate-based authentication.

Building a wireless network can be a tricky task. Well, let me clarify that. Building a secure wireless network can be a tricky task. Due to the aforementioned weakness in WEP, there are a few infrastructure changes you could put in place to ensure a more secure wireless environment. Figure 6.8 shows a diagram of a wireless network with the WAP devices placed in a perimeter network, where the clients are then forced to authenticate against a virtual private network (VPN) server before being allowed access to the internal network. By constructing your wireless access as seen in the diagram, you are ensuring that even if your WEP key is compromised and an unknown client gains wireless access, they are still prevented from causing any harm to your internal resources.

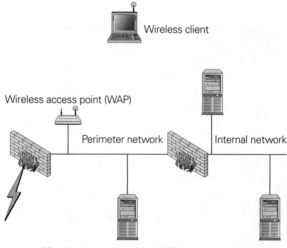

| **FIGURE 6.8** | A wireless network infrastructure with the WAP devices placed on a perimeter network for enhanced security against external attacks |

SSID Security

Every wireless access needs to have a service set identifier to differentiate one wireless local area network (WLAN) from another. All major wireless access point (WAP) vendors have default SSIDs configured on their products. When dealing with SSID security, the obvious first step is to change the SSID to something other than a default. You would be surprised how many default SSIDs on WLANs you can find during a short little war drive around your neighborhood.

Travel Advisory

Commercial wireless products are set with default options to minimize the required setup and therefore are set to broadcast their SSID and not use WEP. It is your responsibility as an administrator to change the defaults as soon as possible.

In addition to changing the SSID value, there is an option on most WAP devices to disable broadcast of the SSID. Broadcasting the SSID makes it easy for users to find the various WLANs configured throughout your network. Of course, this also lets the unauthorized users find out about them as well. Though not considered a strong security feature, disabling this broadcast, as shown in Figure 6.9, still helps prevent rogue access, since only users who know the SSID will be able to establish a connection to it.

Host Name:	Mktg-Wap1 (Required by some ISPs)
Domain Name:	(Required by some ISPs)
Firmware Version:	1.44.2, Dec 13 2002
LAN IP Address:	(MAC Address: 00-06-25-BB-0A-53)
	172 . 16 . 1 . 253 (Device IP Address)
	255.255.255.0 ▾ (Subnet Mask)
Wireless:	(MAC Address: 00-02-DD-84-62-ED)
	⦿ **Enable** ○ **Disable**
	SSID: Marketing
	SSID Broadcast: ○ **Enable** ⦿ **Disable**
	Channel: 6 ▾ (Domain: USA)
	WEP: ○ **Mandatory** ⦿ **Disable** [WEP Key Setting]
WAN Connection Type:	(MAC Address: 00-06-25-BB-0A-54)
	Obtain an IP automatically ▾ Select the Internet connection type you wish to use
	[Apply] [Cancel]

FIGURE 6.9 Disabling the broadcast of an SSID does provide a limited barrier against unauthorized users discovering your wireless.

Advanced Wireless Security

Configuring your wireless network with the highest levels of security, as shown in Figure 6.10, requires a significant amount of administrative effort. To achieve this more secure environment involves merging several rather intense technologies, all for the greater good of wireless security. These technologies include

- Public Key Infrastructure (PKI)
- Wireless hardware that supports 802.1x authentication
- Remote access servers and clients that support the EAP-TLS remote authentication protocol.
- A RADIUS infrastructure (certainly Microsoft's IAS)

Creating a Public Key Infrastructure and distributing certificates to clients and servers creates a more secure means of providing client identification. In most cases, since your WLAN will be limited to only those users within your organization, an internal root certificate authority (CA) with an enterprise subordinate CA will be the more cost-effective CA architecture (more to come on PKI in Chapter 7).

The wireless access point (WAP) and wireless client must support the 802.1x authentication technology, which can use the Extensible Authentication Protocol (EAP-TLS) with certificate-based authentication. Even though EAP-TLS certificate-based authentication is more secure, EAP with the MS-CHAPv2 authentication protocol is a valid solution for smaller organizations without a certificate architecture. The client and the WAP will exchange keys and proceed to

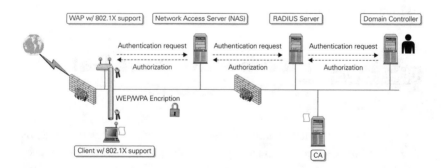

FIGURE 6.10   A highly secure wireless implementation requires merging several technologies.

communicate using either the Wireless Equivalent Privacy (WEP) protocol with an RC4 encryption algorithm or the more secure Wi-Fi Protected Access (WPA) with an option for the stronger Advanced Encryption Standard (AES). AES is capable of using encryption keys with lengths up to 256 bits. For all of you math wizards out there, that is 1.1×10^{77} possible combinations for AES with a 256-bit key.

The Internet Authentication Server or RADIUS implementation helps centralize authentication and accounting and is a required piece to the puzzle when using the 802.1x authentication. The RADIUS server will communicate with an Active Directory Domain Controller to request user authentication and will return the response to the WAP.

Even though it is administratively more difficult to configure security using these technologies, it creates a more secure wireless infrastructure.

Configure Wireless Security Policies

With the growing popularity of WLANs, you just knew Windows Server 2003 would not be complete without including some type of administrative control over wireless access. In fact, administrators of Windows Server 2003 domains can actually manage access to various WLANs using Group Policy. By creating wireless security policies in Active Directory, an administrator can control which WLANs users can access. As with all Group Policy settings, which users will be affected is dependent upon the level at which the policy is placed. The policy shown in Figures 6.11 and 6.12 is created at the domain level to prevent any users from within the domain from accessing WLANs other than the Marketing or Sales WLANs.

As with the rest of our resource administration through Group Policy, the true value here comes in the administrative ease we gain in controlling many users from a single policy.

Objective 6.05   Plan Security for Data Transmissions

Any good book on networking with sections on network security would not be complete without some discussion of the Open Systems Interconnection (OSI) model. The OSI model came about as a way of providing a standard

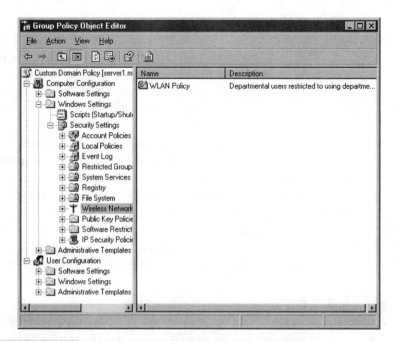

FIGURE 6.11   A domain-level group policy called WLAN Policy

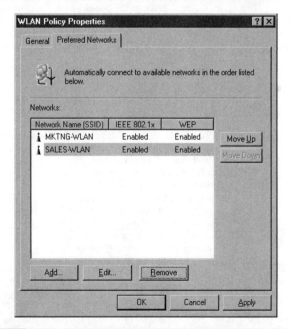

FIGURE 6.12   The details of the WLAN policy reveal that users can connect only to the Marketing WLAN and the Sales WLAN.

of communication across systems. It was built upon the idea of a series of layers for communication that add and remove the layer-specific information and then pass the information to the next layer. The direction the information is passed, up to a higher layer or down to a lower layer, is dependent on the direction of the communication, inbound or outbound, respectively. Table 6.4 shows a diagram of the OSI model and some of the protocols that function at the different layers.

When we talk about securing the data transmissions across the network, we need to factor in the different layers of the OSI model so that we can determine exactly what protocols require the secure communications. From there, it is a matter of finding the utilities or features that provide the data transmission security. IPSec runs at the network layer, which is why it is so commonly used. As data flows down the OSI stack, each layer adds new information to the packet of information given by the layer above. When IPSec is enabled, the data coming into the network layers is encrypted and then handed to the data link layer for

TABLE 6.4 The Open System Interconnection Reference Model

Layer Number	Name	Defined	Common Uses/ Protocols
7	Application	This layer supports end-user applications for things like e-mail, web browsing, file transfer, remote administration, and more.	Common applications: Outlook, Internet Explorer, Telnet
6	Presentation	The presentation layer is responsible for transforming data into a format usable by the application it is providing it to in the application layer.	Common protocols: POP/SMTP, HTTP, FTP, DNS, SNMP, HTTPS
5	Session	The role of the session layer is to initiate, maintain, and end connections between communicating systems.	Common ports: 25, 80, 23, 53, 161
4	Transport	As its name would imply, the transport layer is responsible for the end-to-end communication between systems and manages the flow control of data, while also ensuring successful data transfer.	Common Protocols: TCP, UDP
3	Network	The network layer is the layer that helps us get to all of the different servers we need by performing the necessary routing and switching to get from source system to destination system.	Common Protocols: Internet Protocol (IP) versions 4 and 6
2	Data link	At the data link layer, all of our data gets changed into bits capable of being processed on the wire.	Common protocols: PPP, SLIP
1	Physical	And last but not least, the physical layer is where all of the bits are moved from one location to another over some physical medium.	ADSL, Coaxial Cable, Cat-5, ATM, ISDN

transformation and preparation for delivery. Once the encrypted information reaches its source and the data begins flowing up the OSI stack, information is removed at each layer and passed to the layer above. So as the data gets passed into the network layer, IPSec will decrypt the information and hand it off to the transport layer.

Exam Tip
Though you may not be tested directly about the OSI reference model, you should have a solid understanding of how information flows up and down the stack when sent from source to destination.

Secure Data Transmissions Between Systems to Meet Security Requirements

Earlier, we discussed planning our implantation of IPSec as part of our overall security architecture; however, it is important to understand the significance of IPSec on your network. IPSec adds a considerable amount of overhead to packets transferred between systems. As with anything that you implement for security, every time you gain an advantage in one column, you add a disadvantage to another column. With IPSec, that disadvantage is the added network overhead that causes a drop in communication efficiency.

Once again, this is the reason why we implement a feature like IPSec in locations throughout the network where such implementation has been deemed necessary. Certainly, we could just force IPSec down to every system under our control and be done. But in this "pay me now or pay me later" trade-off with IPSec, you may end up being so secure that your users can't do anything in a timely manner.

Using IPSec to Secure Data Transmissions

It's obvious that using IPSec is a recurring theme in this chapter, but it's only for good reason—IPSec is our easiest and one of the strongest ways to provide security of data.

Exam Tip
For the exam you may be asked to implement IPSec policies. Remember to do only what meets the planned security goals. Never do more than you are asked.

Objective 6.06   Plan Website Security

Pop quiz, you just caught wind of an underground hacker's challenge to deface as many websites as possible; what can you do to ensure you aren't victimized? The real answer depends on how good the hackers are and how mean you have been to them! When it comes to website security, administrators often get caught between a rock and a hard place. The web was originally supposed to be a way to distribute information efficiently to the general public. So security wasn't so much an issue, because the information was free and dispensable. The evolution of the Internet has now driven us to becoming very security conscious, because now that information is very much indispensable. Customer information, including everything from medical information to credit card numbers to financial history, is now stored on servers that are frequently accessed via the public Internet. As a result, we find ourselves walking a fine line between secure information and insecure information.

Authentication

Windows Server 2003 includes the latest version of Microsoft's Internet Information Server (IIS), version 6.0. The product may have taken some time to evolve to where it is today, but a look at the new features confirms Microsoft has certainly put a great deal of effort into increasing the efficiency, security, and manageability of web resources. They have made great strides, particularly in the area of website authentication mechanisms. Table 6.5 summarizes the authentication mechanisms available on Windows Server 2003 web server running IIS version 6.0.

The authentication protocol you opt for is directly related to the level of security you are seeking and how much effort you want to put into it. As with anything else you do on your network, the more security you want, the more administrative effort you will have to put forth. Figure 6.13 shows the possible authentication mechanisms for IIS version 6.0.

Anonymous authentication is your basic zero-security configuration used to allow easy web access to the general public. When you need to add a little security to the site but you cannot control the client types accessing your site, the next step up from anonymous authentication would be basic authentication. Under anonymous authentication, the web server maps your connection to the IUSR_*computername* account that is included in the Guests Windows group by default.

TABLE 6.5 Summary of Authentication Mechanisms Available on a Windows Server 2003 Web Server Running ISS Version 6.0

Authentication Mechanism	Security Rating	Password Encryption	Will Pass Through Proxy Server or Firewall?	Client Prerequisites
Anonymous	None	**	Yes	Will work with any web browser
Basic authentication	Low	Clear text	Yes	Will work with most web browsers
Digest authentication	Medium	Hashed	Yes	IE 5.0 or above
Advanced digest	Medium	Hashed	Yes	IE 5.0 or above
Windows Integrated Authentication	High	Hashed with NTLM. Kerberos TGT used.	No except with PPTP tunnel	IE 2.0 or above for NTLM Windows 2000 and IE 5.0 or above with Kerberos
Certificate authentication	High	**	Yes with Secure Sockets Layer (SSL)	IE or Netscape
.NET Passport authentication	High	Encrypted	Yes with Secure Sockets Layer (SSL)	IE or Netscape

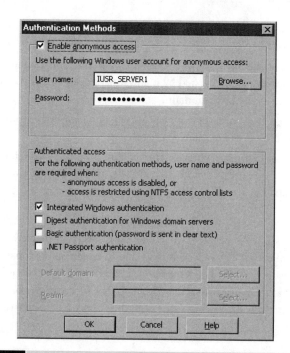

FIGURE 6.13 Web authentication mechanism options on a Windows Server 2003 web server running IIS version 6.0

Basic authentication requires the user to enter a valid username and password (and possibly a domain). The assumed security level for basic authentication is low. The fact that the user is prompted for this information is a bit misleading with regard to the level of security you are providing because the information is sent in clear text over the network and is thus extremely visible to prying eyes. As the administrator, you have the option of specifying a default logon domain so that the user does not have to fill in that information. Obviously, there is some administrative overhead added here because you have to ensure that a valid user account exists for any clients needing access to the site.

As we move up the authentication chain, we hit digest and the new advanced digest authentication. Both mechanisms require a username and password but provide an enhancement over basic authentication by hashing the credentials. The advanced digest authentication adds the feature of storing the user information on the domain controller using an MD5 hashing algorithm. Digest and advanced digest are considered to be of medium security and will allow authentication through a proxy server or firewall. On a web server running IIS 6.0, advanced digest is the preferred authentication mechanism. Advanced digest certainly has its advantages, but you have to be certain that all of the following are in place:

- Clients accessing the website must be using Internet Explorer 5.0 or above.
- The user accessing the web must belong to the same domain as the web server or one trusted by it and must have a valid account in the Active Directory domain.
- Windows Server 2003 must be running on at least one Domain Controller in the domain.
- IIS must be running on a version of Windows Server 2003. If either the web server or the domain controller is not running a version of Windows Server 2003, IIS will default to digest authentication.

As we move into the high levels of web authentication mechanisms, we hit the Windows integrated mechanism, which is largely restricted to providing intranet connectivity to web resources due to its inability to pass through a proxy server or firewall. Unlike with basic authentication, there is no initial prompt for a username and password, as the browser simply passes through your credentials to the web server. The authentication credentials are sent via either NTLM, for the NT4 clients with older browsers, or Kerberos, for the Windows 2000 and later clients using Internet Explorer 5.0 or above.

Certificate authentication is used for clients and servers taking advantage of Secure Sockets Layer (SSL) communication. There is much more to come on SSL in the next few pages.

The .NET Passport authentication is part of Microsoft's new initiative to create a single sign-in environment across the World Wide Web with its varied demands.

SSL Sites

Secure Sockets Layer (SSL) is a security protocol based upon public-key technology (certificates) used heavily by companies wishing to provide confidentiality and integrity of data for user information transmitted over the Web. Utilizing SSL requires a change to the site's URL (uniform resource locator) from HTTP:// to HTTPS://, as well as implementation of certificates and enabling SSL. The level of security is at the discretion of the administrator, with the option for 40-bit SSL encryption or 128-bit SSL encryption, which is stronger and more secure but adds more network overhead.

With a certificate now placed on the web server, a public-key/private-key pair is available for use in encrypting the data. When navigating to a secure site, the following steps take place to ensure data confidentiality:

- The client initiates a connection to the server.
- The server sends the client its public key through its certificate.
- The client verifies the certificate (public key).
- A session key (or encryption key) is created and encrypted using the server's public key.
- Secure communication continues with the new session key, which can be decrypted only using the server's private key.

The process of authenticating the server's public key or certificate involves checking with the list of trusted certificate authorities on the client's machine. As shown in Figure 6-14, clients have default trusts to specific root certification authorities, as listed on the Content tab in the Internet Explorer Tools menu.

The purpose of the default trusted root certification authorities is to avoid users' viewing a warning message regarding the trust level of the website. In the event that you decide a commercial root CA like Verisign is not the road you

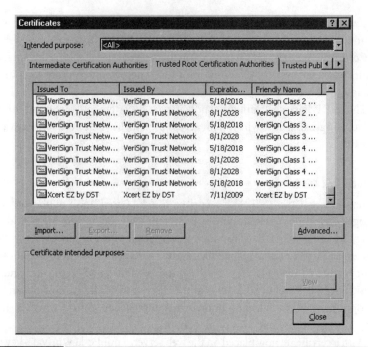

FIGURE 6.14   Systems that run Internet Explorer have predefined trusts to most major commercial root certification authorities.

want to travel, you will need to implement your own certification hierarchy and enable a web server certificate on your server running IIS, as shown in Figures 6.15 and 6.16. Users visiting your website will then experience a warning message regarding the trust level of the certificate applied to the server and must agree to trust your self-issued certification. In actuality, you are saying to your web visitors, "Come on, trust me, I do!" Certainly not something that will fly with the educated consumer. The majority of savvy Internet-goers like the warm and fuzzy feeling that a commercial CA provides for secure sites—especially when it comes to transferring personal information like credit card numbers, addresses, and e-mails. Chapter 7 will go into more detail regarding certificates.

Although the majority of companies and individuals use the web for beneficial purposes, there are those individuals with goals that are, let's say, less than moral or even downright malicious. (We've been a victim to such dishonesty.) To protect against those types of individuals, systems like SSL are put into place so that consumers can feel comfortable using the web for the purpose it was intended.

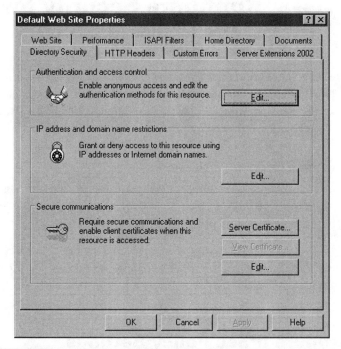

Selecting the Server Certificate option to enable a web server certificate

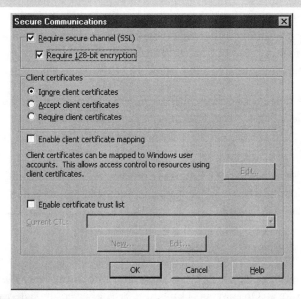

After importing a certificate, you can gain the 128-bit encryption level of SSL by enabling the Require Secure Channel (SSL) and Require 128-bit Encryption check boxes.

Objective 6.07

Configure Security for Data Transmissions

We have discussed in great detail and to great lengths the importance of IPSec for ensuring data integrity and/or encryption. So now we will take you into the task of creating an IPSec policy and how each of the settings in IPSec affects your network security.

Exam Tip

You will certainly need to be comfortable with implementing data transmission security. Keep in mind that placing an IPSec Secure Server Policy at the domain level that requires all systems to use secure communications is certainly a fail-proof way of securing data; however, it is often overkill. Be clear on the differences between needing security all the time (IPSec Secure Server Policy) versus wanting security only when available (IPSec Server Policy).

Configure IPSec Policy Settings

Okay, we have had enough with this planning business already. You have decided you want IPSec and now you have to implement it. IPSec can be configured in several ways and at several different levels with a choice of hashing and encryption algorithms. Which one is right for you is dependent on what traffic you want to secure and how secure you want it to be.

IPSec can be configured and enabled using any of the following tools:

- **Active Directory Users and Computers** Allows configuration of IPSec policies at the domain or Organizational Unit level
- **Active Directory Sites and Services** Allows configuration of IPSec policies at the site level
- **IP Security Policies on Active Directory** Allows configuration of IPSec policies for the local system or domain, or for another system or another domain
- **Local Security Policy** Allows configuration of IPSec policies for the local system only

We are going to step through the process of the IP Security Policy Wizard to create a policy for an Organizational Unit called Secure Servers through Active Directory Users and Computers Group Policy snap-in. At each step the settings that will play the biggest roles on your security implementation are defined. Figure 6.17

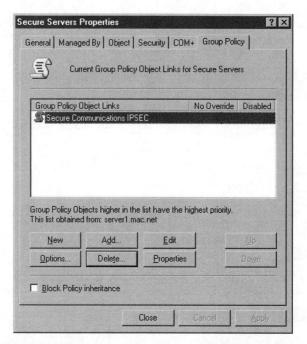

FIGURE 6.17   The Group Policy tab of the properties of the Secure Servers OU

shows the Group Policy tab on the Properties of the Organizational Unit named Secure Servers. Here we are giving a name to the new Group Policy in which we will create our IPSec policy.

As we start the IP Security Policy Wizard, we will be asked for a name and description of the policy as shown in Figure 6.18. For troubleshooting reasons, you should give your policies names that give meaning to the underlying policy. For example, here we have called it Custom IPSec Security as opposed to calling it IPSecPOL14B7364SLR09171973.

In the next window of the wizard, Figure 6.19, we will opt not to keep the default response rule so that we may create our own.

At the end of the wizard, we left the box checked to edit the properties of the policy so that we may further configure our own rules and filters. Choosing to add a new rule on the Rules tab of the policy properties jump-starts another wizard, called the Create IP Security Rule Wizard. The first step in the wizard, Figure 6.20, is to establish the tunnel end point. If the policy should apply only to communication with one specific machine, the appropriate selection is the second option, which allows you to specify the IP address of that machine. This

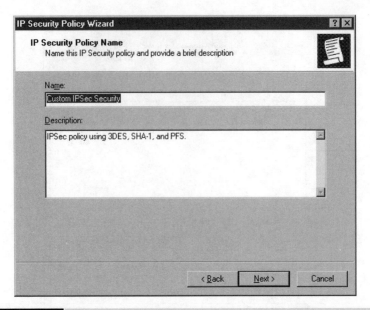

FIGURE 6.18   Naming and describing your IPSec policy with something useful will prove invaluable come time to troubleshoot.

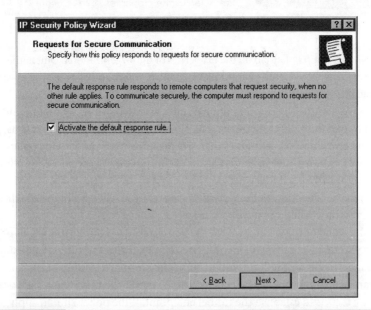

FIGURE 6.19   There is always an option to keep the default response rule for IPSec or create your own custom rules.

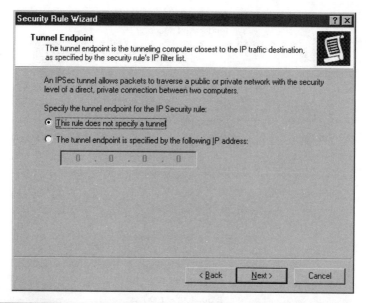

FIGURE 6.20 An IPSec policy can limit the use of IPSec directed to only one specific machine, called Tunnel mode.

is called IPSec tunnel mode and is considered to be point-to-point encryption. If you choose not to specify a tunnel forcing IPSec to all systems that fall under the scope of management of this IPSec policy, then you will not need to specify an IP address. This is referred to as IPSec transport mode and is considered to be end-to-end encryption. Figure 6.21 shows the encryption differences between tunnel mode and transport mode. As it shows, IPSec transport mode ensures end-to-end encryption, where the client sending the data encrypts the information and the client receiving the information performs the decryption. IPSec tunnel mode uses point-to-point encryption, where systems, or routers, in between the source and destination perform the encryption and decryption process.

Exam Tip

IPSec tunnel mode is more favorable in situations where administrators are not so concerned with encryption of data on the internal networks but require the data to be secure when traversing WAN links made up of commercial lines.

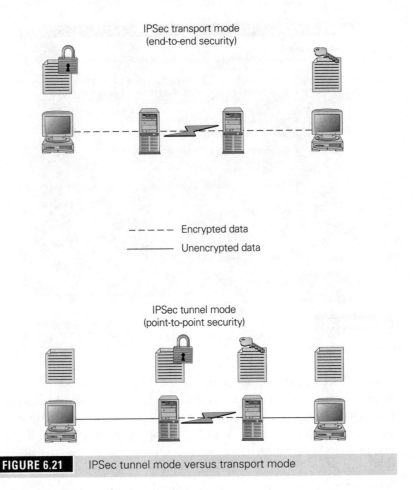

FIGURE 6.21 IPSec tunnel mode versus transport mode

The next step in the wizard is to specify which communications should use the policy. The selections include All Network Connections, Local Area Network (LAN), and Remote Access. We are going to leave the default of All Network Connections, as shown in Figure 6.22.

Now it comes time to specify the IP filter lists, as shown in Figure 6.23. Here we can choose to which particular types of IP traffic this rule applies. We also have the option to create our own using the IP Filter List Wizard. Here we will leave the default selection for all IP traffic to ensure that no traffic will go unencrypted.

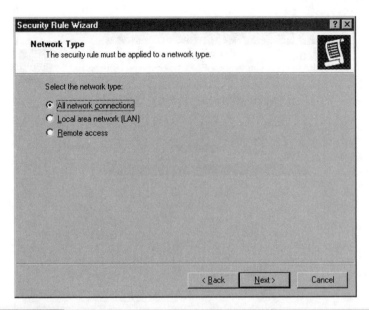

FIGURE 6.22 The wizard enables you to select different types of traffic to utilize the IPSec policy.

After defining the types of traffic to be included, we have to choose the filter action (Figure 6.24) to apply to the traffic that meets the conditions of our filter lists. We are going to use the Add Filter Action Wizard to create our own filter action.

In the IP Filter Action Wizard, we will name and describe a new IP filter action, as shown in Figure 6.25.

Since we are trying to implement security on our Secure Servers OU, our filter action should allow the clients to negotiate security (as in Figure 6.26), as opposed to blocking or permitting traffic.

The wizard now asks how the system should react to clients requesting information when those clients do not support IPSec (see Figure 6.27). Good ol' down-level Windows 98 and Windows NT throw a wrench in our security plans (hence the Microsoft recommendation of upgrading all your client systems to at least Windows 2000). The options here include responding to the requests using unsecured methods or to simply deny communication with the legacy client systems.

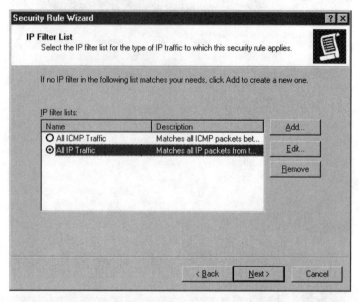

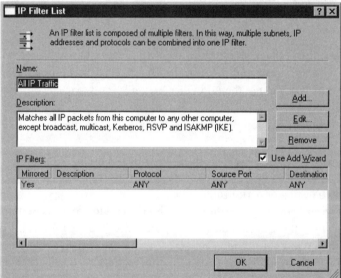

FIGURE 6.23 IP filter lists are used to specify which types of IP traffic are subject to the IPSec filter actions.

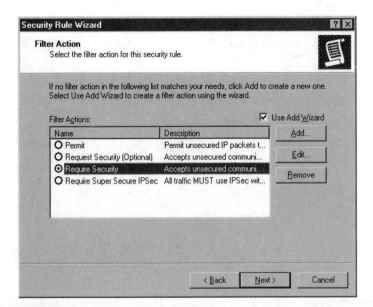

FIGURE 6.24 IP filter actions detail the level of security for the traffic that meets the criteria of the IP filter lists.

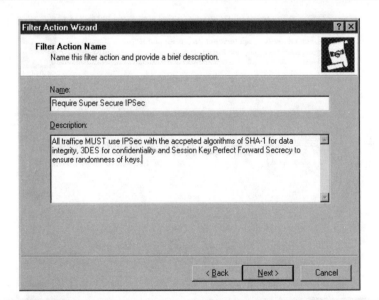

FIGURE 6.25 New filter actions can be created when the default actions and settings of Client (Respond), Server (Request), and Secure Server (Require) do not meet your needs.

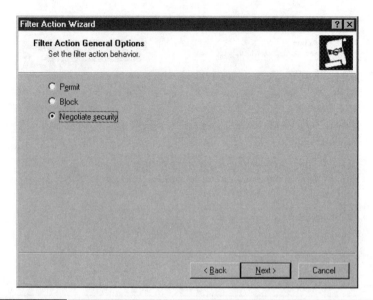

FIGURE 6.26 IPSec policies give you the opportunity to permit, block, or negotiate security for traffic.

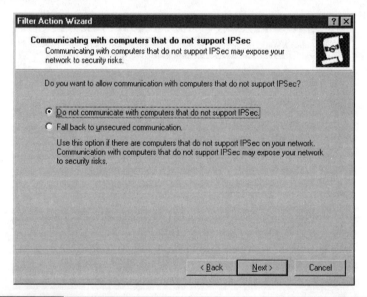

FIGURE 6.27 Leaving the default here effectively cuts off all unsecured communications.

Now we finally get into the nitty-gritty of the algorithm options to use in our new policy. Figure 6.28 shows the custom selection on the IP Traffic Security page of the Filter Action Wizard as well as the detailed view of the algorithm selections. Here we have chosen the 160-bit SHA1 algorithm over MD5 to maintain the integrity of the data. This algorithm will be used to ensure that the data sent between systems does not get changed along the way. For our data confidentiality, we have chosen 3DES, which uses three 56-bit keys to encrypt the data three times. The other choice is DES. You can see here that you also have the option to alter the key lifetimes by forcing a new key to be generated when a given amount of traffic is sent or when systems have remained in communication for a given length of time.

Going back to the original analogy about security regarding childhood club days, we can think of IPSec policies as the final rules for securing our club. If we relate this to the encryption and integrity algorithms and Perfect Forward Secrecy (PFS) configured in IPSec, it would be like having to create a secret language, for a secret language, for a secret language (3DES) in order to talk to other members of the club, and at the same time we would need to have a 160-word phrase based on the original message that summarizes our message to

FIGURE 6.28	By customizing the implementation of the hashing and encryption algorithms, you can make IPSec as secure as you wish.

ensure the message wasn't changed (SHA1), and on top of all that, we couldn't reuse the same secret language for future communications.

Travel Advisory

Choosing to use the algorithms with greater key lengths, SHA1 and 3DES, incurs additional overhead on IPSec, as it takes longer to prepare the data to ensure the integrity and confidentiality.

After finalizing the Filter Action Wizard, looking at the properties of the Filter Action, we note an important check box that relates to the creation of session keys between systems using this IPSec policy. By checking the box Use Session Key Perfect Forward Secrecy (PFS), you are configuring IPSec to prevent the reuse of a session key between systems. Enabling this box, as shown in Figure 6.29, enhances the security of your IPSec policy, however it also detriments your transfer efficiency.

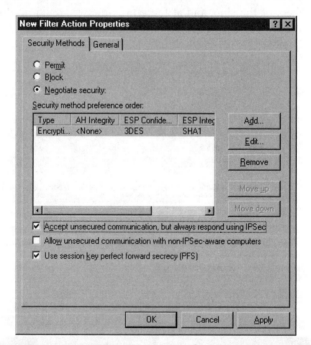

FIGURE 6.29   Use of SHA1, 3DES, and Session Key Perfect Forward Secrecy (PFS) creates a highly secure environment at the expense of efficient network communication.

You can see that configuring your IPSec policies is no small task. Proper implementation requires planning, evaluating, implementing, and reevaluating on a regular basis, or else all your hard work could be wasted.

Objective 6.08 Troubleshoot Security for Data Transmissions

In a perfect world, there would be no need for troubleshooting because everything would work exactly as we planned from start to finish. Then we wake up. Then we realize troubleshooting will always be an issue that we will have to contend with. To put icing on the cake, the troubleshooting problem gets exponentially more tedious as we add more and more functionality to the products and services we implement on our network. To stick with the theme of the chapter, we are just going to focus here on troubleshooting data transmission security, in particular IPSec.

Tools

IPSec has several tools available for creating, managing, and monitoring IPSec policies, each with its own advantages and purposes. These tools include

- Active Directory Users and Computers (ADUC) group policy editor
- Group Policy snap-in
- IPSec Policy management console
- Event Viewer
- Resultant Set of Policies (RSOP)
- IPSec Monitor

While you may not use all these tools all the time (as you may not be frequently creating policies), you will find that you often use RSOP and the IPSec Monitor to monitor and maintain the policies you have created.

IP Security Monitor MMC Snap-in

The Microsoft Management Console (MMC) named IPSec Monitor is a tool intended for administrators who need to monitor or troubleshoot their IPSec implementation. As shown in Figure 6.30, you can see the active IPSec policy applied locally to the machine or to the domain or Organizational Unit (OU)

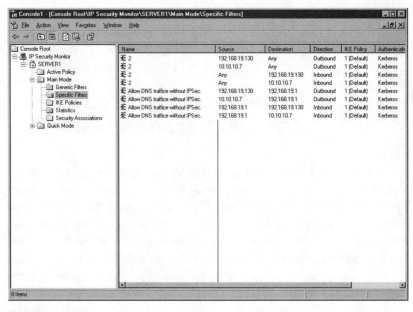

FIGURE 6.30   The IPSec Monitor MMC snap-in shows the active IPSec policy for a given machine.

that the system belongs to. This utility also gives you information regarding the statistics of IPSec use with respect to that machine. Figure 6.31 shows a listing of all the statistical information you can review on the statistics node under the server being monitored.

A definite plus for administrators who despise leaving their desks to perform tasks on systems in different locations is the ability to use IPSecmon to monitor remote systems. The catch here is that when remotely monitoring, you can monitor only systems running the same flavor of Windows operating system. So if your network is made up of a mixture of Windows 2000, Windows XP, and Windows Server 2003 systems, you will need to monitor the Windows 2000 clients separately from the newer versions of Windows. Hey, that is what remote desktop administration is for! It's great when a plan comes together.

Resultant Set of Policy (RSOP) MMC Snap-in

For an administrator of a Windows 2003 domain, perhaps one of the most common headaches is troubleshooting group policies. Policies can be set at the local system, site, domain, or Organizational Unit level, thereby complicating the

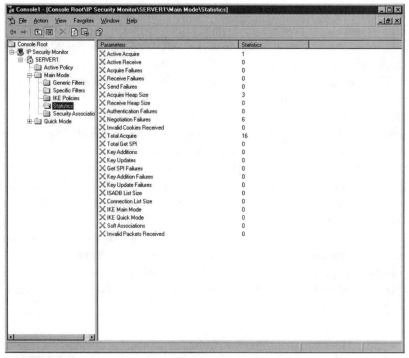

FIGURE 6.31 The IPSec Monitor MMC can provide statistical information regarding active connections, failed connections, and more.

troubleshooting process. Add to this the block policy inheritance and no override options, and troubleshooting becomes even more problematical. Toss in the administrator's ability to apply security filters to groups, users, and computers, and now troubleshooting can get downright nasty. All of these potential settings and options create a complex web of conflicts among policies placed at the various object levels.

Inevitably, the first step in troubleshooting the group policy process for a given security principal (user or computer) is to identify the effective policies for that principal. Enter the Resultant Set of Policy (RSoP) management console. The RSoP is an MMC snap-in that allows administrators to easily query an object to determine what group policies are being processed by that object. Through the RSoP, the policy precedence can easily be concluded. RSoP returns a result that outlines all the effects of policies, including settings like Software Installation, Folder Redirection, Administrative Templates, Scripts, and of course IPSec. When a computer boots up or a user logs on, each will authenticate and retrieve all of the information regarding group policy that comes from the local policy, site policy, domain policy, or OU policy stored in the Common Information Management Object Model (CIMOM). It is the CIMOM database that provides the RSoP query with resulting data.

The RSoP can be accessed by running rsop.msc or by adding the snap-in to a new or existing management console. When stepping through the RSoP, you are given the option to run in one of two modes—logging or planning—as seen in Figure 6.32. The logging mode polls through the existing policies on a machine and returns the current effective settings. The planning mode can be extremely useful for administrators looking to implement new policies, as it will simulate a results set for a security principal as a "what if" scenario. The planning mode effectively allows you to determine if new policies are going to adversely affect current settings or if they will achieve your desired goal.

As an administrator, you will most likely find yourself using the RSoP on many occasions. As Figure 6.33 shows, the RSoP will show the policies affecting a user or computer by showing the name of the policy setting, the effective setting (enabled or disabled), and the name of the Group Policy Object propagating the setting, the user, or the computer.

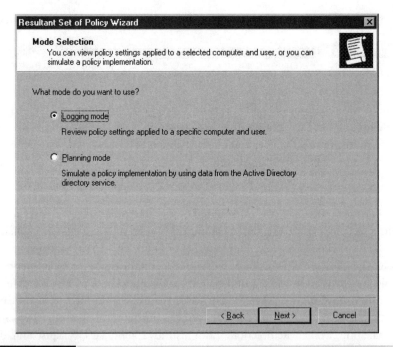

| FIGURE 6.32 | The Resultant Set of Policy (RSoP) snap-in has a logging mode for looking at existing settings and a planning mode for looking at "what if" scenarios. |

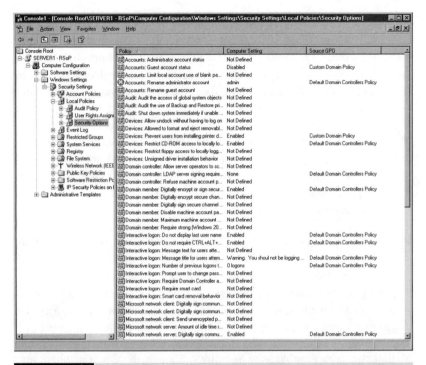

The RSoP snap-in helps administrators determine what the effective policy settings are and where they originate.

CHECKPOINT

✔**Objective 6.01: Plan for Network Protocol Security**   Planning your network protocol security is a time-critical process that exacts an administrator's due diligence to provide sufficient network documentation. Even after implementation, the process itself is dynamic and requires constant reevaluation, design, testing, and implementation.

✔**Objective 6.02: Plan Secure Network Administration Methods**   Terminal services might be going through a naming crisis, now being called Remote Desktop Administration, but it is still a fantastic utility for remote administration. As today's networks become more and more geographically dispersed, remote administration will become a daily ritual and a much relied-upon service.

✔**Objective 6.03: Configure Network Protocol Security**   Security. Security. Security. IPSec. IPSec. IPSec. There is obviously a strong push toward putting this industry-standard protocol in the forefront of network protocol security. With the ability to push IPSec to one, some, or all of your systems through Group Policy, obtaining data integrity and encryption for your network has never been easier.

✔**Objective 6.04: Plan Wireless Network Security**   If you plan on joining the wireless wave, just be sure you plan on developing a secure wireless wave. Along with the great growth in wireless technology comes the growth of new hacking methods. The common and simple practice of war driving could leave you vulnerable to unwanted visitors.

✔**Objective 6.05: Plan Security for Data Transmissions**   The war of administrators versus unauthorized users seems never ending. As security measures become more sophisticated, so do the hacking tools. The smarter the administrators get, the smarter the hackers get. Given this ongoing and seemingly never-ending battle, it is crucial to your environment that your security plan constantly evolve to meet the specifications of the corporate security policy.

✔**Objective 6.06: Plan Website Security**   Though the dot com phase may have crashed, there is no doubt that the Internet is still a crucial communication medium. And though it may not be doing so as rapidly as it did three or four years ago, Internet technology continues to evolve. For administrators of networks that function with and require access to both intranets and internets, website security is a must. From the insecure anonymous setting to the highly secure certificate-based authentication, every web presence warrants a look at security.

✔**Objective 6.07: Configure Security for Data Transmissions**   Hello, my name is IPSec. I am your friendly network neighborhood data security protocol. Your entire network may not require the additional overhead of IPSec, but you may want to secure those files on the servers in the research department. IPSec enables you to get as secure as you wish. Data encryption options of DES or 3DES and integrity algorithm choices of MD5 or SHA1 give administrators plenty of flexibility in their implementation of data transmission security.

✔**Objective 6.08: Troubleshoot Security for Data Transmissions**   Inevitably, you will encounter problems. But that's a good thing. Maybe? If things worked all the time, then we'd be out of jobs. When it comes time to diagnose data transmission problems, you have a handful of tools at your disposal.

REVIEW QUESTIONS

1. The Research department in your company has stumbled upon a new liquid compound that allows genetically altered hairless mice to regrow hair with a single drop of the liquid. As the IT manager, you are tasked with making sure that all the information regarding this finding, which is stored on a server named ResFS1, is always accessed using secure communication and is never accessed by unauthorized systems outside of the Research department. All systems that need access to the information are managed within an Organizational Unit named Research. Which of the following steps should you take? Choose three.

   A. Configure a local security policy on ResFS1 to have IPSec Secure Server enabled.

   B. Create a new Group Policy Object named SecureComm at the domain object in Active Directory Users and Computers.

   C. Create a new Group Policy Object named SecureComm at the Research OU in Active Directory Users and Computers.

   D. Configure the SecureComm Group Policy Object with the IPSec Secure Server policy.

   E. Configure the SecureComm Group Policy Object with the IPSec Server policy.

   F. Configure the SecureComm Group Policy Object with the IPSec Client policy.

2. You have set up an internal web server, using Windows Integrated Authentication, to easily deliver company information to all employees. All the employees are notified via e-mail about the new site. Within the first few minutes of sending the e-mail, you get a call from the Macintosh-using Graphic Design department about not being able to hit the website. Adding additional services to the network is not permitted. What should you do? Choose one.

   A. Convert your web server to Windows Server 2003 and use Advanced Digest Authentication.

   B. Use certificate-based authentication for the Macintosh client systems.

   C. Enable the Digest Authentication option on the properties of the website.

   D. Create accounts with access to the site for the Macintosh users and enable the Basic Authentication option on the properties of the website.

3. After reading a recent article regarding network security, you are suspicious about your own internal users running packet-sniffing utilities and viewing information that they shouldn't be using. What can you do to ensure the highest level of confidentiality for data transmissions on your network? Choose one.

   A. Implement an IPSec policy that uses the 56-bit DES algorithm for data encryption.

   B. Implement an IPSec policy that uses the 3DES algorithm for data encryption.

   C. Implement an IPSec policy that uses the 160-bit SHA-1 algorithm for data encryption.

   D. Install a web server certificate on all servers with confidential information and require 128-bit SSL communication.

4. You are hired as a network security consultant for a company that manufactures transistors for microprocessors. The company has ten offices spread across the United States that communicate securely via directly connected wide area network (WAN) links. Each office has a Windows Server 2003 system running the Routing and Remote Access service and has been configured to use IPSec. The chief information officer has brought you in because on several occasions their IPSec policy has been compromised and information has leaked into a competitor's hands. What can you do to help prevent this from happening again? Choose one.

   A. Edit the IPSec authentication method to use Kerberos v5.

   B. Edit the IPSec authentication method to use certificates and import a certificate on each Windows 2003 Server connected to the WAN links.

   C. Edit the IPSec authentication method to use a preshared key and input the identical string on each Windows 2003 Server connected to the WAN links.

   D. Configure the servers to use IPSec tunnel mode.

5. You are the network administrator for a traditional software company that has decided to begin selling its products via the Internet. You are worried about users' reluctance to enter personal information to be sent to your server. What can you do to ensure that all personal information sent from a user is not passed to the web server in clear text? Choose one.

A. Import a web server certificate from a commercial certificate authority and enable 128-bit Secure Sockets Layer (SSL) communication.

B. Configure the server to use Digest Authentication.

C. Enable the IPSec Secure Server policy in the local policy of the web server.

D. Configure a certificate-based L2TP VPN connection from the client to the server.

6. Your Windows Server 2003 network has about 50 users that frequently connect to and disconnect from the network. Often they are in different areas of the network and can't find an open RJ-45 Ethernet port to plug into. You are looking into the possibility of using several wireless access point (WAP) devices to create a wireless local area network (WLAN) named TrueMobile for these highly mobile users. You are concerned, however, about the possibility of a security breach by malicious users. What can you do to help prevent unauthorized users from getting to your WLAN? Choose one.

A. Create a Group Policy Object at the domain object that prevents all systems in your domain from connecting to any WLAN other than TrueMobile.

B. Implement the wireless access points and place them all on their own IP subnet.

C. Configure the wireless access point (WAP) devices to disable the broadcasting of their secure session ID (SSID).

D. Configure the wireless access point devices to disable Wired Equivalent Privacy (WEP).

7. One of the web servers in your Windows Server 2003 network has been configured to allow traffic only through the standard HTTP port of 80. The box normally runs fine, but every once in a while, the wwwservice stops and your website goes down. You are annoyed with having to get up at three o'clock in the morning to go restart the service. What should you do? Choose one.

A. Configure the wwwservice to start automatically if it stops.

B. Use Task Scheduler to create a job that restarts the wwwservice every eight hours.

C. Open port 3389 and configure the web server to allow remote desktop administration and start the service from home when it stops.

    D. Open port 443 and create a special administrator website that uses SSL and a certificate from your own enterprise certificate authority.

8. Which of the following provide the highest level of security for IP Security policies needing data integrity and data authentication? Choose two.

    A. DES

    B. 3DES

    C. MD5

    D. SHA1

REVIEW ANSWERS

1. **A** **C** **F**   When implementing IPSec, you should never apply more security than you need, as doing so causes degradation in network efficiency. The question only requires IPSec for traffic against one machine from one particular department. So a local policy on the machine requiring IPSec and a Group Policy on the OU for the clients set to IPSec Respond will provide exactly what is needed.

2. **D**   The Macintosh clients are unable to authenticate using an authentication mechanism that is looking for a Windows login. In order to allow them to authenticate with the easiest administrative effort yet still require authentication with username and password, you should enable Basic Authentication.

3. **B**   3DES is the strongest encryption algorithm for IPSec confidentiality.

4. **B**   Certificate-based authentication is the strongest form of authentication for two systems authenticating one another for the purposes of IPSec communication.

5. **A**   SSL requires importing a certificate. To ensure that the users do not get a warning message about trusting the certificate, you should use a certificate from one of the predefined commercial certificate authorities.

6. **C**   Disabling the SSID on a WAP helps prevent unauthorized users by not making the WLAN readily available. This is not considered strong security, however, because unauthorized users could still connect if they found out the SSID through other methods.

7. **C**   Remote desktop administration, aka Terminal Services, requires the use of port 3389. Since the issue here is simply the service stopping and does not require you to physically stand in front of the box, this is a problem that can easily be resolved using remote administration.

8. **B** **D**   The highest levels of data confidentiality and integrity are achieved with 3DES, which uses three 56-bit keys to encrypt data, and SHA1, which uses a 160-bit algorithm to create the message hash.

Security and Performance

Planning Network Security Infrastructure

	NEWBIE	SOME EXPERIENCE	EXPERT
ETA	6+ hours	3+ hours	1 hour

Perhaps you have just finished reading the title of Chapter 7, then looked back at the title of Chapter 6, compared the two, then pondered what's the difference? Yes, Chapter 6 did focus on security; however, our focus was primarily on network security as it relates to protocol security and communication between systems. This chapter will focus more on the overall security of the network, including the implementation of a public key infrastructure using certificate services.

Objective 7.01 Network Security

IPSec, SSL, and remote administration may be an important part of your network security; however, they are only a portion of the due diligence required by the network administrator to ensure proper data security and a network environment. Network security extends beyond these features to include things like authentication, remote access, folder permissions, certificates, physical environment, and end-user education.

Objective 7.02 Plan a Framework for Security

Networks are not built by sitting down in front of a group of PCs and installing software. Or that would be better put, *good* networks are not built by sitting down in front of a group of PCs and installing software. Good networks are built through proper planning and documentation. Before any physical network infrastructure is implemented, a network diagram should always be laid out. This diagram should include the various subnets, servers, workstations, routers, and switches to be placed throughout the environment. This diagram should be part of what is referred to as your *network plan*. The network plan will be your guide for establishing the network design, deployment, and evaluation. In most cases, this plan will be developed by a team of engineers working together to provide a solid foundation for a network that is scalable, efficient, and manageable. The network plan will also include information regarding your documentation procedures, security planning, capacity planning, and deployment planning.

As suggested in Chapter 6, documentation will play a crucial role in the event that something goes wrong during the implementation phase and you must roll back to a functioning production environment within a limited amount of time. This documentation builds effective communication between team members so that everyone on the team can identify and understand how changes somewhere in the network will cascade through the remainder of the network and potentially cause problems. This process also affords you the opportunity to make note of the person or persons responsible for specific segments or services available on the network.

The security portion of the network plan should focus on how you will provide access to files, folders, printers, services, and other resources that users need to perform their daily duties. It should also include how to prevent unauthorized access as well as how to react to security breaches such as improper data updates and deletions, loss of data due to hardware failure, and lack of authorized access to an authorized user.

After the network planning phase is complete, your team can move into the development phase. In this phase, you will build an infrastructure as agreed upon in the network planning phase. This new infrastructure will remain a test environment until you are certain it will withstand the strains of being implemented as a production environment. Your test environment should mirror your existing or envisioned production environment and should in no way be a part of the actual production network. This will be a good time and place to try new technologies or implement new hardware or software solutions.

Travel Advisory

When creating development or test environments, you should keep them separate from the production environment. This should be done by implementing separate physical networks that do not communicate with each other. You may even go so far as to separate them with a firewall.

One of the more valuable pieces of information that comes from the deployment of a testing environment results from what is called capacity planning. Capacity planning is the method of ensuring that your systems will handle the workload of the production environment. For example, will your domain controller handle the morning login requests, will your file servers handle sufficient amounts of data in a manner that is acceptable to the user, and will your remote access servers handle the number of dial-up users in your network?

The development phase is not just about capacity planning but should also include the planning and testing of your backup and restore procedures. Before moving to a production environment, you should always be sure that your roll-back plan will function when you need it to. The last place and time you want to find out that your rollback plan does not work is when you really need to use it. Otherwise, your next step may be to visit www.monster.com.

When capacity planning, security testing, rollback testing, and new hardware/software tests are finished and the test environment has been sent through the ringer, you will then be faced with creating a deployment plan.

The deployment plan will guide you through the transition of converting the test environment into the production environment. The strategy you use will be dependent upon the amount of risk you are willing to undertake during the process. Your team may be risk-averse, and so you may plan your deployment in small steps as opposed to a more aggressive and quicker deployment plan. The deployment plan will also be affected by network operations. If you have an environment that sees substantial use 24 hours a day seven days a week, you may be limited in the amount of downtime that you can suffer. This type of environment would require a slower, more gradual deployment; perhaps starting out with a limited subset of more advanced end users who could provide valuable feedback about the new network environment. In the event that your network is not heavily used and experiences periods of little or no use, your deployment plan can take advantage of these times to move your development environment into production much faster.

Plan a Change and Configuration Management Framework

Once you have successfully completed the move from development and testing to production, your work has only just begun. Now it is time to manage and maintain the production environment so that it continues to run securely and efficiently. The common day-to-day tasks and the intermittent updates you perform should all follow a predefined set of guidelines for implementing and distributing the changes. This process, commonly referred to as the Change and Configuration Management Framework, will utilize things like Active Directory, Group Policy, and the Distributed File System (DFS). Or you may step to one of the heavy-hitting products like Systems Management Server (SMS) or a similar third-party product.

Your daily network management will lead to periodic reevaluation of the infrastructure, which in turn could lead to further planning, development, testing, and implementing; such will be your network life cycle. Without this evolution of the network, your business productivity is sure to remain stagnant or perhaps even degrade. If you compare the work habits and duties from even ten years ago, it is easy to see how much change has occurred from the standpoint of worker accountability. Businesses are dependent on every employee now more than ever due to the widespread acceptance of the separation of services and the technologies that allow collaboration across large geographic distances. For example, companies rely on employees for very specific job functions forcing the accountability for network operation to be shared. This prevents any one individual from being the sole administrator and prevents a single point of network administration failure.

Plan for Security Monitoring

How will you know when your network is secure? How will you know if all your planning and testing efforts have actually mitigated the threats you suspected they would? Truth is, you won't know. Not unless you implement a consistent methodology for monitoring your network security. There are many third-party intrusion detection systems that can provide some exponential number of reports, but some of your best and easiest tools come straight from within the Microsoft Server 2003 product suite. This means your everyday tools: IPSec monitor, the Event Viewer, RSoP (see Chapter 6), the network monitor, and the Microsoft Baseline Security Analyzer. We will discuss the last-named of these tools toward the end of this chapter. However you approach monitoring, just by default, you have a highly functional security monitoring tool set provided to you.

Once you find the right tools, the monitoring process should be planned and documented. You're probably ready for us to get off your back about documenting and planning, but it's a concept that is easily overlooked and severely underrated. We can tell you that walking into an undocumented network as a consultant sometimes makes you not want to accept the contract. We can't tell you how many networks and servers we have run across with all kinds of ad hoc installations done without documenting why things have been done. If you can't provide a baseline analysis with a regularly recorded performance chart, how can you make an informed or even half-way educated decision about how to approach a problem?

Suppose someone calls you and says, "We need you to help us, our systems have been hacked." Your immediate response would most likely be "What happened?" If the other person came back and said "I don't know, it just stopped working like it used to," how would you begin to solve the problem? On the other hand, with proper security monitoring, if that same person were able to present something like audit logs or Performance Monitor data, you could take a much more efficient approach to the problem.

The moral of my story, then, is twofold: 1) monitor often and 2) document everything. Inevitably, every administrator learns these lessons. Unfortunately, some learn them the hard way.

We don't mean to scare you into monitoring and documenting, although in fact the task is getting increasingly easier with products like Microsoft Visio for planning and documentation and Microsoft Internet Security and Acceleration Server to monitor security around the perimeter of your network. In fact, you need look no further than the Windows Server 2003 or Windows XP product. These products now offer a built-in Internet Connection Firewall and logging feature that can be enabled on any LAN interface or modem connection.

Objective 7.03

Plan a Public Key Infrastructure (PKI) Using Certificate Services

"Ladies and gentleman, I proudly introduce to you, the new and improved Microsoft Certificate Services! The Windows Server 2003 product family includes brand new features never seen before in a Microsoft Certificate implementation. Hurry in now to pick yours up or simply install it yourself."

Alright, alright. So maybe it doesn't warrant a formal announcement of this sort, but there are certainly some new features and improvements to the Microsoft PKI. These new features include

- A new Certificate Template management console snap-in that enables editing of certificate templates.
- Autoenrollment and autorenewal for computers *and* users. Whereas Windows 2000 certificate services allowed only computers to autoenroll, now users can do so.
- Ability to publish Certificate Revocation List (CRL) deltas (changes). Not having to publish the entire list of revocations at every publication interval allows you to maintain a more current CRL.
- Auditing of the activities occurring on a certificate authority.
- Archiving and recovery of keys by using a recovery agent certificate.

- Qualified subordination, which gives you administrative control over the namespaces a CA can issue certificates to and what type of certificates they can issue.
- The Certutil.exe utility for managing certificates from a command prompt.

There is very little question that when it comes time to stepping up the security of your network infrastructure, you turn to certificates as the answer. Of course, as with everything else we have discussed regarding security, there is an inverse relationship between efficiency and overhead. The more security you add to the network, the less efficient the network becomes. Certificate Services can be installed through the Add New Windows Components on the Add/Remove Programs node in Control Panel.

Travel Advisory

Microsoft Certificate Services is heavily grounded in the machine name and its domain when installed. For this reason, you will see a warning message when you choose to install, stating that you will not be able to join or disjoin from a domain or change the name of the machine. Be certain that the system you are installing the service on is configured exactly the way you want it to be and will not require modifications. The only way to make changes is to uninstall Certificate Services.

Certificates can be issued to users, computers, or even services running on your network and are often used for things like these:

- **User authentication** Ensuring user identity for resource access
- **Web server authentication (SSL)** Used for secure processing of online transactions that include personal information
- **Secure e-mail (SMIME)** Offering digital signature for nonrepudiation, and encryption for confidentiality
- **IPSec** Computer authentication for secure communication
- **Code signing** To ensure customers that the downloadable code is valid
- **Encrypted File System (EFS)** For encryption and recovery of files
- **Smart cards** Higher security authentication by requiring the user to have a smart card device for authentication

The implementation of certificates brings a high level of security but an exponentially greater amount of administrative overhead. The concept of certificates and their use for authentication relies heavily on the idea of trust. When a user authenticates themselves to a server by providing a certificate, that certificate holds meaning only if the server has an established trust with the entity that issued the certificate, or what is called the certificate authority (CA).

When a system trusts a particular CA, it is transferring, to that CA, the burden of proof about the identity of a user. If you revisit the Chapter 6 example of Secure Sockets Layer communication for web services, you'll get the idea. When you connect to a website that has been issued a certificate by a major commercial vendor that you trust, you are not directly trusting the website; rather, you are trusting that the commercial vendor has verified the identification of the website owners and issued a certificate for that reason. If you ever want to see just how much goes into this, visit the website for a commercial CA, like Verisign, and pick yourself up an e-mail certificate or something of the like. You'll experience first hand just how badly they want to ensure that you are you. On the other side of the coin, you are trusting that the CA also knows who not to give out certificates to, so you know not to trust them.

Let's look at an example that may hit a little closer to home. Imagine that today you just bought a brand-new car. Imagine now that your boss is the best thing since sliced bread and you *trust* him very much. (This is just pretending, remember!) So you are standing in the parking lot showing your new car to your friends and one of them asks to drive it. You quickly respond with a "NO" and a surprised look on your face, thinking what audacity this person has. Then up walks a complete stranger that you don't know, who says, "Your boss gave me this special card that says I can drive your car." You hand the stranger your keys and off they roar. "Why do they get to drive it but I don't?" your friend asks. "Because I trust my boss and my boss said it was okay to let them drive."

In this example, you don't have a direct trust relationship with the stranger/potential carjacker, but you do trust your boss and therefore authorize the service. In this analogy, the carjacker presented you a certificate issued to them by someone you trusted. Your boss, in this sense, was listed among the Trusted Root Certification Authorities, but your friend wasn't.

This list, the Trusted Root Certification Authorities, forms the basis for trust in a particular CA, which is stored in what is called the certificate store. Planning a public key infrastructure (PKI) can be an overwhelming task, as you have really four types of CAs to choose from:

- Stand-alone root CAs
- Enterprise root CAs

- Stand-alone subordinate CAs
- Enterprise subordinate CAs

Even within those types, the subordinate CAs can be further delineated as subordinate intermediate CAs or subordinate issuing CAs.

Certificates are made up of various attributes, which include a public key, an expiration date, a usage purpose, and more. The most popular form of certificates you will find follow the X.509v3 standard.

Stay tuned for the next session to see which CA goes where and why. When do we use which one? Find out in the next section.

Identify the Appropriate Type of Certificate Authority

As noted at the end of the preceding section, there are four types of certificate authorities that can be implemented. Figure 7.1 shows the Certificate Services installation wizard offering each of the four options. Which of these you implement will depend upon your needs, but no matter which you choose, you will always find it easier and more manageable to implement a certificate authority hierarchy. By this, we mean you will implement multiple tiers of CAs, each designated to provide a specific function in the hierarchy. The CA hierarchy will undoubtedly start with a root CA and trickle down to lower-level subordinate CAs.

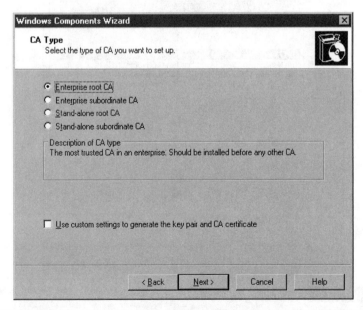

FIGURE 7.1   Microsoft's Certificate Services Installation wizard offers you four choices for installation.

The critical distinction between the stand-alone CA and the enterprise CA lies in how the certificate information is stored, how certificate requests are processed, and how the Certificate Revocation List (CRL) is published. The stand-alone CA requires much more administrative overhead, as it requires all certificate requests to be approved or disapproved manually by an administrator. The enterprise CA utilizes information from Active Directory to automatically process a pending certificate request.

When it comes time to publish information about revoked certificates, the stand-alone CA requires it be manually published to a shared folder called the CRL Distribution Point (CDP), located by default in the C:\WINDOWS\system32\CertSrv\CertEnroll directory. The enterprise CA automatically publishes the CRL to Active Directory as well as to CDP, as seen in Figure 7.2. The clients can then access this information in multiple ways to make certain they are not authorizing a certificate that is no longer valid. The differences between the enterprise CA and the stand-alone CA are reason enough to perform careful planning before implementation, as you can see in Table 7.1.

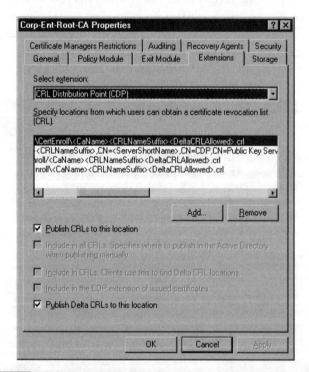

FIGURE 7.2   The CRL Distribution Point (CDP)

TABLE 7.1	Differences Between the Enterprise CA and the Stand-Alone CA	
Setting	**Enterprise CA**	**Stand-Alone CA**
Requires Active Directory?	Yes	No
How are requests processed?	Automatically	Manually
How and where is the CRL published?	Automatically to AD and to a shared folder (CDP)	Manually to a shared folder (CDP)
Can it be configured as offline root?	No	Yes
Can it be used with smart cards?	Yes	No
Can it be used to issue certificates automatically through Group Policy?	Yes	No

Exam Tip

The enterprise certificate authority requires Active Directory be present. The enterprise CA processes requests automatically; the stand-alone CA requires manual processing. As you progress through this chapter, be sure you understand the additional features you gain from implementing an enterprise CA.

The very names "root CA" and "subordinate CA" define these entities' relationship. The root CA is the start of the CA hierarchy. Its main function is to hold the highest trusted certificate and to provide additional certificates to the underlying subordinates. The subordinate CA, the real workhorse in the relationship, is responsible for issuing certificates to users and computers submitting requests. Within the subordinate type, you may find implementations that include intermediate subordinates between the root and the issuing CAs. Figure 7.3 shows how a two-tier CA hierarchy differs from a three-tier one.

A glance at the diagram may lead you to think that the three-tier version looks like more administrative work and exposes a greater number of servers to attack. You are right on both counts. The advantage you gain by having a CA hierarchy of more than two levels helps from a manageability standpoint but more so from a recovery standpoint. When a CA becomes compromised, an administrator should revoke its certificate, thereby revoking all certificates given out by that CA. Figure 7.4 shows the same two CA hierarchies from Figure 7.3, except this time, a CA has been revoked. Assuming that each of the two hierarchies issued the same total number of certificates, you can see that in the two-tier version, when we

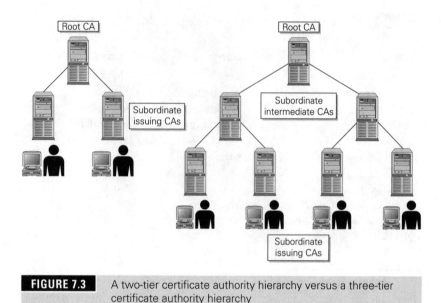

FIGURE 7.3 A two-tier certificate authority hierarchy versus a three-tier certificate authority hierarchy

revoke the certificate of the subordinate, we are also revoking a higher number of certificates (1,000), and thus must issue new ones. In the three-tier architecture, revoking the subordinate or issuing CA's certificate causes less commotion in the overall public key infrastructure by causing a lower number of certificates to be

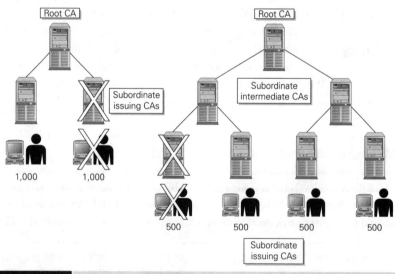

FIGURE 7.4 The CA hierarchy with a greater number of CA "tiers" gives you the opportunity to secure your higher-level CAs.

revoked (500). By adding the extra layer of intermediate CAs you are adding an additional administrative layer that can ease the management of your certificate deployment.

You may well ask, "What if the intermediate is compromised, or worse yet, the root?" A very valid thought indeed. But we have a solution nonetheless. Since the root CAs and the subordinate intermediate CAs provide certificates only to other CAs and do not directly respond to requests issued by users and computers, they are not needed during everyday network communication. And thus was born the offline CA. An offline CA is one that is just that: offline. There is no communication to the network; you could even remove the network adapter for increased security. The significance of the offline root is that since the root heads the whole CA hierarchy, should it be compromised, the entire structure crumbles. This server is therefore taken offline and locked up to prevent malicious attempts to compromise it.

The offline CA is needed only when a new subordinate request must be resolved. The answer here is to use the sneakernet. You have certainly heard of the sneakernet. This is the communications medium in which you put on your sneakers and use a floppy disk or other removable medium to transfer a certificate request from a new subordinate to its closest intermediate CA. Once the request is processed, the certificate can be saved back to the floppy or other medium, walked back over to the requesting system, and imported. we know this may sound like a true headache, but the reality is that you should not be adding CAs daily. In fact, you may not install one weekly, monthly, or even annually. Since your offline CA does not have connectivity to the network (hence the term offline), it is not recommended to make it an enterprise CA, because of the enterprise CAs reliance on Active Directory.

Obviously, planning a certificate hierarchy begins with the root CA and deciding between stand-alone and enterprise forms. Now the question remains whether you should utilize a commercial CA or build your own root. The answer here is simple: If your network infrastructure needs include public trust of any sort, then you should utilize the commercial root CA. If you are providing e-commerce via the web, or offering ActiveX controls on your web page, or perhaps offering free games for download, these are all scenarios where your image is on the line with public trust. Since the popular web browsers come preconfigured to trust the big commercial CAs, there is nothing further for your clients to perform. If, however, you feel that you want your own root CA, your clients will likely be subject to a warning message stating that the site or code or control they are downloading does not have a certificate from a trusted authority. There went your corporate image!

Just having a commercial root CA does not mean you have to give up the administrative ease of the enterprise CA. It is quite common, in fact, to create an enterprise subordinate CA with a commercial root, thus giving you the best of both worlds—public trust and administrative ease.

> **Exam Tip**
>
> A certificate hierarchy with a commercial root and an enterprise CA gives you significant advantages with regard to ensuring public trust and at the same time gaining administrative ease with the integration of Active Directory.

Plan Enrollment and Distribution of Certificates

With some knowledge of certificate hierarchies and the different types of CAs you can now consider exactly how you plan to deliver certificates to the users. With the stand-alone CA, of course, you are a bit limited by the manual processing of certificate requests.

In either case, you have the ability to enroll for certificates via a web page and the Certificate Authority Management Console snap-in. When using an enterprise CA, in addition to the website and snap-in, you can take advantage of an autoenrollment feature available through a Group Policy Object in Active Directory. Figures 7.5, 7.6, and 7.7 show the Certificate Services web enrollment page, the Group Policy autoenrollment in Active Directory, and the Submit Request option on the Certificate Authority snap-in. In the case of web enrollment, depending on the type of CA the request is sent to, the user may get an immediate response or may be asked to come back at a later time to check the status.

The method you use for enrollment is highly dependent upon the demographic of your client operating systems. For environments running all Windows 2000, Windows XP, and Windows Server 2003, the Group Policy automatic request would be your easiest distribution method. In a mixed-OS environment, the web page seems to make the most sense. Of course, the issue with the web page is security. We are sure you don't want just anyone walking up and getting a certificate. The website, then, comes with default permissions of Basic Authentication and Windows Integrated to allow the non-Microsoft clients access to the site.

As we have preached over the last few pages, the enterprise CA is much easier to manage from an administrative standpoint because of its communication with Active Directory.

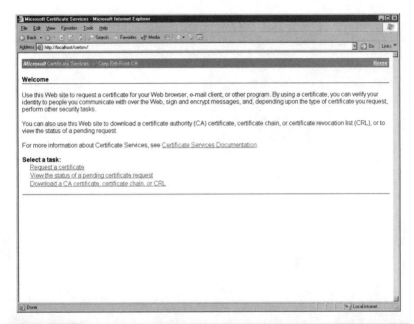

FIGURE 7.5   Obtaining a certificate can be as easy as visiting a web page and issuing a request for one.

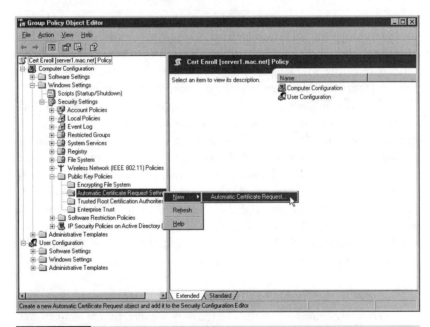

FIGURE 7.6   Systems within a domain can be configured to automatically request a certificate from a specific enterprise CA.

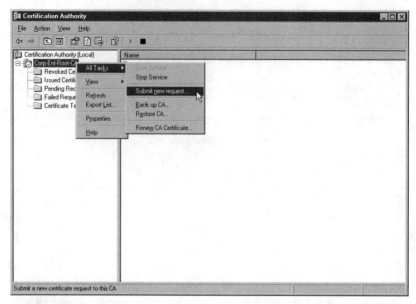

FIGURE 7.7   Certificates can also be requested at the Certificate Authority Management Console snap-in.

As an administrator, you'll probably agree that not everyone should be able to obtain any type of certificate they want. So something must establish what users can enroll to what certificates. When the enterprise CA option is selected, a series of certificate templates are added to the services node in Active Directory Sites and Services. Figure 7.8 shows the different template types.

A common example is how the Encrypted File System (EFS) recovery agent is assigned. This is one or more individuals who have the right to decrypt files encrypted by other users using EFS. By default, you can enable the domain administrator account as a recovery agent. However, you may wish to give these rights out to a few specific users who you trust with them. With a stand-alone certificate authority, you would be forced to manually grant the certificate to the individuals you wish to have this right. For ten users to be recovery agents, you would have to manually grant the certificate ten times, and each additional user would require additional administrative overhead. With the enterprise CA, this assignment can be accomplished rather easily by taking the following actions:

1. Place the users in a group. We'll call ours EFSRAs (Figure 7.9).

2. Edit the permissions on the EFS recovery agent certificate template to include the Enroll permission for the EFSRAs (see Figure 7.10).

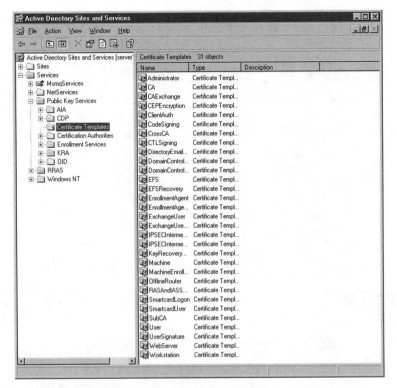

FIGURE 7.8   Enterprise CAs use the template permissions to decide whether or not a certificate gets issued to a user or computer.

3. Once the users have obtained a certificate, import the certificates to the Encrypting Files System node in Group Policy (Figure 7.11).

Travel Advisory

It is Microsoft's recommendation that recovery agent certificates not remain in the certificate store. Suggested practice is to enroll for the certificate, export it to a secure location, and import it only when needed for recovery purposes. If imported for the sake of recovering documents, it should be deleted from the store once the recovery is complete.

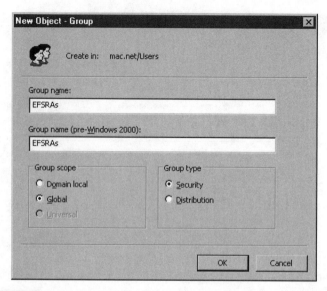

FIGURE 7.9 Creating a group to use for Recovery Agent Certificate enrollment

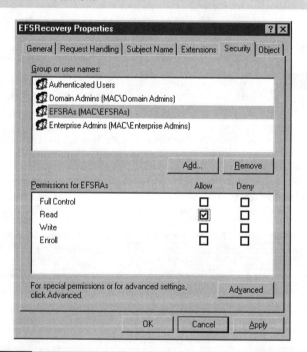

FIGURE 7.10 A user or group must have the enroll permission to obtain a certificate from an Enterprise Certificate Authority.

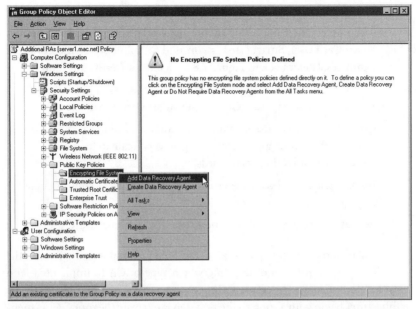

FIGURE 7.11 Adding an EFS recovery agent through Group Policy in Active Directory

Planning and Implementing for Smart Cards

Smart cards are becoming an ever more popular solution for administrators looking for enhanced security. They provide a highly secure and portable method for providing user authentication, code signing, or digital signatures for nonrepudiation (integrity). Smart cards enable what is known as "two-factor" authentication; users must provide something they have (the smart card) and something they know (a pin code). This form of authentication is much more secure than the traditional username and password authentication, which are simply two things the user must know. The Windows Server 2003 and Windows XP product family supports many plug and play smart cards from several major vendors, including American Express, Compaq, HP, Omnikey, and more.

Implementing a smart card solution is quite involved and requires careful planning (yes, we said it again). We will talk in more detail about each of these steps throughout this section. The steps include these:

1. Create a certificate authority hierarchy by starting with a root CA. Of course, the preference here is to create the offline CA.

2. For each domain in the forest that will need to be a part of the smart card implementation, configure the appropriate permissions on the Smart Card User, Smart Card Logon, and Enrollment Agent certificate templates. (Refer back to Figure 7.8 for a look at Certificate Template configuration.)

3. Enable each participating CA to issue Smart Card certificates.

4. Configure a smart card enrollment station by installing a smart card reader and granting an enrollment agent certificate to the user responsible for issuing smart cards.

5. Install a smart card reader on each participating user's computer and configure a smart card for user logon.

6. Educate users on the policies and procedures for smart card use.

Let's take a look at each step in more detail. Step 1 is what was discussed in the preceding section in terms of deciding which type of CA to implement. You must have certificate architecture to implement smart cards, and all certificate architectures begin with a root, so the first step is to create the root CA. As mentioned earlier, the recommended root CA is a stand-alone offline root CA. If you also need to issue certificates to web servers where public trust is a concern, you can take advantage of a commercial CA as your root CA.

Step 2 involves configuring the appropriate permissions for the different certificate templates involved in a smart card implementation. These are

- **Smart card user**   Used for authentication and digitally signing e-mail
- **Smart card logon**   Used only for authentication
- **Enrollment agent**   Used to authorize the user responsible for creating or enrolling smart cards

Step 3, shown in Figures 7.12 and 7.13, is the process of enabling a CA to issue any of the three certificates assigned permissions in Step 2. As you can see in Figure 7.12, a certificate authority must be configured to provide smart card certificates by adding the appropriate template types to the list of certificate templates available. As Figure 7.13 shows, a certificate authority responsible for smart card certificates needs to be configured with the smart card logon, smart card user, and enrollment agent certificate templates. The smart card logon and the smart card user do not both have to be enabled. The one you choose is dependent upon your proposed smart card use.

Step 4 consists of setting up the system, called the enrollment station, where the smart cards will be created. It will be the location where certificates will be

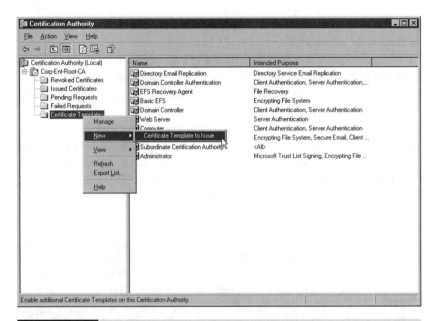

FIGURE 7.12 Choosing a new certificate template to issue

stored within the smart card itself. This step requires that you install a smart card reader and obtain an enrollment agent certificate for the user or users responsible for smart card creation and distribution. Smart cards are not free-for-all gifts given to random users. They should be treated with caution and discretion, just as you would treat the distribution of identification badges for building access.

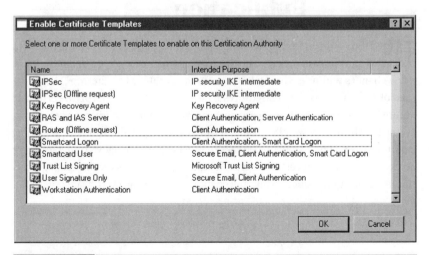

FIGURE 7.13 Enabling a certificate template

Step 5 is to set up the smart cards for the users and install your smart card readers on their systems.

The last step, Step 6, is more of a formality than anything, but if users are not educated in the proper use and care of the smart cards, your duties as an administrator may become increasingly difficult as you have to consistently work with uninformed end users.

Once the process is complete and your implementation has gone to the production environment, your users that are taking part in the smart card rollout will no longer need to use the CTRL-ALT-DELETE keystroke to initiate a logon. This function is replaced by simply inserting the smart card into the reader and then prompting the user to enter their PIN code.

Exam Tip

Remember that using smart cards for interactive login does not require a change in the authentication protocol; however, when using smart cards for remote access authentication, it is still necessary to enable the Extensible Authentication Protocol (EAP) on both the client and the server running the Routing and Remote Access Service (RRAS). The RRAS server must also hold a certificate to perform the certificate-based mutual authentication of the remote access client.

Objective 7.04

Configure Active Directory for Certificate Publication

In the preceding section, we covered the steps required to plan and implement a smart card infrastructure. The third step in the process required us to make a few changes within Active Directory. The fact that we are altering AD for the sake of utilizing smart cards requires us to work with an enterprise certificate authority, since a stand-alone certificate authority does not utilize AD.

In that third step, we altered the permissions to specific templates regarding smart card use. The permissions on these templates are what allows or denies a user access to that particular certificate type. It is these permissions within AD that a certificate authority will query while automatically processing a certificate request.

Plan a Security Update Infrastructure

It's no secret that the Microsoft operating system is the most widely used in the world. Given this fact, it's no surprise that it's the one most hackers try to break. Call it a virus, a Trojan, an exploit, or anything else; the fact remains that there are a lot of individuals in the world spending a lot of time discovering these vulnerabilities. For this reason, as administrators of environments that run the Windows operating systems, we must continually apply security patches and service packs to our computers.

Maintaining system security, then, must be a part of our network plan. This security update infrastructure must include a documented methodology for applying hot fixes, patches, and service packs to the network. Without creating a standard practice for implementation, there will most certainly be circumstances where applying a hot fix, patch, or service pack could have an unforeseen interaction with another application on your network and cause even more trouble than without having the additional installation. It is your responsibility to build a structured method to accomplish all of the following steps:

1. Evaluate the security level of your clients and servers.

2. Download the latest and greatest updates.

3. Test the updates against the current network environment (preferably in a test environment, not the production environment).

4. Deploy the tested updates into your production network.

With these procedures properly included in your administrative routine, you will find that your overall network security scheme will be up to date and certainly more manageable.

Tools

Now that you are familiar with the procedural requirements for developing a security update infrastructure, we can discuss some of the more valuable tools that you can build that infrastructure upon. The two tools that appear to be rapidly gaining in popularity are the Microsoft Baseline Security Analyzer (MBSA) and the Microsoft Software Update Services (SUS).

> **Exam Tip**
>
> You should be extremely familiar with all the functionality available on both the MBSA and the SUS. Microsoft seems very proud of these utilities and wants to be sure that they are part of your existing administrative arsenal. So learn them *and* use them.

These tools can be downloaded from Microsoft's website; just make a simple keyword search on either acronym at www.microsoft.com/downloads. MBSA and SUS are complementary tools and should be used together.

Other tools work with these two utilities to help build a secure environment. The Internet Information Server (IIS) Lockdown tool is a wizard that helps secure a system running IIS with any of the popular Microsoft web products: Exchange, Commerce Server, FrontPage Server extensions, and more. Another Microsoft-provided tool, also specifically for web servers, is the URLScan security tool. This tool helps administrators separate valid HTTP traffic from bogus or malicious requests against a web server.

Microsoft Baseline Security Analyzer

The Microsoft Baseline Security Analyzer (MBSA) is a graphical utility as well as a command-line tool to scan for operating system configuration errors and unapplied security updates. The MBSA scan can be run against a single system by name or IP address, as shown in Figure 7.14, or a group of systems by specifying a domain name or a range of IP addresses, as shown in Figure 7.15. MBSA can be executed against the update catalog available on the Web or against your own internal Software Update Services (SUS) server

Once you have downloaded MBSA, it can be installed by executing mbsasetup.msi. MBSA version 1.1.1 is the latest version (as of August 2003) and runs on the Windows 2000, Window XP, and Windows Server 2003 operating systems. Even though it can be initiated only from one of these operating systems, it will scan any of the following:

- Windows NT 4.0
- Windows 2000
- Windows XP
- Windows Server 2003
- Internet Information Server (IIS) 4.0 and higher
- SQL Server 7.0 and 2000
- Internet Explorer 5.01 and higher
- Office 2000 and 2002

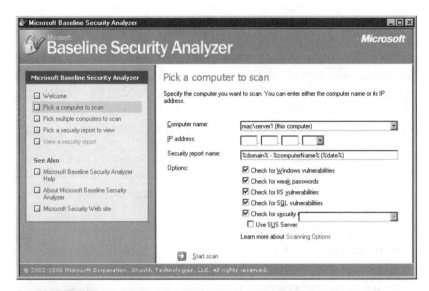

FIGURE 7.14 The Microsoft Baseline Security Analyzer can be used to scan a single system.

- Exchange 5.5 and 2000 (security updates only)
- Windows Media Player 6.4 and higher (security updates only)

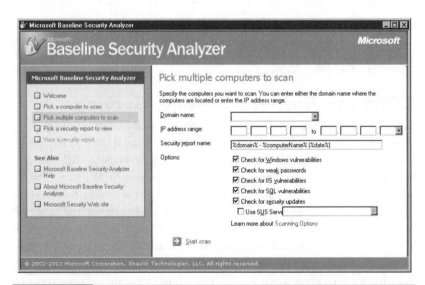

FIGURE 7.15 MBSA can also be used to scan multiple systems by specifying a domain name or a range of IP addresses.

Running MBSA does not take a great deal of time for any given machine and can be customized to scan only for specific items. Running the full MBSA on a system functioning as a domain controller could require a longer period of time, just as running MBSA against an entire domain of systems would incur additional network overhead. The time needed for the MBSA to complete can be reduced by customizing the checks that are performed; however, if run in its entirety, MBSA will check all of the following items:

- **Windows vulnerability checks**   Scans items regarding Guest account status, type of file system, shared folders availability, Administrator group membership, availability of anonymous access, autologin, and expired passwords.
- **Weak password checks**   Scans for weak or blank passwords.
- **IIS vulnerability checks**   Scans for security problems and queries whether or not the IIS Lockdown tool has been run.
- **SQL Server vulnerability checks**   Scans for weaknesses in SQL Server 7.0 or 2000 security. MBSA returns information regarding authentication mode, status of the sa account, and SQL service account membership.
- **Security updates check**   Scans for missing security updates using the HFNetChk utility. The current system configuration is compared against a frequently updated database to see if any current updates are missing.

Figure 7.16 shows a completed full MBSA scan against a system running Windows XP Professional.

Microsoft Software Update Service

Arguably one of the most tedious tasks in network management is maintaining an updated operating system for the numerous clients and servers. By this, we are not referring to moving all your Windows 98 systems to Windows XP. That may be tedious, but at least it's a one-shot deal (if you do it right, of course). We are talking about delivering service packs and updates to all the systems. Sure, we have the capability of software deployment via Group Policy, but there is still a good bit of manual labor in obtaining the updates, patches, hot fixes, and service packs. Well, my astute certification seeker, those days are no longer, because now we have Microsoft's Software Update Service, or SUS. We pronounce it as if it rhymes with Zeus, but we don't know if that is an industry thing or just me not wanting to say the whole string of words. Yes, the whole three-word string is what we are avoiding. We call it efficiency!

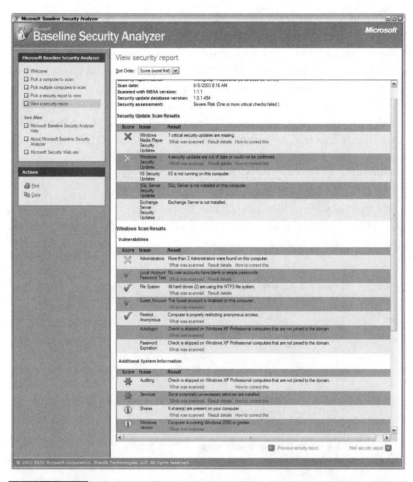

| FIGURE 7.16 | A completed full MBSA scan shows all vulnerabilities and weaknesses in a system as well as what hot fixes or security updates are missing. |

SUS is an automated means of downloading, storing, and delivering the latest and greatest hot fixes and service packs directly from Microsoft's website. We are sure that you are familiar with the Windows Update option, as it used to be right in front of our faces every time we hit the Start button! It has now been reduced to an option on the left side of the page on the Control Panel. Don't get me wrong, it's not that Windows Update is less important than it was in the earlier Windows versions, We just think that too many administrators didn't want users seeing it so readily. Of course, that has been replaced with the wonderful little reminder for

"Stay up to date with Automatic Updates" that shows up until configured. The Windows Automatic Updates feature can be integrated with SUS, in that the clients can be directed to your own internal SUS server instead of venturing out to the Internet to grab the latest updates. Windows Update and Automatic Updates are methods for obtaining the most current updates from Microsoft; however, they are only for a single system and require administrative privileges. In your world, that means either you walk around to all the systems and click Start | Windows Update or you make someone an administrator and tell them to do it. We just don't see either of these approaches as being too practical.

With SUS on the network, your clients can be configured through Group Policy as shown in Figures 7.17 and 7.18.

Group Policy is, of course, a great tool for deploying service packs; however, you still must make the manual effort to search and download the latest updates. SUS automates the whole process for us.

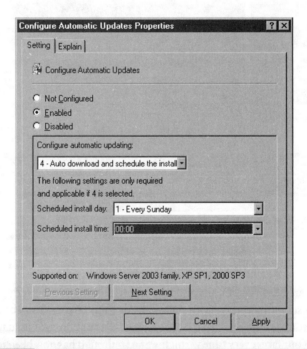

FIGURE 7.17   Group Policy can be used to schedule clients to obtain updates.

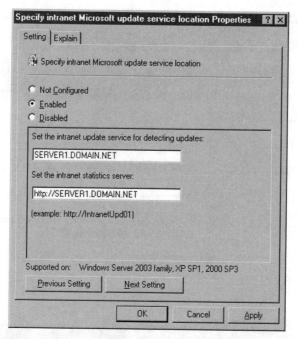

FIGURE 7.18   Clients can be configured to install the updates from an internal server instead of traversing the Internet to one of Microsoft's Update servers.

Currently, the server-side SUS with Service Pack 1 and the SUS client can be downloaded from Microsoft's website by going to www.microsoft.com/downloads and performing a search. We'd give you the link, but it would take to long for you to type. The server-side component will run under Windows 2000 and Windows Server 2003 with Internet Information Services installed, while the client side runs on any system using Windows 2000 with Service Pack 2, Windows XP (home or pro), and Windows Server 2003. The server-side component includes all the following features:

- Security is built in, as only administrators local to the SUS server are able to bring down the latest updates from Microsoft's website.

- Automatic synchronization with the Windows Update catalog, shown in Figure 7.19, allows your SUS server to pull down the latest updates to a local directory for easier deployment to clients. For larger network environments, multiple servers can be configured to run SUS to allow clients to be load-balanced across SUS servers.

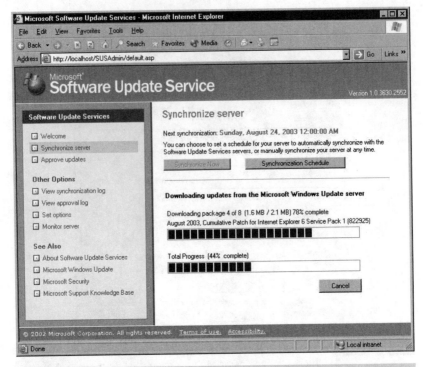

FIGURE 7.19 Microsoft's Software Update Service can be synchronized with the Windows Update Catalog to bring down all the latest updates to a local directory.

- Information about the updates is held in cache on the SUS server, shown in Figure 7.20, to increase performance of client queries.

- Updates are not made available to clients until they have been approved by an administrator, as shown in Figure 7.21. SUS can be managed remotely by administrators via HTTP or HTTPS.

- Administrators can keep logs and statistics, as shown in Figure 7.22, about the client downloads and the updates that have been approved. SUS is highly customizable, allowing you to choose settings such as where clients will obtain updates, from which server to synchronize updates, if updates should wait for approval, if the updates should be stored locally or maintained on a Microsoft Windows Update server, and even which languages to download.

- Administrators can choose different languages for the hot fixes and service packs that are downloaded.

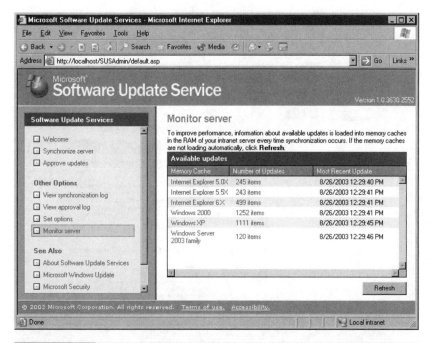

FIGURE 7.20   The server(s) offering SUS hold the information about available updates in cache for performance enhancements.

The client side of the SUS deployment includes an install that works much in the same way that the Windows Automatic Updates works. The client pulls the updates down from a specified location, either the Internet or an internal SUS server. The client component of the SUS technology includes features like these:

- Security is built in, as administrators are the only ones with sufficient rights to configure the Automatic Updates functionality. Surely, we don't want responsibility for updates to be placed on the end user.

- Clients are automatically configured using the Windows Automatic Updates functionality. Clients with built-in support for Automatic Updates include Windows 2000 systems with Service Pack 3, Windows XP systems with Service Pack 1, and systems given the stand-alone Automatic Updates application. Group Policy can be used to configure the Automatic Updates on the client systems.

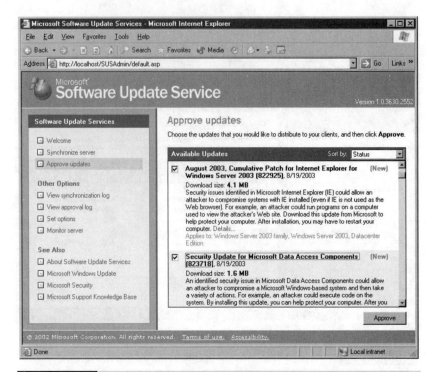

FIGURE 7.21 Updates downloaded to an SUS server can be configured to be held until an administrator approves them for delivery to client systems.

Travel Advisory

Systems running Windows 2000 Service Pack 2 require the installation of the wuau.adm administrative template in order to configure the automatic updates for client systems.

- Only updates pertinent to the system at hand are downloaded. Understandably, it wouldn't be efficient for a Windows XP system to attempt an installation of the Windows 2000 Service Pack 4 update or for a system to apply the latest Windows Media Player fix if Windows Media Player was not even installed.

- Updates occur without any user interaction and can even be configured so that the user is unaware of updates being installed from the SUS server. Bandwidth allocated to the updates is dynamic, in that it will be reduced when a competing request is made and so have no detrimental effect on the users' foreground applications.

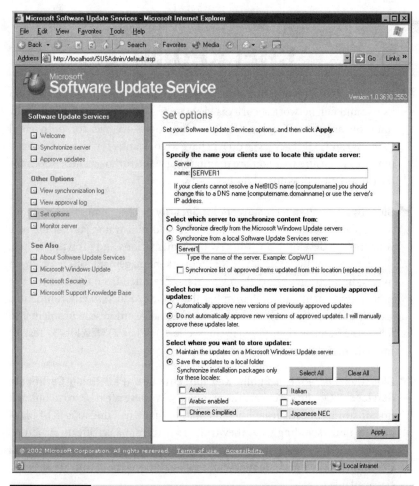

FIGURE 7.22   SUS is highly customizable.

- Updates that require reboots are installed together to prevent multiple reboots. This happens automatically.

As shown over the last page or so, SUS is a highly functional deployment tool for administrators needing to maintain a large number of systems with a centralized and automated process. It is, of course, not without its limitations. SUS does not work with down-level clients like Windows 98 or Windows NT. SUS is also without an uninstall feature, making update testing an even more crucial part of the approval and deployment process.

CHECKPOINT

✔**Objective 7.01: Network Security**   Unlike the dot com phenomenon with its rise and fall, network security is likely to be a concept that will only continue on an upward swing. As the technologies change, for both good (admins) and evil (hackers), you will have to constantly revisit your security practices to ensure that you are maintaining a network with little room for the exploitation of vulnerabilities.

✔**Objective 7.02: Plan a Framework for Security**   The man (or woman) with a plan. That should be you. As a diligent administrator, you should take your time to develop plans for new implementations and growth. Ad hoc, shoot-from-the-hip-type styles of network management often result in more administrative effort than would have resulted from taking the extra time to document a plan. Remember that your production environment is sacred, and inserting new variables can often cause unforeseen problems. So follow the framework outlined in this section: 1) Plan, 2) Develop, 3) Test, 4) Implement, 5) Evaluate, 6) Start over.

✔**Objective 7.03: Plan a Public Key Infrastructure (PKI) Using Certificate Services**   Oh the joy of certificate services! We have often heard people tell horror stories of certificate implementations gone bad due to lack of planning or understanding what they truly needed from a certificate structure. Be sure that once you decide to use a certificate architecture, you understand the administrative and functional differences among the certificate authorities available to you.

✔**Objective 7.04: Configure Active Directory for Certificate Publication**
Active Directory was created to ease management of resources. And it does its job quite well. The incorporation of Active Directory into the Windows product has significantly reduced the spectrum of control needed to manage a network environment. Don't let that statement hit you in a negative way. It doesn't mean that we don't have as much control as we did with NT 4.0, because we certainly have that and more. The point is that we don't need to spread ourselves all over the place now. We can use Active Directory for its intended purpose of providing a centralized location for the management of all resources. By integrating applications and services such as certificate services into Active Directory, we are simplifying our network management scheme.

✔**Objective 7.05: Plan a Security Update Infrastructure**   Once the network is planned, developed, tested, and deployed, an ongoing maintenance schedule will most certainly fill all of your days (and maybe nights and weekends too). A large chunk of these routine duties will inevitably fall under the category of security. Planning a streamlined security update infrastructure with tools like MBSA and SUS will ease your mind, your worries, and best of all, your administrative tasks.

REVIEW QUESTIONS

1. One of the web developers for your online banking website has created a new ActiveX control that runs a financial calculator for people wanting estimated loan payments based on different interest rates and payment schedules. You are worried about clients not wanting to download it for fear of a virus being embedded into the code. You want to ease the clients' fears but at the same time make it easy to distribute code-signing certificates to your developers. What should you do? Choose one.

   A. Create a stand-alone offline root certification authority and manually distribute code-signing certificates to your developers.

   B. Use a third-party company to investigate the backgrounds of all your developers and allow the third-party company to issue code-signing smart cards to all approved developers.

   C. Create an enterprise subordinate certificate authority with a commercial root certificate authority and give the developers permission to enroll for the code-signing certificate.

   D. Use the Dynamic Host Configuration Protocol to deliver code-signing certificates to developers. Obtain the code-signing certificates from a trusted commercial certificate authority.

2. Your network infrastructure consists of a stand-alone offline root certification authority and four enterprise subordinate certification authorities. This morning, you realized that one of your enterprise subordinate certification authorities was compromised by a disgruntled employee. Which of the following steps should you take to prevent any further use of the certificates distributed by the compromised certificate authority? Choose two.

   A. On the compromised certification authority, revoke the certificates that were compromised.

    B. On the root certification authority, revoke the certificate of the compromised certification authority.

    C. Use Active Directory to publish the Certificate Revocation List.

    D. Use a floppy disk to publish the Certificate Revocation List (CRL) to the CRL distribution point.

3. Your Windows Server 2003 network consists of a single forest with seven different domains. You are part of an elite group of administrators who belong to the Enterprise Administrators group. Your team has decided to implement smart card authentication for all domain controllers to ensure the highest level of security. You have created your certificate hierarchy with an enterprise offline root and two enterprise certification authorities and assigned permissions for the smart card user and enrollment agent certificate templates. Next you establish the enrollment station. You attempt to obtain an enrollment agent certificate, but it is not available as an option. What should you do?

    A. Configure the offline root to issue enrollment agent certificates.

    B. Configure a subordinate certificate authority to issue enrollment agent certificates.

    C. Authorize your enterprise certificate authority on a domain controller that belongs to your forest root domain.

    D. Import a certificate from a commercial certificate authority.

4. Your network consists of a single domain with six subnets using several of the different internal addressing ranges. Recently, some of your systems have fallen victim to several vulnerabilities that, as you have since found out, had fixes available more than eight months before you were affected. What can you do to monitor the status of your systems' security level?

    A. At each of the affected systems, run the Microsoft Baseline Security Analyzer to identify the missing updates.

    B. On any system within your network, run the Microsoft Baseline Security Analyzer against a valid range of IP addresses that includes the addresses of the affected systems.

    C. On any system within your network, run the Microsoft Baseline Security Analyzer against all the systems within your domain.

    D. Create a Group Policy Object on the domain to deploy the Microsoft Baseline Security Analyzer.

5. Your network consists of 100 Windows XP Professional clients and 15 Windows Server 2003 servers. You have been experiencing a large number of problems with updates that have not been checked for compatibility. What can you do to prevent unknowing administrators from installing untested updates and to prevent excessive traffic? Choose two.

   A. Configure a server on your network with the Software Update Service and set the option to allow only approved updates.

   B. Use a Group Policy to disable the automatic Windows update functionality.

   C. Configure the latest updates to be stored on a local server.

   D. Configure your Internet connection server to prevent Windows Update packets from leaving the internal network.

REVIEW ANSWERS

1. **C**   When your infrastructure requires both public trust and ease of administration, your certificate hierarchy should include a commercial certificate in conjunction with an enterprise subordinate certificate authority.

2. **B** **D**   When a subordinate certificate authority is compromised, its certificate should be revoked at the certification authority that issued the certificate. Since the root certification authority in this situation is offline, the Certificate Revocation List (CRL) must be published manually.

3. **B**   Since your certificate hierarchy is in place and the permissions have been set, it seems likely that you have not yet enabled the certificate authority to give out the necessary enrollment agent certificates.

4. **C**   When a group of systems need to be analyzed using MBSA and the systems span different IP subnets, the easiest method of monitoring many systems is to use the domain name as the common denominator for systems included in the scan.

5. **A** **C**   The Software Update Service is a great administrative tool for downloading and deploying updates from the Microsoft Update Catalog. Two options that make SUS attractive to an administrator are the ability to deploy only tested and approved updates and the option to store the catalog on a local server, thereby preventing internal systems from traversing the Internet to obtain updates from Microsoft's servers.

Planning Server Availability and Performance

ETA	NEWBIE	SOME EXPERIENCE	EXPERT
	6–8 hours	3–4 hours	1–2 hours

Keeping your machines running is not just a case of installing them and occasionally checking that everything is okay. Despite assurances to the contrary by manufacturers and software engineers, computers do have hardware failures, and there are bugs in the system. Worse, there are elements outside of your control—fire, theft, human error—that you can't predict any more than you can predict a hardware or software failure.

For all of these reasons and more, you will need to consider the effects of a failure or problem somewhere in your system and plan to be able to cope with the problem so that your users and clients are either unaware of the issue or are not unduly affected by it.

Windows Server 2003 provides a number of solutions that can help, and in this chapter we'll be examining these solutions. We'll start by looking at the highest level of protection, which, unfortunately, is a solution not always available to everybody. Clustering technologies, including fail-over clusters and Network Load Balancing systems, offer the best level of protection by providing partial or complete replacement servers and functionality in the event of a problem with one or more of the servers in your network. The problem is that the Cluster Service requires very careful configuration and the use of a shared disk device for a proper installation. This can make Cluster Service expensive to install, especially when there are other, simpler solutions available such as NLB (Network Load Balancing).

Network Load Balancing also enables us to spread the load of the requests around a network of machines so that they all share the load of the request process. NLB can be used in this way only for certain solutions—web serving for example works, while file serving does not—unless of course we also combine it with the distributed file system.

To determine whether Network Load Balancing is necessary, we can use the Performance system monitoring tool to identify and report on system bottlenecks and therefore recognize the areas of a system that need to be addressed.

Our last stop is to look at probably the most fundamental of all the solutions when it comes to recovering from some kind of failure: backups. Simple backup and recovery procedures allow you to recover from most failures by rebuilding your servers or simply recovering files in the case of failure.

Objective 8.01

Plan Services for High Availability

In Windows Server 2003, there are two clustering solutions: Network Load Balancing (NLB) and Cluster Service. Both systems were available in Windows 2000, but they have been updated in Windows Server 2003. In this section we'll look at how these systems work so that you can plan to implement services based on either solution.

Although both are technically classed as cluster solutions, Cluster Services and NLB work in different ways and have different advantages and potential uses:

- Cluster Service can be used to provide machine-level backup to a system in the event of failure. Typically it's used within datacenters and enterprise server configurations where you need 100 percent availability. Clusters can be configured in a number of different ways, but always have one goal in mind—for one machine to take over the responsibilities of another in case the first fails.

- Network Load Balancing is a software-only solution for distributing requests over a number of servers within an NLB cluster. This provides basic failover support, by redirecting a request only to a currently active machine, and also implements load balancing by spreading the requests among the machines to make the best of the overall horsepower.

A third technology exists that can also be added to Windows Server 2003 through Microsoft Application Center 2000, which is called Component Load Balancing (CLB). Unlike the other technologies that provide support for clusters irrespective of the specific applications you might be supporting, CLB works at the application level.

Using CLB, individual Common Object Model+ (COM+) components reside on a number of separate servers within a COM+ cluster. This enables you to distribute the workload of an application across multiple servers running a single business application. CLB automatically routes calls to individual COM+ components within the COM+ cluster. It can also be used with a combination of NLB and Cluster Service to provide an additional tier of load balancing within a large web farm.

Travel Advisory

Refer to the documentation on Microsoft's site for more information on Application Server 2000.

Supported Editions and Services

Clustering of one form or another is now supported by all versions of Windows Server 2003. If you need true clustering services, then you need Enterprise or Datacenter Editions as these are the only two editions to support the Clustering Service. NLB is supported by all editions. You can see the full breakdown in Table 8.1.

TABLE 8.1	Clustering Support in Windows Server 2003 Editions	
Edition	**NLB**	**Cluster Nodes**
Standard Edition	Yes	Not Supported
Enterprise Edition	Yes	8
Datacenter Edition	Yes	8
Web Edition	Yes	Not Supported

NLB is basically only applicable to IIS and related web-serving solutions. This is because NLB must redirect requests to an appropriate server when a request is accepted. For IIS and web serving, where a request is accepted, processed, and responded to, this is a fairly simple process. For most services, the sequence of connection, request, process, and response is not so clear. With file services, for example, the connection typically stays open for the duration that a file or directory is open on a client—you could redirect the request to another server when one server is already handling the communication.

Clusters, on the other hand, are more flexible—they can support many more services—but they are able to support only fail-over, not load balancing. That said, there are still some services that either cannot be clustered or cannot effectively share the information to provide 100 percent availability. For example, file sharing services can be clustered, but you cannot retain the open files between the two cluster servers. When one server fails and the new one takes over, any open files on clients will be unavailable. Thus you get a backup service, but not a transparent backup service.

Local Lingo

Fail-over: When one machine fails to perform and its services and availability are automatically shifted to an alternative machine within a cluster, it's referred to as a fail-over.

Cluster services concentrate on two main areas:

- Internal services, such as distributed file systems, DHCP, and WINS.
- Public services, such as IIS and message queuing.

For a full list of the services that can be clustered, see Table 8.2.

TABLE 8.2	Services Supported by Clustering Services	
Service	**NLB**	**Clustering**
Internet Information Service	Yes	Yes
DHCP Service	No	Yes
Distributed File Service roots	No	Yes
Distributed Transaction Coordinator	No	Yes
File shares	No	Yes
Message queuing	No	Yes
Printer spools	See Note	Yes
Volume Shadow Copy service tasks	No	Yes
WINS Service	No	Yes

Exam Tip

You will be expected to know which services are supported by both clustering and NLB and be able to identify which solution should be used.

Travel Assistance

Technically, you can NLB print spools by having two servers that both print to the same network-attached print device. In practice, of course, you've still got only one device actually handling the printing, so the benefits are never really fully realized.

Network Load Balancing

In an NLB installation, each computer within the NLB cluster is a separate individual machine connected to the other members by only a network connection—cluster members don't share information or storage space through a shared device as they do with Cluster Service.

Therefore, you configure the network to send requests to an NLB cluster. For example, you might configure www.mydomain.com to point to an IP address that is configured as the IP address for your cluster. User requests sent to this IP address are actually received by all members within the cluster, but only one cluster member processes and responds to the request. You can see this more clearly by looking at Figure 8.1.

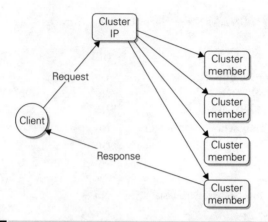

FIGURE 8.1   Requests and responses in NLB

The decision for which machine should respond is based on a set of internal rules and customizable affinity rules. These can be summarized as follows:

1. Any members who are offline or haven't recently responded to other cluster-member activity requests are removed from consideration.

2. If the request has been received by a known client and affinity between the client and server are configured, then that server handles the request.

3. If the request is from a new client, then the least busy member with the highest priority handles the request.

Because of this constant communication between the machines, and especially because of the results of decision 1 in the preceding list, NLB provides both load balancing and fail-over protection within a network. If a member server is unavailable, for whatever reason, it is automatically taken out of the equation and routed to a server that can handle the request.

NLB Management

Network Load Balancing is administered through a single administration application, called the NLB Manager. An NLB cluster is created on one machine. Individual members of the cluster can be added from within NLB Manager without you needing to visit each machine. The NLB Manager handles all aspects of the configuration for all members within the cluster, automatically propagating changes to each member. Furthermore, NLB Manager enables you to manage multiple clusters, simply by connecting to an existing cluster.

To create a new cluster with NLB:

1. Open NLB Manager by selecting Start | Administration Tools | NLB Manager.

2. To create a new cluster, select Cluster | New. You will be presented with the Cluster Parameters dialog box shown in Figure 8.2.

3. You need to give the cluster a unique IP address, which should be separate from the IP address of any member servers. You'll also need a suitable netmask and name for the new cluster—this will be automatically registered in the DNS/AD for you. Remote administration is disabled by default, and you should leave it like this. You can still connect to a monitor/administer cluster using NLB manager, even with this option switched off. You also need to specify whether the cluster should work in Unicast or Multicast mode—see "Planning Your NLB Cluster," later in this chapter, for more information.

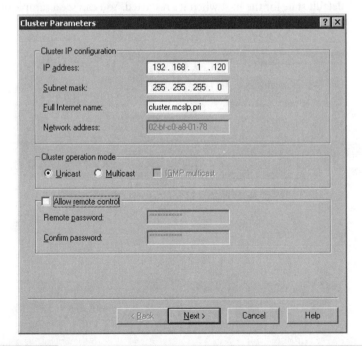

FIGURE 8.2   Creating a new cluster

4. Figure 8.3 shows the next step: adding the IP addresses of the member servers for the domain. NLB Manager will connect to these machines and configure them automatically for you to handle cluster requests.

5. Figure 8.4 shows the Port Rules dialog box. Here you can define which ports are handled by the cluster—typically this will be port 80 for an NLB cluster—as well as set different affinity rules for different ports and cluster members. See the next section, "Port Rules and Affinity," for more information.

6. The next stage is to choose the physical interface for a given machine that will be used to handle requests for the cluster. This enables NLB to set the appropriate cluster IP address on the interface. In servers with multiple network adaptors, you can use this to specify a single adaptor, or you can use different adaptors to handle different cluster traffic. After you've selected the interface and clicked Next, you will be able to specify the host priority—which you should choose based on the host's speed and its expected load according to the affinity settings—and the default state for the host when it's restarted. You can see a sample of the configuration window in Figure 8.5.

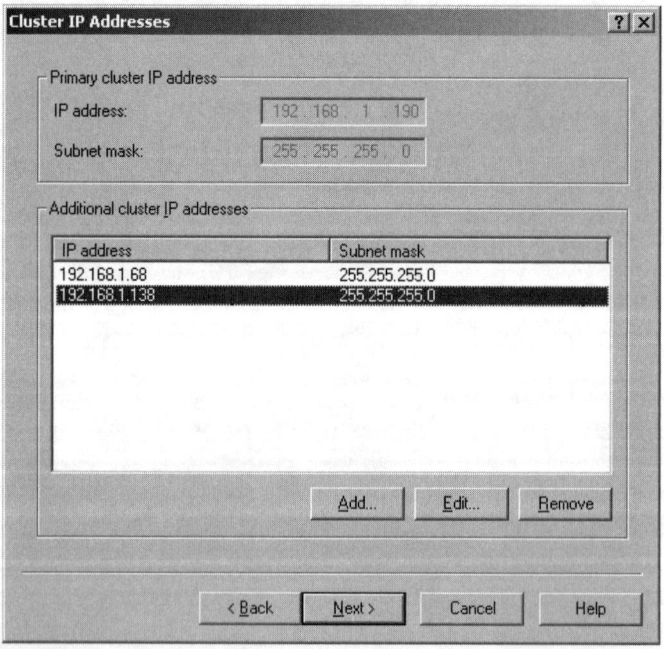

FIGURE 8.3   Adding member servers to a cluster

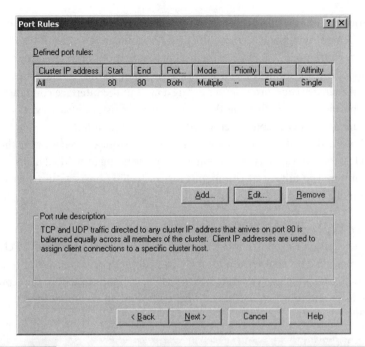

Setting port rules and affinity details for the cluster

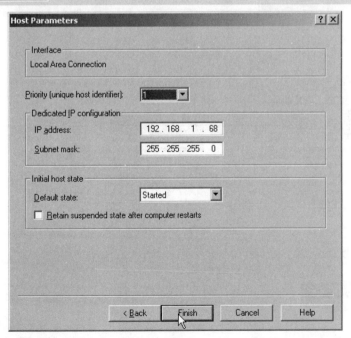

Setting cluster member parameters

You should now be ready to monitor and use your cluster. The main cluster management window is shown in Figure 8.6. You can see here all the clusters that are configured. You can add further clusters to monitor by selecting Cluster | Connect To Existing. You can see from the example that we have a problem with the cluster configuration, signifying a fault in the interface configuration. This probably means that the IP address for the cluster already exists or that NLB manager was unable to set the IP address on that interface.

From within NLB Manager you can also start, stop, and reconfigure the entire cluster as well as starting, stopping, and suspending individual hosts within the cluster. The full list of commands for controlling hosts within a cluster is shown in Table 8.3.

Port Rules and Affinity

NLB clusters allow you to control to which TCP and UDP ports the NLB cluster will respond. This enables you to finely control the specific network protocols and therefore which services a cluster member responds to within the scope of the cluster and to which it can continue to respond on an individual basis.

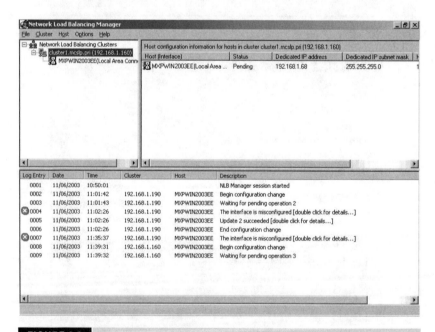

FIGURE 8.6 Monitoring a cluster in NLB Manager

TABLE 8.3	Controlling Clusters and Cluster Members

Command	Effect on Host
Start	Host starts and operates normally.
Stop	Host stops and any existing requests are simply dropped.
Drainstop	Host stops but processes any existing requests before coming to complete stop.
Suspend	Host stops processing requests, and any existing requests remain pending.
Resume	Resumes after suspension, processing any requests that were suspended.

To control a cluster's ports, right-click the cluster within NLB manager and select Control Ports from the pop-up menu. For each configured port range you can do the following:

- *Enable or disable the port range.* Disabled port ranges are ignored by the cluster, even if an enabled port range includes the disabled port range. For example, if you enable ports 1 through 65535, but disable ports 450 through 6500, then this is equivalent to enabling ports 1 through 449 and 6501 through 65535.

- *Drain the port range.* Draining a range enables existing connections to complete their operations but disables any new connections. This is the best way to take an NLB cluster offline as it allows existing clients to continue to function.

To configure the port settings, either configure them during cluster setup, or right-click the cluster, select Properties, and then the Port Rules tab. From here you can configure individual port ranges and set each range's properties, as follows:

- **Affinity Setting**   Controls how NLB load balances incoming requests to this port range. Options are as follows:
  - **None**   No specific IP address or range is applied, and the load is balanced across the cluster.
  - **Single**   New requests are balanced normally, but from then on the same server will always handle requests from the client IP address. This is useful if a server holds state information for a connection as it allows the client to continue talking to the same server during

their conversation, and therefore retain the correct state information.

- **Class C** New requests are balanced normally, but from then on clients on the same Class C subnet are handled by the same server.
- **Port Range** The range of ports to include in this affinity setting.
- **Protocol** The protocol or protocols (TCP/UDP) to be handled with this affinity setting.

Command-Line Management

You can also manage and monitor the cluster from the command line using the wlbs command-line tool. The wlbs tool provides many of the same facilities as NLB manager but can of course be used from within a remote telnet session. Some of the key commands of the wlbs command-line tool include

- **reload** Reloads the driver's parameters from the registry for a cluster.
- **display** Displays all the configuration parameters for a cluster, including the current status and last few log messages.
- **query** Displays the current cluster state for the current members of the cluster.
- **suspend** Suspends the cluster operations (start, stop, and so on) until resume is used.
- **resume** Resumes cluster operations.
- **start** Starts cluster operations on a specific host.
- **stop** Stops cluster operations on a specific host.

Travel Assistance

Running wlbs without any options will show the available commands and options available to you within wlbs.

Virtual Clustering

If you are familiar with NLB in Windows 2000, then you already know that past versions of NLB spread requests across a cluster according to the IP address and port address range on a whole-cluster basis. Although technically this made administration of the cluster easier, it also limited a cluster to a very specific range of websites. In particular:

- Each member of the cluster was limited to supporting the set of traffic defined by the cluster.

- All members of the cluster had to support traffic for all the websites or applications they hosted, even if you didn't want all websites to be load balanced.

- You had to block all applications on a cluster member, not just specific applications.

To address these problems, Windows Server 2003 includes a new feature called Virtual Clusters. Virtual Clusters take into account the preceding problems and provide a number of solutions:

- Cluster IP addresses can be configured with different port address ranges, allowing one cluster IP address to redirect to a particular application being hosted on a specific port on each member. For example, IP address 192.168.1.20 could refer to port 80 hosted websites on the cluster members, whereas 192.168.1.21 refers to port 8080 sites.

- Traffic for a website or application can be filtered out on a cluster member basis, allowing upgrades on a single member with the cluster to take place without shutting down all other applications on that member.

Cluster member–level affinity allows you to assign different hosts within the same cluster to handle specific web sites or applications. For example, AppOne could be hosted by members one, two, and four, while AppTwo is handled by members two, three, and five.

Planning Your NLB Cluster

When planning an NLB cluster, you first identify the reason for wanting an NLB cluster. What is it that you need to accomplish? NLB clusters provide two different types of functionality: fail-over support, by automatically redirecting requests to an available server, and system load balancing, by spreading requests over two or more machines.

When looking primarily at fail-over support, you can use Table 8.4 to determine whether NLB is suitable.

TABLE 8.4	Fail-Over Support Provided by NLB	
Failure Point	**NLB Suitable**	**Alternative Solution**
Network hub	No	Redundant networks (may be achievable if using multiple network adapters and multiple NLB layers—that is, two NLB networks that are themselves protected by a secondary NLB that provides the public interface.
Power outage	No	UPS/Generator.
Server connection	Yes	Second network interface.
Disk failure	Yes	Hardware/software RAID.
Other hardware failure	Yes	Hot swap components.
Server software failure	No	Cluster Service
IIS failures/interruptions	Yes	
Web application failure	Yes	
WAN links	No	Redundant links

For determining whether NLB is appropriate for traffic loading, we have to look deeper at the specific application and how NLB can be used to spread the load. NLB can distribute TCP and UDP requests, and its primary use is in distributing the following protocols:

- **HTTP**   Web services handled by IIS, typically on port 80.
- **HTTPS**   Secure web services, port 443.
- **FTP**   Ports 20/21 and 1024–65535.
- **TFTP**   For BOOTP and similar services, port 69.
- **SMTP**   For email transfer, port 25.
- **RDP**   For Terminal Services, port 3389.

How you use NLB depends on the exact application and requirements. There are, however, three main aspects to the successful configuration of an NLB cluster: the execution model, capacity planning, and optimization.

Execution Model

NLB clusters support four execution models, based on the number of network adapters and the operating mode for the cluster:

- **Single network adapter per server in unicast mode (SU)** This model is suitable for clusters where direct communication between nodes is not required and where there is limited traffic to specific member nodes outside of cluster traffic—that is, the server is wholly dedicated to servicing the cluster.
- **Multiple network adapters per server in unicast mode (MU)** This model is suitable when communication with other members is required. You can also use this model when you want to separate inter-member and client/cluster communication.
- **Single network adapter per server in multicast mode (SM)** This model is suitable when inter-member communication is required but where there is limited cluster-related traffic handled by each server. This is ideal for individual servers that have a higher usage in an individual capacity, but where clustering is used for a specific low-use fail-over application.
- **Multiple network adapters per server in multicast mode (MM)** This model is suitable when inter-member communication is required and where there is a high level of cluster-related traffic.

We can actually resolve this down further by looking at specific examples, shown in Table 8.5. I've used the two-letter abbreviations from the preceding list as column headers. In the table, Yes means the model is ideal, No means the model is unsuitable, and Possibly means that it may suitable, but is not ideal.

| **TABLE 8.5** | Choosing an Execution Model Based on Application Usage |

Situation Description	SU	MU	SM	MM
Standard (static) web service	Yes	Possibly	No	No
Dynamic/application led web service	No	Yes	Possibly	Yes
Intranet	No	No	Yes	Yes
Exchange based e-mail/ collaboration services	No	Yes	Possibly	Yes
FTP service using DFS to share directories	No	No	No	Yes
WWW service using DFS to share directories	No	Yes	No	Yes
Fail-over for low-load service	Yes	Possibly	Yes	Possibly
Fail-over for high-load service	No	Possibly	No	Yes

Capacity Planning

In addition to choosing the correct execution model, capacity planning enables you to identify the ideal size of your cluster. In general, you should add members to your cluster until your machines can adequately cope with the demand without saturating the network connection used for the cluster communication.

For example, in a high-load web environment, you may have determined that you need four computers to handle the load. Each computer would be a member of the NLB cluster, with each handling approximately the same number of requests. If, however, the network load is such that four machines do not have the network capacity to handle the requests, you may need to increase the number of servers. Conversely, if the overall network transfer is low, but CPU time is high, it may be possible to replace four servers with two more powerful ones, perhaps using multiple CPUs.

Also bear in mind that in a fail-over situation, your remaining servers should be able to cope with the increased load for the period when the other server or servers are unavailable. This calculation should include both unplanned and planned downtime for your cluster members. You therefore need to over-compensate for the total expected load in your server calculations.

For example, a four-node cluster runs at a maximum of 60 percent—that is, each node has an average loading of approximately 60 percent of the total cluster loading. If one member is out of service, the remaining three members must handle an additional 20 percent of the load, making a total of 80 percent for each member.

You can determine and monitor the loading of individual members using Task Manager (on an individual basis) or System Monitor (on an individual and cluster basis).

Optimization

Bearing the calculations and requirements in mind during the capacity planning stage, the optimization of individual machines within the cluster will have an effect on the overall cluster performance and the cluster member's abilities to support the services of a failed member. There are three main areas to consider:

- **Hardware** The hardware for each machine will depend on the expected application. For servers that provide many files or share printer resources, the disk is the limiting factor, so using RAID is a must. You may also need to use a higher rate network card than normal due to the large amount of data being transferred. Conversely, a highly processor intensive application—such as dynamic web serving, e-commerce sites, and so on—may require more RAM and higher rate processors, with disks and network cards having a lower priority.

- **Paging file**   The location of the paging file will have an effect on all applications. Ideally the file should be placed either on its own drive or a low-use drive to help boost access. Also, consider setting the minimum and maximum sizes to the same value to prevent resizing the paging area constantly and increasing the risk of disk defragmentation.
- **Network performance**   Switches off network services that are not required. Use a switch rather than a hub, and consider using a second, dedicated network adapter purely to handle cluster traffic.

Cluster Service

Cluster service provides fail-over capability for two or more servers within a given cluster. It cannot be used to improve the performance or response times for an application.

Typically, the nodes in a cluster are connected to the same shared storage solution, such as a RAID device, which is used not only to store user data, but also to share the quorum, which contains information about the cluster and how it operates. Nodes are not attached to each other except through the network and the shared storage device.

Local Lingo

Quorom   This is a service used to store information about the cluster, including information about the cluster's resources, which node owns each resource, and other data.

Each machine in the mode communicates a heartbeat to the other nodes, which indicates the node's availability. The moment the heartbeat of the primary node dies, the next available node in the network takes over the services the primary node was handling.

Cluster Service Features

Both Enterprise Edition (previously Advanced Server) and Datacenter Edition support 8-node clusters. However, the Cluster Service will only create clusters of nodes running the same OS edition,—that is, all nodes in a cluster must be running either Enterprise or Datacenter Editions. You cannot mix and match the two.

Other new enhancements, briefly, are

- 64-bit memory support in both Enterprise and Datacenter Editions, allowing for up to 4TB of memory per node. This is particularly useful for SQL Server installations.
- Terminal server support, although active sessions cannot be migrated during a failover.
- Majority Node Set (MNS) clusters allow clusters to be set up without using a shared storage device. Instead, Microsoft supplies the quorum resource. This allows for geographically dispersed clusters—for example, two database servers in different locations, cities, or even countries. You can use the same system in installations in which the ultimate storage requirement is not critical; for example, in a network-oriented system where data is ultimately transferred to or logged to another device. However, because there is no shared storage device, it's not possible to share user data across the cluster.
- The Cluster Service is also now installed by default but not activated; you don't need to separately install the Cluster Service. Instead, just open the Cluster Administrator and configure a new cluster.
- Remote Administration allows all aspects of the cluster to be configured remotely. Changes to drive letters and physical disks are also replicated to active terminal server client sessions.
- The command-line tool, cluster.exe, enables scripting and automation for cluster management.
- Support for a larger quorum, 4MB instead of just 64KB, allows for more file and/or printer shares.
- Active Directory (AD) integration. Clusters can now be registered in AD as a single computer; clusters can be identified, published, administered, and accessed by their cluster name, not their individual node names. Because a cluster is a single node, Kerberos authentication can be enabled on the cluster.
- Network status is taken into account when deciding which node to switch to in the event of fail-over. Previously, if a node lost network communication, it retained control of the cluster, even though other nodes in the cluster couldn't connect to it. Now, a node must have an active public network interface before gaining control of a cluster.
- Rolling upgrades allow nodes to be taken offline and upgraded while the other nodes continue to provide fail-over support, meaning that there is less downtime.

Identify System Bottlenecks

Sometimes your machine is just going to run slow for apparently no reason whatsoever. The only way you are going to find out what is causing the problem is to monitor the system and find out what's wrong. There are two potential solutions provided with Windows Server 2003. The first is the Task Manager, which provides basic functionality for examining running processes, RAM, and network performance. If you need to go deeper and examine whether the problem is with a particular process or service or a hardware limitation, then you need to use the built-in Performance monitoring tool.

> **Exam Tip**
>
> You may be asked to identify what might be wrong with a given machine according to different facts and figures. Although these are typically somewhat subjective, read the question and answers carefully as the examples given should give relatively clear solutions for the suggested faults.

We're going to look at both solutions in this section and try to identify what signifies a potential problem and what the solution might be. We'll also take a look at the different counters and monitors that are available to monitor your system.

> **Travel Advisory**
>
> There is an art to monitoring performance, and it can only really be gained through a combination of hard work, sleepless nights, and a deranged sense of attention to detail. Regardless of what tool you use, the ultimate decision or conclusion is typically a case of personal experience and opinion, rather than hard-and-fast rules.

Using Task Manager

The task manager provides some basic system monitoring functionality that can be easier to use and identify than using the full Performance application. However, the information provided is relatively simplistic and concentrates on only three elements: processor, RAM, and networking.

The Processes Tab

The Processes tab provides you with a list of active processes, including subprocesses, along with the user name, current CPU usage, and memory usage for each process. You can see a sample of the dialog box in Figure 8.7.

You can use this tab to identify which services and processes are using the most CPU and memory. If you click the table headers, you can sort the list by each column. Typically, a service or process that is running at more than 75 percent CPU usage indicates either that it is taking too much CPU time or that your machine is potentially underpowered. However, more investigation will be needed before you can make a reasoned decision on this information.

Similarly, excessive memory usage can also indicate a problem, but be aware that some applications—particularly databases or database-led applications like Exchange—may legitimately use significant amounts of memory.

The Performance Tab

The Performance tab gives you a more active interpretation of the current CPU and memory usage. You can see a sample of the window in Figure 8.8.

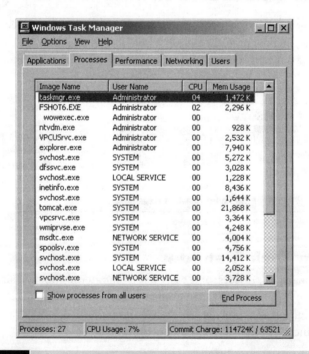

FIGURE 8.7   The Processes tab within Windows Task Manager

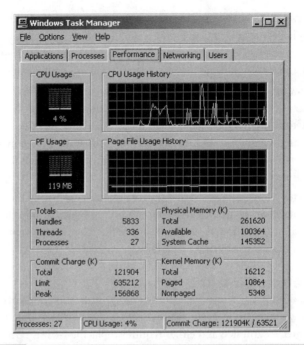

FIGURE 8.8   The Performance tab within Windows Task Manager

The different sections give the following information:

- **CPU Usage**   Shows the current CPU usage in percentage points for all active processes within the system. If you have more than one CPU, this display shows the current usage for both CPUs as individual bar graphs.

- **CPU Usage History**   Shows a graph of the CPU usage over time. If you have more than one CPU, a graph for each CPU is given here. You can use this to monitor the CPU usage over a particular event or while a particular application is executing.

- **PF Usage**   Shows the current paging (swap) file usage. A high value here may indicate that you need to increase the size of the swap file on your machine. If your paging file is already set to between two and four times your physical RAM, then you may need to increase your physical RAM to compensate.

- **Paging File Usage History**   This shows the history of paging file usage. High, intermittent spikes can indicate a reliance on paging files when RAM is required.

- **Totals**   This shows the total number of handles, threads, and processes currently active on the machine.

- **Physical Memory (K)**   This shows the amount of physical memory available, the amount currently available, and the amount used for the system cache. Particularly low values of available memory, system cache, or both indicate that you may require more physical memory.

- **Commit Charge (K)**   This shows the total amount of memory currently in use, including that used by the system cache. The Limit is the total memory available, including swap, while the Peak value shows the highest amount of memory used by your system. A figure here that exceeds your total physical memory may indicate a lack of RAM in your server.

- **Kernel Memory (K)**   Shows the total memory in use by the kernel. Values here are unlikely to change and don't typically indicate any useful information. However, be aware that page kernel memory is available for use by other programs.

The Networking Tab

The Networking tab shows you the network utilization for each network adapter in your machine. You can use this to gauge whether your current network adapter is saturated and either requires replacing—say a 1GB in place of an existing 100MB—or adding to by increasing the number of adapters.

You can see a sample of the Networking tab in Figure 8.9.

System Monitor

The System Monitor is the built-in monitoring tool for examining the internal execution of different components within the server. The System Monitor within Windows Server 2003 is called Performance. In addition to the basic information we've already seen, Performance can monitor a number of internal objects not accessible through Task Manager. These performance objects are named according to the object they monitor; for example, the Processor object monitors CPU performance.

In addition to the internal objects provided by the operating system—including those for monitoring memory, processors, and networking services—other applications and services can provide their own counters and objects for monitoring. For example, Performance is able to monitor the WINS service or the Microsoft Exchange service through the performance objects that these systems provide.

Performance objects are further subdivided into counters that monitor specific data. For example, the Pages/sec counter provided by the Memory object tracks the rate of memory paging.

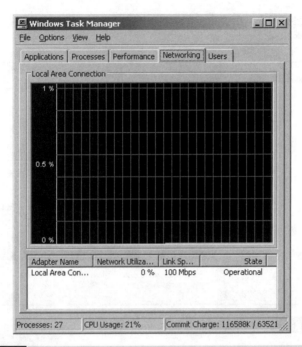

FIGURE 8.9   The Networking tab within Windows Task Manager

Although your system might typically make available many more objects, the following are the most frequently used objects:

- Cache
- Memory
- Objects
- Paging file
- Physical disk
- Process
- Processor
- Server
- System
- Thread

You can see a sample of Performance in action in Figure 8.10. To open Performance, click Start | Control Panel, double-click Administrative Tools, and then double-click Performance.

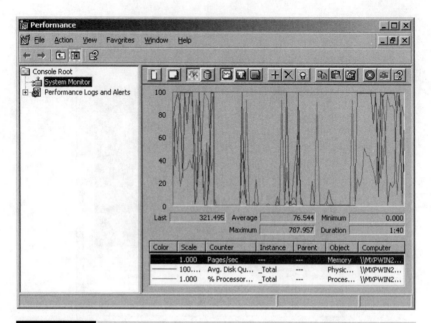

FIGURE 8.10 Performance, the internal System Monitor application

To add counters to System Monitor:

1. Open Performance.

2. Right-click the System Monitor details pane and click Add Counters.

3. To monitor any computer on which the monitoring console is run, click Use Local Computer Counters.

4. Or, to monitor a specific computer, regardless of where the monitoring console is run, click Select Counters From Computer and specify a computer name or IP address.

5. In Performance object, click an object to monitor.

6. To monitor all counters, click All Counters.

7. Or, to monitor only selected counters, click Select Counters From List and select the counters you want to monitor.

8. To monitor all instances of the selected counters, click All Instances.

9. Or, to monitor only selected instances, click Select Instances From List and select the instances you want to monitor.

10. Click Add, and then click OK.

To perform this procedure, you must be a member of the Administrators group, the Performance Log Users group, or the Performance Monitor Users group on the local computer, or you must have been delegated the appropriate authority.

As you can see from Figure 8.10, by default, the following four counters are displayed in System Monitor:

- Memory\Pages/sec
- PhysicalDisk(_Total)\Avg.
- Disk Queue Length
- Processor(_Total)\%Processor Time.

If you select an object on a remote computer, you might notice a short delay as System Monitor refreshes the list to reflect objects present on that computer.

The range of objects available depends on the system you are monitoring. For example, some objects have several instances; in a system with multiple processors, the Processor object type will have multiple instances. The Physical Disk object type has one instance per physical disk. Some object types such as Memory and Server have only a single instance. If an object type has multiple instances, you can add counters to track statistics for each instance, or in many cases, for all instances at once.

You can use this facility to monitor CPU usage, for example. You could monitor all CPUs and determine whether a performance issue could be solved by spreading the load across the CPUs or whether you need to add another CPU to your system.

By default, counters are shown with both the instance name and an instance index. To turn off this feature, right-click the details pane, click Properties, select the General tab, and clear the Allow Duplicate Counter Instances check box.

When you select two instance indexes of the same counter—for example, if you are monitoring multiple threads of a process—note that the instance index number assigned to that instance changes over time as the instance, such as a thread, starts and stops. The index number does not necessarily correspond to the same thread over the life of the process.

When creating a monitoring console for export, make sure to select Use Local Computer Counters. Otherwise, System Monitor will obtain data from the computer named in the text box, regardless of where the console file is installed.

For a description of a particular counter, click the name of the counter in Add Counters, and then click Explain.

You can change the default display characteristics assigned to a counter such as the color, line style and width, and graph scale by using the Data tab in the System Monitor Properties dialog box. To access the Data tab, right-click the details pane, and then click Properties.

Objective 8.03

Plan a Backup and Recovery Strategy

There is nothing worse as a user than to discover you've lost an important document, invoice, or e-mail during your work. Worse, you certainly don't want to lose the ability to use one of your servers, especially if it's providing critical files or services, such as Active Directory or file/printer sharing.

There are lots of reasons that failures and loss of systems can occur. The most obvious, and typically the most difficult to cope with, is a hardware failure. Hardware failure is particularly hard to deal with because it presents additional problems beyond simply recovering the information—you need to find replacement parts or components to get your machine working again.

Actually, we can probably get much worse than that—imagine that your building burns down, there's a chemical leak, or worse, a serious explosion such as that experienced by companies in terrorist attacks. In this type of catastrophic situation, you have more to do than just find a replacement component—you have to find a complete replacement machine and probably a new location.

At the other end of the scale is the simple accidental deletion of a file or component—it can be done as simply as highlighting the wrong file and pressing the DELETE key too quickly, but it happens.

In any of these situations, having a backup enables you to recover from the accident, mistake, or machine failure. But a backup solution is good only if you have a comparable recovery strategy to get your machines working and back online as quickly as possible.

For the exam, Microsoft expects you to know the significance of the backup process, the best ways to back up your machines and networks, what items you should back up, and how frequently these backups should take place. They will also expect you to know how best to build a recovery strategy to get your machines working again in as little time as possible, including the steps required to rebuild an entire machine or its critical system state data to get your servers back online. We'll look at all these issues in this section.

Backup Planning

Ignoring specifics for the moment, you should plan your backup system according to your recovery requirements. For example, if, in the event of a machine failure, you need to get your server working again within a few hours of its original failure, then your backup strategy, including frequency and contents, should reflect this requirement.

The critical element in this situation is the period of downtime that your company can afford to live with and how much time you are willing to spend bringing systems back into operation and recovering or reproducing the data that you lost between the time of the last backup and the time of the incident.

To give an example, imagine the accounting department's machines are backed up each night at 10 P.M., and you have a failure at 3 P.M. in the afternoon. The recovery time will be the time it takes to recover the information from the backup plus an additional seven hours it will take for your accounting department to process the information they worked on between 8 A.M. and 3 P.M.

Exam Tip

You'll be expected to make decisions about when and how frequently to back up, as well as make decisions based on the times, type, and recovery requirements, all of which are covered in this section. Some of the questions will even give the backup parameters and expect you to make judgment decisions on the best solution.

This section covers the three main areas of consideration when determining the appropriate backup strategy:

- Backup type
- What to back up
- When to back up

Armed with the details on these areas, we'll then be able to translate these settings into a number of methodologies that are frequently used to define your backup strategy.

Backup Types

Most backup software, including Microsoft's own Backup Utility, support the three basic backup types: full, incremental, and differential. Each type backs up the files you select and, depending on the backup type you select, optionally clears the archive attribute on each file. When a file is modified, the OS sets the archive attribute. The incremental and differential backup types use this information to determine which files should be backed up.

The full range of backup types include the following:

- *Full* (normal) backups copy all the files you select, clearing the archive attribute bit after each file has copied to the backup set. The attribute is ignored for selecting files.

- *Incremental* backups copy only the files that have changed since the last normal or incremental backup (by examining the archive attribute setting); that is, they copy only the files that have changed since the last backup.
- *Differential* backups copy only the files that have changed since the last full or incremental backup (by examining the archive attribute setting), according to the setting of the archive attribute. The attribute is not updated when each file is backed up.
- A *copy backup* copies all the files you select but does not update the archive attribute for each file. You can therefore perform a copy backup without it affecting the operation or execution of your main backup set or sequence.
- A *daily backup* copies all the files that have been modified on the day the backup takes place. As with a copy backup, the archive attribute bit for each file is not updated.

Exam Tip

Microsoft considers that most companies perform a full backup each week and an incremental or differential backup each day in between. However, you should be aware of the different types of backup and how the combinations of backups work together.

Choosing the right backup combination is important because it affects not only how you back up but also how quickly and easily you will be able to recover in the event of failure. You should make the decision based on a combination of the speed at which you need to recover from a failure coupled with the rotation of tapes—so that you can have copies offsite for example—and the efficiency of tape usage. For example, when using a combination of a full backup and incremental backups, you will need the full backup tape set and each incremental tape, but you will also be able to easily ship older incremental tapes offsite and have more efficient tape usage as you are backing up a relatively small amount each evening. However, if using a full backup in combination with differential backups, you need only the full set and the last differential tape. You will, however, use more tape progressively each day and potentially lose the ability to go back to a specific day within the backup set.

We'll look at this in more detail in the "Backup Methodologies" section later in this chapter.

Using Volume Shadow Copy Service

In addition to the main backup types given in the preceding section, there is an additional backup type called Volume Shadow Copy Service (VSCS, occasionally shorted to VSS), which works in tandem with the operating system. Really, it's a completely separate entity to the backup service, but it's an important part of your backup strategy.

With the VSCS, Windows Server 2003 reserves space on a disk to record the changes in files as they are used and saved. This means that as users open and save files, a sequence of different versions is created by the VSCS system at set periods of time. Windows Server 2003 does this on a fixed schedule. At each period, the server creates a shadow copy (or snapshot) of the disk at a particular point in time, with the changes between this snapshot and previous snapshot being recorded on a file-by-file basis. This means that you can go back to a previous version of a file, or even recover files and entire folders that were deleted, without you ever having to perform a specific backup process.

Older versions of the files are automatically disposed of to make room for newer versions, so the system becomes self-managing.

You can then go back to a previous version of the file (by viewing the previous versions within the file's Properties dialog box). Users can do this even without the intervention of the IT department as the different versions of the file are stored and recorded by the VSCS system. Support for recovery and viewing of previous versions is provided only with Windows XP clients.

However, what this means is that your users are able to handle their own recovery of files when they have made a mistake and saved over a version of a file that they needed to keep. This reduces the load on your IT department having to handle the recovery process themselves.

Volume Shadow Copy Service obviously uses more disk space than just using a standard disk and backup routines, but it gives the added benefit of making restoration of particular files much easier. VSCS can also be used to create backup copies of other core files such as the Active Directory databases, DNS, DHCP, and WINS databases and other configuration files—the VSCS works with the services in question to temporarily delay writes to the database files while the copy is created.

VSCS also works with professional storage solutions such as Storage Area Networks to allow you to create copies of files on larger storage volumes than those used within a networked server environment.

VSCS does *not* make a copy of the volumes but takes a snapshot of what parts of the hard disk have changed. It then uses this information to restore these parts to the previous state to bring the data back to a previous point in time. VSS is very handy to get a quick snapshot of a system and its files and can be used to recover previous versions of documents on shared volumes—something that many administrators will find very appealing.

Exam Tip

The exam will expect you to know the pitfalls and problems of using Volume Shadow Copy Service. You may be asked to make a recommendation based on the backup or file/application type.

Using Automated System Recovery Sets

If you have a system failure that prevents you from booting up correctly, you can normally recover from the situation by using safe mode, the last known good configuration, or by rolling back drivers to a previous version.

If these techniques don't work, the usual solution would be to rebuild and recover from a backup. If you use the standard backup and recovery techniques (that is, just using the Microsoft Backup or a similar utility), you will have to perform a number of operations manually, potentially including re-installation of the operating system and applications before you can even start to recover the data and system configuration.

Automated System Recovery (ASR) provides a solution when normal recovery options are exhausted. During re-installation from a Windows Server 2003 CD, you can use ASR to recover the system without having to manually re-install and restore information.

ASR backs up the system state data, system services, and all disks that contain operating system components. It also creates a backup disk that contains information about the disk setup and volumes plus information about the backup and how the restore process should proceed.

Exam Tip

You may be asked in the exam to identify the components backed up by ASR and how and when to use ASR to recover your system.

You can create an ASR backup using the Automated System Recovery Preparation Wizard, or by selecting All Information On This Computer in the simple backup wizard within the Backup utility.

You should create an ASR set regularly, at least every three months, and if possible, every month. You should also update the ASR set if you change the configuration of the machine significantly, including changes to volume configurations, additional disks, or changes in server roles.

Choosing What to Back Up

What you back up is probably the most important consideration you'll have—if you don't back up the right files or objects, it doesn't matter when or how you back them up, you'll never be able to recover the files correctly. The result will be a backup that is of no use to anybody.

There are two primary concerns when considering what to back up: the system files required to bring a server back into availability as quickly as possible and the data files in which your company stores its information and data.

Critical Files

The critical files on any machine, including a Windows Server 2003 computer, include the registry, the Active Directory files if they exist, and any other configuration files required to bring your machines back on line as quickly as possible.

Within Backup, these critical components are conveniently available as a single backup source called the system state data. The information included in the system state data is reliant on the machine and its roles. You can see a summary of the information included in the system state data in Table 8.6.

Local Lingo	
Boot files These files include the files required to start Windows and include Ntldr and Ntdetect.com.	

TABLE 8.6	Components Included in the System State Data During a Backup
Component	**Included in System State Data?**
Registry	Always
COM+ Class Registration Database	Always
Boot files, including the system files	Always
Certificate Services Directory	If the server is a Certificate Services server
Active Directory directory service database	If the server is a domain server
SYSVOL directory	If the server is a domain controller
Cluster service information	If the server is part of a cluster
IIS metabase	If IIS is installed/configured
System files under Windows File Protection	Always

> **Local Lingo**
>
> **System files**   These files incorporate the files required to load, configure, and run the operating system.

If you select Backup for the system state data, then the relevant components will automatically be backed. It's not possible to select individual components within the system state data.

> **Travel Advisory**
>
> You cannot back up the system state data of a remote machine. This type of backup works only on a local machine when using the standard Backup utility. To back up the system state data of a remote machine, you will need to purchase special backup software such as Veritas Backup Exec, Dantz's Retrospect, or Legato's Networker.

Data Files

Your data files should be easy to identify—they'll probably be located in one or more folders on your system that are probably shared out to other users—unless you are terribly untidy, in which case you'll need to select each location individually. Also remember to back up your database files, IIS websites and associated data.

Applications and OS

Typically you don't back up applications and operating system files; you should have these readily available on installation CD-ROMs. It's nearly always faster to recover these files from the CD by completing a normal installation. There are exceptions to this rule—applications that you have created and installed, web applications and components, or applications that are heavily patched may be better backed up for a quicker recovery.

That said, Microsoft recommends that you back up your boot and system volumes in addition to the system state data. This ensures that you also back up any drivers, configuration files, and system updates that would otherwise be ignored.

Servers and Clients

In a small network it's possible to use the Windows Backup Utility to back up remote servers and clients, but it's not necessarily recommended as you have to enable sharing on each machine. It's also impossible to back up the system state data in this manner. There are, however, other tools available that can be used to back up all the servers and clients on your network, including remote servers and clients, from a single machine.

In a multisite installation, backup of remote servers will generally not be either time or cost effective. However, if you are using separate domain servers at each site and you have relatively fast connections between sites, then you may want to back up the system state data and AD information remotely in the case of failure.

If you do decide to back up servers or clients, remote or otherwise, then the same basic rules apply—you need to back up the system state data, user data, databases, and so on, just as if they are local. Also keep in mind the list of items not to be backed up—the same items and rules apply. What are those rules, you ask? Let's visit those next.

What Not to Back Up

There are some files that you can accidentally back up that serve no purpose other than to take up space on your backup tapes. Backing these files up achieves nothing but wasting space and will never be used to recover information in the event of a failure or problem.

The Windows Backup Utility and most other backup applications have the ability to include and exclude different directories—you can use this to specifically exclude information that you know does not need to be backed up.

For example, in most situations you should avoid backing up

- **Operating systems and applications**   Except in the examples already given above (that is, during an ASR backup or when backing up system state data), avoid backing up applications and operating systems. Remember that you should keep your installation CDs in the same secure location as you keep your backup tapes, so that in the event of failure, you have everything you need to recover the machine.

- **Temporary files**   The temporary files directory within your Windows installation doesn't contain anything useful, and in fact, probably contains information that you could easily delete whether you are running a backup or not.

- **Internet cache files**   Generally these contain no useful information, only the downloaded HTML and graphics components of the websites that a user has visited. The exception to the rule is that these files can also include the cookies used to store site data and login details.

- **Paging files**   A paging file usually takes up at least 512MB, and on a large server may take up significantly more. Because paging files are transient files, they are modified every day, which means you'll be backing up a single large file every time you run a backup. But they are of no use to anybody—a paging file is composed of applications and data paged out by the OS while it's running and the contents can change from second to second—the moment you restart the machine, the paging file is effectively re-created. Even if you could back up the paging file, recovering it would be impossible, and the information contained in it would never match the state of the system at the time the file was created.

Choosing When to Back Up

The company, its environment, and how it operates will govern when you back up your machines. There are two considerations that affect every backup decision—which days (and therefore how frequently) a backup is done and at what time on those days. The combination of the two will determine your recovery time and also your recovery frequency and backup types.

Days of the Week

It should be pretty obvious that you should back up your machines at least once each working day. A common implementation is to perform one full backup on one day, usually Friday, and then to perform an incremental or differential backup on each following day.

Which type of backup you perform again depends on the specific needs of the company. I prefer a weekly backup on a Monday, because then I have a reference point to the start of the week and can restore back to pretty much any day within the week from that starting point. Others prefer to have a Friday backup that closes off the end of the week.

Time of Day

The time of day is the easiest of the two time parameters to consider—you should choose a time that fits in the company's normal operating times and schedules. The issue with choosing a time is not to ensure the open files are backed up, but that you back up the latest copy. You can ensure that files are backed up, even if open, using Volume Shadow Copy Service.

For example, if the company has normal office hours between 8 A.M. and 5 P.M. and you know that you have staff working late some evenings until 9 P.M., you could assume that at 10 P.M. each evening, it's safe to do a backup that captures the latest version of each file.

For companies that operate in shifts over a longer period, even up to 24 hours, you should try to take your backups at the shift crossover time. For example, if you have three eight-hour shifts that cross over at 1 A.M., 9 A.M., and 5 P.M., you should back up your files at those times—there should be a 15–30 minute period of relative quiet when you can back up information, although don't necessarily expect to achieve a full backup in that time!

In some situations you might need to make more than one backup each day. For example, in companies where the information and transactions are time and particularly financially critical, waiting until the end of the day could be fatal if there is an accident, hardware failure, or other problem. In these situations, you should choose a time that fits in with the company's availability requirements.

If you need to be able to restore your machines to a working state quickly with as little a loss of information as possible, then you can increase the frequency of your backups, even down to the space of a couple of hours or even less. Be aware, however, that performing backups this frequently will have an impact on your server's performance.

Backup Methodologies

We can take combinations of backup types and backup times and create a number of methodologies that create suitable backup solutions for most companies. We've already covered some of these details throughout this section, but it's worth taking a closer look at the various advantages and disadvantages of some potential solutions.

> **Exam Tip**
>
> You will be expected to work out what has been backed up and what is required to recover a machine from the sequence of backup types. Only a sample of these combinations has been shown here, so make sure you know the different backup types and how they interrelate.

The most common backup solution is a simple weekly full backup with an incremental backup each day.

You can also alternate backup sets and create multiple sets so that you have up to four weeks or more of effectively individual backups each day. It's also a good idea to alternate sets within a given week—for example, use one set on Monday, another on Tuesday, and so on, so that you can store individual night tapes securely.

The benefits of this system are

- A weekly backup of everything.
- A daily backup of all the changes.

- The ability to go back to a specific day within a given period.
- Efficient use of tapes and available storage.

The pitfalls are

- To recover from a failure, you need to recover not only the full backup but also each incremental between the full backup and the day of the failure. For example, if you have a failure on Wednesday, you must recover the full backup, plus the incremental from Monday and Tuesday. A failure on the morning of the full backup would require you to recover from five tapes.

We can improve on this by using a differential backup each evening in place of an incremental, as shown in Table 8.7. Because a differential backs up everything since the last full or incremental backup, in this scenario each daily backup records all the changes since the last full backup.

As with incremental backup, in a differential backup we can combine the basic parameters with multiple tape sets and tape rotation.

The benefits of this system are

- A weekly backup of everything.
- A daily backup of all the changes.
- Recovery can be completed using only two tapes, the full tape and the last differential tape.

The pitfalls are

- Inefficient use of tapes and available storage.
- Inability to go back to a specific day.

We can, of course, combine the two solutions to alternate between incremental and differential backups, leading to the solution in Table 8.7.

TABLE 8.7   Combined Incremental/Differential Backups

Day	Backup Type
Friday	Full
Monday	Incremental
Tuesday	Differential
Wednesday	Incremental
Thursday	Differential

The benefits of this system are

- A weekly backup of everything.
- A daily backup of all the changes.
- Ability to recover from a specific day
- Recovery can be completed using at minimum only two tapes, the full tape and the last differential tape. At maximum, recovery can be completed using three tapes: the last full, last differential, and last incremental.

The pitfalls are

- Relatively inefficient use of tapes and available storage.

Media Storage

Although not a requirement for the exam, it is considered best practice to know how to store your backup devices and media. Remember that a good backup contains everything you need to bring your organization back online as quickly as possible.

If the tapes are stolen, destroyed by fire or another accident, or if they are stolen, their effectiveness and usefulness to you are reduced significantly—probably to zero. If the tapes get into the wrong hands, you've potentially given away all of your company data to a competitor or worse.

Tapes, and the original installation CDs for your operating system and applications, should at least be stored in a safe that is not only physically secure but also protected against damage in the event of fire. You should also have more than one copy of your backups—the copy backup mode in the Windows Backup Utility will help here.

For even better protection, the tapes should be stored off-site; better still, you could use one of the many off-site tape storage companies that deliver and pick up your backup tapes each day.

Recovery Practices

The exact pattern of recovery that you choose will depend entirely on how you backed up your machines and the reason for your recovery. Assuming you have an adequate backup in place—and you should have if you've followed the guidance given here—then your primary concern is how to get your machines and network working again as quickly as possible.

In this section we'll look at some of the major issues affecting recovery of data in the event of hardware or other failure. You will be expected to know the primary methods.

Testing Your Backups

You should always plan to test the quality of your backups. Not only will this confirm that your tapes or other media are in good working order, it will also confirm that you are backing up the correct files and components and that you can correctly bring your systems back online in as quick a time as possible.

The easiest way to test the backups is to actually try a recover to a new machine or have a server or desktop computer dedicated to the task of restoring data from a tape for the purposes of testing the tape and backup quality. This will require an additional machine to handle the testing, but it doesn't have to be equivalent to your servers—it could be a cheap or older machine not doing anything. In any case, $500 compared to the thousands or millions you could lose from a bad backup is a small price to pay.

Recovering System State Data and User Data

Performing a restore operation is a fairly simple and straightforward process. Within Backup you just select the restore option, choose the tape set you want to restore from, and then choose the files you want to restore. You can also choose to overwrite existing files—which you will want to do if you have re-installed an OS and want to recover the system state data.

Recovering Entire Networks

If you have had a complete systems failure across your network due to a fire or similar catastrophe and have to start from scratch, then you should plan to restore the systems in the following order:

1. Primary domain controllers
2. Member servers and data
3. Non-member servers and data
4. Clients

This ensures that you get your servers up and running as quickly as possible without having to worry about missing domains or services. In general, for member servers, restore the key servers first; for example, when restoring IIS services and applications, restore the server primarily responsible for the IIS connectivity, and then any message servers or processors followed by the relevant application servers. The aim is to prevent individual servers or clients trying to access servers and resources that aren't there. By restoring your domain controller first, you ensure that other servers will not fail during startup with authentication errors.

Using Automated System Recovery (ASR)

You can access the ASR recovery process by pressing F2 after booting up from a Windows Server 2003 CD-ROM. The recovery process will use the floppy disk to reconfigure the disks and volumes, and then it will install a basic system before recovering data from your tape backup on to the system.

Note that you will have to restore your data files manually—ASR only stores and recovers system and system state information.

Recovering Server Clusters

To recover a single node, the best solution is to use ASR to recover the node data and configuration. The restored node can then rejoin the cluster.

Recovering Active Directory Databases

Generally if you have a failure bad enough that you need to recover the information on a domain controller, you must start up the machine in Directory Services Restore Mode, which you can do from the Startup options menu when booting a machine by pressing F8. This starts the controller without starting up the Active Directory service and initializing the database. You can then restore system state data from a backup and reboot as normal. To restore the AD database in this fashion, you must use the directory services restore password (created when you created the domain) and use the local administrators account to log into the machine.

Restoring from a Volume Shadow Copy Backup

If you have backed up a machine using a Volume Shadow Copy Service, you can recover the previous version of the file by selecting the file properties and using the Previous Versions tab to view the previous versions of a file. That's it—there are no other stages involved, and we don't need to use backup tapes or other solutions to recover the information. It's right there on the disk.

CHECKPOINT

✔**Objective 8.01: Plan Services for High Availability**   You should know the basics of how the two primary clustering technologies work and what services they can be applied to. NLB is used to share and provide fail-over support of TCP/IP services. Cluster Service is used to provide an immediate fail-over backup to an alternate machine in the event of failure. You should also know how to plan to use these clustering technologies to provide a high-availability service.

✔**Objective 8.02: Identify System Bottlenecks**   From the information in this section, you should be able to use and monitor both local and remote systems in terms of their disk, memory, processor, and other parameters. By monitoring these objects, you should be able to identify potential bottlenecks in the system and then make decisions about which element of a server you should correct to alleviate or eliminate the problem.

✔**Objective 8.03: Plan a Backup and Recovery Strategy**   You should know the basic backup types including Volume Shadow Copy Service, what to back up, when to perform a backup, and how to use a combination of these parameters to create a backup plan suitable for your needs. You should also understand the difference between a differential and incremental backup and how this relates to the files that are backed up. Remember that Volume Shadow Copy Service backs up open files, but at the cost of potentially breaking applications when the backup is used to restore the files. You should also be able incorporate regular uses of the Automated System Recovery system to perform backups in event of a serious system failure. When the backup has been completed, you should be able to create a suitable plan to recover the information on a single server, across a network, and even within a cluster.

REVIEW QUESTIONS

1. You're an administrator for a network that includes a server used to provide developing and beta websites for your company's clients. Because developers are regularly installing updated software components and websites on the machine, it is often down during the day when your clients are trying to use it. To alleviate this, you want to

install two servers so that one can be taken out of action and updated while the other continues to provide existing websites to your clients. You do not want the machines to share information. What should you do? (Choose one.)

A. Set up two identical machines with the same IP address.

B. Set up two identical machines with a shared RAID device and the Cluster Service.

C. Set up two identical machines and configure a Network Load Balancing cluster.

D. Set up two identical machines each using a RAID device.

2. The server supporting your website is over capacity. By checking the logs and using System Monitor, you are able to determine that your machine is under-powered by at least 25 percent. You decide to add another identical machine and configure Network Load Balancing to share the load. You also know that you expect the load to increase by 50 percent over the next six months. The developers have also indicated that they need to install a number of updates within the same period. You must ensure that the cluster is able to cope with the extra load and the updates. How should you continue with the reconfiguration? (Choose all that apply.)

A. Add one identical server to the cluster.

B. Add two identical servers to the cluster.

C. Change the priority of the initial server to be higher than the second.

D. Add one identical server and configure its priority lower than the existing nodes.

3. You are running a demo application from a supplier on your test server. The test server has 512MB of RAM, a 2GB paging file, and a RAID device with 80GB of storage. During execution, the system seems to lock up. You manage to open Windows Task Manager and identify that the application is using 350MB of RAM and using up all the available CPU time. The memory graph also shows a number of large spikes in swap space usage that coincide with spikes in the CPU load. You need to upgrade the machine to test the software effectively. What component should you upgrade? (Choose one.)

A. Install more RAM

B. Install a faster CPU.

C. Install an additional disk drive.

D. Install a second CPU.

4. A server in your company provides web services but appears to have sluggish performance. You need to monitor the CPU and memory usage over a week so that you can provide the performance graphs to management to get approval for upgrades to the machine. Which tool should you use to generate this information? (Choose one.)

A. Task Manager

B. Performance

C. System Monitor

D. Event Viewer

5. You have a machine that is running Exchange Server, which you need to back up each evening. Exchange is used to handle all of your e-mail for your site and is required to be in operation 24 hours a day, although there is a quiet period very early in the morning. You configure Backup Utility to run a full backup each Friday evening and an incremental backup every other evening. When you test the backup you find that many of the files critical for Exchange are not on the backup set. What should you do? (Choose one).

A. Configure Exchange to shut down while the backup completes.

B. Configure Backup to create a Copy backup each evening.

C. Configure Backup to use Volume Shadow Copy Service when backing up the machine.

D. Configure Backup to back up Exchange in the morning, instead of the evening.

6. The primary file server in your organization needs to be backed up. There is a gap in usage of the machine in the middle of the night that enables you to perform backup, but there is room to back up only about 50 percent of all the data at this time. On weekends, the server is not in use. How should you configure your backup strategy to ensure the machine is backed up correctly? (Choose two.)

A. Run a weekly full backup.

B. Run a daily full backup.

C. Run daily incremental backups.

D. Run daily differential backups.

7. You server is backed up each evening using an incremental backup and each weekend using a full backup. As part of your account procedures, you must create a separate backup of the accounting files onto a separate tape at the end of each month. You need to include this requirement in your plan, but must ensure that the separate backup you create does not upset the daily and weekly backup. What should you do? (Choose one.)

   A. Run a full backup of the accounting files on the last day of each month.

   B. Run a copy backup of the accounting files on the last day of each month.

   C. Run a daily backup of the accounting files on the last day of each month.

   D. Run a differential backup of the accounting files on the last day of each month.

REVIEW ANSWERS

1. **C**   NLB is the obvious choice here as it's easy to set up and still provides fail-over support if one machine has to be taken out of service. D won't work as you can't do this without using Cluster Service, while B is overkill for what are relatively simple needs. A will cause an error on the second machine you configure, as you can't have two machines with the same IP address.

2. **B**   The current under capacity, expected growth, and requirement to have one machine down during an update means that you need two machines, not one, to solve the problem. The others answers might alleviate the problem, but they won't solve it.

3. **A**   A large memory requirement like this, coupled with large disk and CPU spikes, indicates an overuse of the paging file space.

4. **C**   Only System Monitor can reliably store information for this long so that it can be analyzed.

5. **C**   Volume Shadow Copy Service will copy open files to the backup. A isn't valid because we need the server up. A Copy backup is identical to a normal backup—it just creates a copy without updating the archive attribute, and it still won't copy open files.

6. **A** **C**   A full backup followed by incremental backups ensures that over time the entire server will be backed up, even if all the files are not backed up in one evening. Differential backups required progressively more time, while full backups require the most time.

7. **B**   Running a copy backup will not update the archive attribute, so we can use it to create a copy of the files without affecting the rest of the backup. A differential backup doesn't update the archive attribute, either, but it won't back up all the files you select, only those that have been modified.

Appendixes

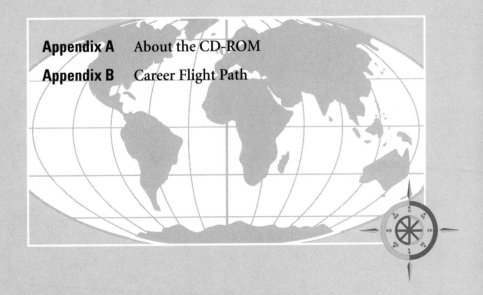

About the CD-ROM

Mike Meyers' Certification Passport CD-ROM Instructions

The CD-ROM included with this book comes complete with MasterExam. The software is easy to install on any Windows 98/NT/2000/XP computer and must be installed to access the MasterExam feature. To register for the second bonus MasterExam, simply click the link on the main page and follow the directions to the free online registration.

System Requirements

The software included on the CD-ROM requires Windows 98 or higher and Internet Explorer 5.0 or above, as well as 20MB of hard disk space for full installation.

Installing and Running MasterExam

If your computer CD-ROM drive is configured to autorun, the CD-ROM will automatically start up upon inserting the disk. From the opening screen, you may install MasterExam by clicking the MasterExam or MasterSim buttons. This will begin the installation process and create a program group named LearnKey. To run MasterExam, select Start | Programs | LearnKey. If the autorun feature did not launch your CD-ROM, browse to the CD-ROM and click the RunInstall icon.

MasterExam

MasterExam provides you with a simulation of the actual exam. The number of questions, types of questions, and time allowed are intended to be a representation of the exam environment. You have the option to take an open-book exam (including hints, references, and answers), a closed book exam, or a timed MasterExam simulation.

When you launch the MasterExam simulation, a digital clock will appear in the top-center of your screen. The clock will continue to count down to zero unless you choose to end the exam before the time expires.

Help

Select the Help button on the lower-left corner of the main page to access the help file. Individual help features are also available through MasterExam.

Removing Installation(s)

MasterExam is installed to your hard drive. For best results in removing the programs, use the Start | Programs | LearnKey | Uninstall options.

If you want to remove RealPlayer, select Add or Remove Programs from the Windows Control Panel. You may also remove the LearnKey training program from this location.

Technical Support

For questions regarding the technical content of the MasterExam, please visit www.osborne.com or e-mail customer.service@mcgraw-hill.com. For customers outside the United States, e-mail international_cs@mcgraw-hill.com.

LearnKey Technical Support

For technical problems with the software (installation, operation, or removal installations), please visit www.learnkey.com or e-mail techsupport@learnkey.com.

Career Flight Path

The Microsoft Windows certification program that you will be joining when you take your 70-293 exam includes an extensive group of exams and certification levels. Passing the Planning and Maintaining a Microsoft Windows Server 2003 Network Infrastructure exam is all that is required for Microsoft's baseline certification—the Microsoft Certified Professional (MCP).

Microsoft's premier certification is the Microsoft Certified Systems Engineer (MCSE), and the 70-293 exam is a core requirement for this certification.

Core Exams

There are seven exams that every MCSE candidate must pass. These exams test your knowledge of Windows Server 2003 and include four required networking system exams, a client operating system exam, and a design exam. You can choose between exams to fulfill the client operating system and design exam categories, as long as you complete one for each category. Additionally, you will be required to pass one elective exam.

Networking Systems Exams

The four required tests on the Networking Systems are

- **70-290** Managing and Maintaining a Microsoft Windows Server 2003 Environment
- **70-291** Implementing, Managing, and Maintaining a Microsoft Windows Server 2003 Network Infrastructure

- **70-293**   Planning and Maintaining a Microsoft Windows 2003 Network Infrastructure
- **70-294**   Planning, Implementing, and Maintaining a Microsoft Windows 2003 Active Directory Infrastructure

Core Elective Exams

At this point you can begin to customize your MCSE to your personal areas of expertise. For both the client operating system and the design exam requirements, you can choose between exam options.

For the client operating system requirement, you can choose between the following exams:

- **70-270**   Installing, Configuring, and Administering Microsoft Windows XP Professional
- **70-210**   Installing, Configuring, and Administering Microsoft Windows 2000 Professional

---

Exam Tip

For those who opted to take the 70-240 exam, Microsoft Windows 2000 Accelerated Exam for MCPs Certified on Microsoft Windows NT 4.0, you have already met the MCSE exam requirement for 70-210.

For the design requirement, you can choose from the following exams:

- **70-297**   Designing a Microsoft Windows Server 2003 Active Directory and Network Infrastructure
- **70-298**   Designing Security for a Microsoft Windows Server 2003 Network

---

Exam Tip

In the next section, you'll also see these two exams listed as electives. These exams can count once each as either a core design exam or as an elective choice.

Elective Exam

With the core client operating system and design exams, you are given a bit of choice; but with the last elective exam, you can really customize your MCSE around your interests and knowledge. Microsoft currently offers eight exams to choose from:

- **70-086**   Implementing and Supporting Microsoft Systems Management Server 2.0
- **70-227**   Installing, Configuring, and Administering Microsoft Internet Security and Acceleration (ISA) Server 2000, Enterprise Edition
- **70-228**   Installing, Configuring, and Administering Microsoft SQL Server 2000, Enterprise Edition
- **70-229**   Designing and Implementing Databases with Microsoft SQL Server 2000, Enterprise Edition
- **70-232**   Implementing and Maintaining Highly Available Web Solutions with Microsoft Windows 2000 Server Technologies and Microsoft Application Center 2000
- **70-297**   Designing a Microsoft Windows Server 2003 Active Directory and Network Infrastructure
- **70-298**   Designing Security for a Microsoft Windows Server 2003 Network
- **70-299**   Implementing and Administering Security in a Microsoft Windows Server 2003 Network

Upgrade Paths

Microsoft offers upgrade paths for those holding MCSE credentials on either NT 4.0 or Windows 2000. These paths allow the MCSE to credit previous exams toward the requirements for the Server 2003 credential.

NT 4.0 Upgrade Options

If you are an MCSE holding an NT 4.0 credential, you are given credit for the elective exam requirement by simply having the MCSE credential on NT 4.0. However, to upgrade to a Windows Server 2003 level, you still must complete the following:

- All four of the networking systems exams (70-290, 70-291, 70-293, and 70-294).

- For the client requirement, either the 70-210 or the 70-270 exam. If you've already passed either of these exams as part of your previous certification path, then you will receive credit for this requirement.
- For the design requirement, either a Windows 2000 design exam or a Windows Server 2003 design exam.

Windows 2000 Upgrade Paths

If you currently hold a Windows 2000 MCSE certification, you have the option of taking either of two networking systems exams:

- **70-292**   Managing and Maintaining a Microsoft Windows Server 2003 Environment for an MCSA Certified on Windows 2000
- **70-296**   Planning, Implementing, and Maintaining a Microsoft Windows Server 2003 Environment for an MCSE Certified on Windows 2000

or the full four networking system exams listed previously (70-290, 70-291, 70-293, and 70-294).

For the client exam requirement, you're already in good stead because your Windows 2000 credential required that you pass either 70-210 or 70-270.

The same goes for the design requirement. The design exam you passed to obtain your Windows 2000 credential now counts toward your Windows Server 2003 credential.

And finally, that Windows 2000 MCSE will count as fulfillment of your elective exam requirement as well!

For All the Latest Info

You should check Microsoft's Training and Certification site frequently to make sure that you're aware of any changes to the program or to specific exams. You can find all the latest information on the MCSE track at http://www.microsoft .com/traincert/mcp/mcse/default.asp.

Good luck with your certification pursuit and thank you for allowing us to travel with you through this small region of the world of certification. Enjoy the trip!

Index

Numbers

0.0.0.0 IP address, advisory about, 55
0 and 255 IP addresses, advisory about, 56
3DES algorithm, using with IPSec Security Policy
    Wizard, 277–278
32-bit and 64-bit processing, explanation of, 7
70-240 exam, advisory about, 380

A

account policies security area in Group Policy
    system, explanation of, 17
Account Policy area of Group Policy, description
    of, 25
account security, significance in customizing
    security templates, 24–26
AD (Active Directory)
    compatibility with BIND, 110–111
    configuring for certificate publication, 314
    creating structure for, 31
    integrating with DNS, 96–97
AD databases, recovering, 369
AD-integrated domain, primary and secondary
    servers in, 99
AD-integrated zones in DNS, advantages of, 90
addressing. See IP address entries
ADSL (Asynchronous Digital Subscriber Line),
    explanation of, 161
ADT (actual data throughput), calculating for
    networks, 151–152
advanced digest authentication, using, 263–264
advanced switches, overview of, 134–135
affinity settings for ports, changing, 341
algorithms, using with IPSec policies, 277–278
AND logical operator, explanation and example
    of, 58
anonymous authentication, using, 262–263
APIPA (Automatic Private IP Addressing), role in
    DHCP IP allocation, 81
AppleTalk network protocol, overview of, 142
application layer of OSI reference model,
    explanation of, 260
[Application Log] template section in Group
    Policy system, description of, 25
application server role
    overview of, 29
    purpose of, 27
    security group role affiliation for, 28
applications, backing up, 362
ARP (Address Resolution Protocol), purpose of, 51

ASR (Automated System Recovery), using, 369
ASR sets, using, 360
Audit Policy area of Group Policy, description
    of, 25
authentication methods
    planning, 262–265
    planning for remote access clients, 218–220
    role in IPSec policies, 244–245, 254
    two-factor authentication, 311
authentication provider, role in remote access, 219
authoritative servers, relationship to DNS and
    queries, 90
authorization vs. authentication, 218
automatic partner discovery, role in WINS,
    118–119
Automatic Update system, features of, 38–39
automatic updates, considerations when using
    SUS, 42
AXFR zone transfers, explanation of, 90

B

B-node in NetBIOS, description of, 115
backup methodologies, overview of, 365–367
backup planning, overview of, 356–360
backup types
    copy backups, 358
    daily backups, 358
    differential backups, 358
    full backups, 357
    incremental backups, 358
backups
    of applications and OS, 362
    choosing frequency of, 364–367
    components in system state data during, 361
    of critical files, 361–362
    of data files, 362
    omissions from, 363–364
    of servers and clients, 362–363
    testing for recovery, 368
bandwidth, role in measuring network
    performance, 151
baseline installation, securing, 14–22
Baseline*.inf policies, purpose of, 26
basic authentication, using, 263–264
Basic*.inf templates, descriptions of, 19
binary
    converting to decimal, 54
    IP address in, 54
BIND implementations, compatibility with, 110
boot files, explanation of, 361
bottlenecks, identifying, 349–355
bridges
    overview of, 138–139
    vs. routers, 198
burst mode handling, relationship to WINS,
    113–114

P

INTERNATIONAL CONTACT INFORMATION

AUSTRALIA
McGraw-Hill Book Company
Australia Pty. Ltd.
TEL +61-2-9900-1800
FAX +61-2-9878-8881
http://www.mcgraw-hill.com.au
books-it_sydney@mcgraw-hill.com

CANADA
McGraw-Hill Ryerson Ltd.
TEL +905-430-5000
FAX +905-430-5020
http://www.mcgraw-hill.ca

**GREECE, MIDDLE EAST, & AFRICA
(Excluding South Africa)**
McGraw-Hill Hellas
TEL +30-210-6560-990
TEL +30-210-6560-993
TEL +30-210-6560-994
FAX +30-210-6545-525

MEXICO (Also serving Latin America)
McGraw-Hill Interamericana Editores
S.A. de C.V.
TEL +525-1500-5108
FAX +525-117-1589
http://www.mcgraw-hill.com.mx
carlos_ruiz@mcgraw-hill.com

SINGAPORE (Serving Asia)
McGraw-Hill Book Company
TEL +65-6863-1580
FAX +65-6862-3354
http://www.mcgraw-hill.com.sg
mghasia@mcgraw-hill.com

SOUTH AFRICA
McGraw-Hill South Africa
TEL +27-11-622-7512
FAX +27-11-622-9045
robyn_swanepoel@mcgraw-hill.com

SPAIN
McGraw-Hill/
Interamericana de España, S.A.U.
TEL +34-91-180-3000
FAX +34-91-372-8513
http://www.mcgraw-hill.es
professional@mcgraw-hill.es

**UNITED KINGDOM, NORTHERN,
EASTERN, & CENTRAL EUROPE**
McGraw-Hill Education Europe
TEL +44-1-628-502500
FAX +44-1-628-770224
http://www.mcgraw-hill.co.uk
emea_queries@mcgraw-hill.com

ALL OTHER INQUIRIES Contact:
McGraw-Hill/Osborne
TEL +1-510-420-7700
FAX +1-510-420-7703
http://www.osborne.com
omg_international@mcgraw-hill.com